D0028624

Bourbon for Breakfast

Living Outside the Statist Quo

Bourbon for Breakfast

Living Outside the Statist Quo

By Jeffrey Tucker

© 2010 by the Ludwig von Mises Institute and published under the Creative Commons Attribution License 3.0.

http://creativecommons.org/licenses/by/3.0/

Ludwig von Mises Institute
518 West Magnolia Avenue
Auburn, Alabama 36832

mises.org

ISBN: 978-1-933550-89-3

For Murray N. Rothbard

Introduction

The title of this book is drawn from one of those defining moments in life in which a small phrase* shatters the social-cultural convention and reveals completely new possibilities. I tell the story herein in the essay on morning drinking.

A great scholar and Southern gentlemen—a man who has written the ultimate guidebook to the writing of the King James version of the Gospels—invited me for an early breakfast, 7:00 A.M. and then offered me coffee.

I said, "yes, thank you."

He then added: "would you like bourbon in that coffee?"

What is revealed in that sentence and the shock it elicited? We believe, for whatever reason, that drinking hard liquor in the morning is unseemly, contrary to social norms, something to hide, a habit of the lower classes that is dangerous or even evil.

But are any of these assumptions true? A new form of prohibitionism has swept the country, imposed on us by our government masters and their cultural backers, even as alcohol consumption rises and rises. Evidently, we live two realities: the one the government imposes on us and the one we adopt in our real lives.

What struck me about this man's phrase was how it presumed that he and I were among the rebels against the prevailing ethos—that together we would reject the government's edicts and create our own norms and reality. This is a wonderful model for living a full life. This book is about seeing that just because government mandates certain things and forbids others does not mean that we must follow or even tolerate the official roadmap for our lives.

The seed of truth to the morning-drinking taboo is that doing this every morning would contribute to a less productive life. But on the weekends or when it is not necessary to be at your sober best, or when you are celebrating some special guest, there is surely nothing wrong here.

In any case, there must be some lost aristocratic tradition of adding a splash, else this highly cultivated, highly educated and scholarly Southern gentleman would not have suggested it. In doing so, he was revealing some lost history with a sense of freedom and possibility. To contemplate the suggestion is to imagine a world that does not exist, one that breaks from the status quo and plays with the pluses and minuses of adopting a new way of living.

Most of the essays in this book do just this. They imagine radical new possibilities of living outside the status quo. Or perhaps we should say "statist" quo because it is the state that is responsible for shaping our world, in brazen ways and also subtle ones that we do not fully realize.

Examples from the book include how and why the "hot" water in our homes became lukewarm and what can be done about it, how our toilets stopped working properly because of legislation that reduced toilet-tank size, how traffic-law enforcement became a racket for extracting wealth from the population to feed the overlords, how copyright and patent legislation is depriving us of cultural and technological innovation, and how politicians who we think are protecting us are really just taking away our own rights to protect ourselves.

To see the costs of statism is to see what Frederic Bastiat called the "unseen." It is about imagining the existence of some possibility that the state has forbidden from existing, playing with that possibility in your mind, and then acting on what has previously been an abstraction and making it a reality. Art helps us accomplish this mental feat, which is why many of these essays deal with literature, movies, culture, and the arts.

But seeing what is wrong with the world—Chesterton's phrase—is only the beginning. Finding the solution, the workaround, is the next necessary step. I try not to highlight problems without also offering a solution of sorts, simply because there is nothing productive or enlightening about despair. Hope comes from imaging a better future that does not yet exist.

Most of the essays in here deal with what are often considered trivial or light topics. But the trivial is quite often very serious, while what we think is serious is often quite trivial, as I try to show. At the same time, I deal with topics that libertarians of my stripe don't often write about, like the ghastly reality of jail (yes, the article is autobiographical) and the problems connected with intellectual property. I make no apology for the fact that the topics are all over the map. Maybe that will make this book more interesting.

An underlying apparatus here is my own formation in economic theory, drawn from my many years of work at the Mises Institute in Auburn, Alabama, and the way that the friendships I've formed in this connection have gradually led me away from the poison of politics as a viable means of social and economic management.

A parallel part of my life involves the study and practice of music, with a particular focus on what is called "early music." Exploring the interaction between culture broadly speaking and political economy is something that happened inadvertantly as I've been plugging away on thousands of articles over the years, of which this book represents only a sample.

We all need to be part of the project of reimagining freedom—of living outside the statist quo—else we will go the way of many societies and civilizations before us: host to a massive apparatus of power and imposition that strangles the growth and ingenuity of people, leading to a stasis that hardly anyone notices until it is too late.

I would like to offer a special note of thanks to Lew Rockwell, who has encouraged the publication of this kind of econo-cultural analysis, and ran many of them on his website, LewRockwell.com. Doug French suggested, even insisted, on collecting them in a book. Many friends, co-workers at the Mises Institute, associates, and loved ones will notice incidents, ideas, and phrases in here that draw from shared experiences and conversations; indeed, there are many senses in which this book is not my own but the result of a community enterprise. They should all know of my gratitude.

Contents

Water and Life

Commerce

Technology

Crime

Health and Manners

Food

Books

Movies

1

The Bureaucrat in Your Shower

January 10, 2006

The Department of Energy may soon be paying a visit to a certain shower head manufacturer in Arizona. The company is Zoe Industries Manufacturing. It runs Showerbuddy.com, a popular site that sells amazing equipment for bathrooms.

Consumers love the company but one man doesn't. He is Al Dietemann, head of conservation for the Seattle Water Board. Al ordered some products and sent them to BR Laboratories in Hungtington, California, according to the Seattle Post-Intelligencer. And sure enough, Bureaucrat Al gained enough data to report Zoe to the feds, accusing Zoe of "blatant violations of environmental protection laws." Now the heat is on.

What's the big deal? What critical matter of American public life is at stake? It's all about water flow and gallons per minute.

You might have some vague memory from childhood, and perhaps it returns when visiting someone who lives in an old home. You turn on the shower and the water washes over your whole self as if you are standing under a warm-spring waterfall. It is generous and therapeutic. The spray is heavy and hard, enough even to work muscle cramps out of your back, enough to wash the conditioner out of your hair, enough to leave you feeling wholly renewed—enough to get you completely clean.

Somehow, these days, it seems nearly impossible to recreate this in your new home. You go to the hardware store to find dozens and dozens of choices of shower heads. They have 3, 5, 7, even 9 settings, from spray to massage to rainfall. Some have long necks. Some you can hold in your hand. Some are huge like the lid to a pot and promise buckets of rainfall. The options seem endless.

But you buy and buy, and in the end, they disappoint. It's just water, and it never seems like enough.

Why? As with most things in life that fall short of their promise, the government is involved. There are local regulations. Here is one example of a government regulation on the matter, from the Santa Cruz City Water Conservation Office: "If you purchased and installed a new showerhead in the last ten years, it will be a 2.5 gpm [gallons-per-minute] model, since all showerheads sold in California were low consumption models beginning in 1992."

You mean they regulate how much my shower sprays? Yes indeed they do. Government believes that it has an interest in your shower? Yes it does.

And it is not just crazy California. The Federal Energy Policy Act of 1992 mandates that "all faucet fixtures manufactured in the United States restrict maximum water flow at or below 2.5 gallons per minute (gpm) at 80 pounds per square inch (psi) of water pressure or 2.2 gpm at 60 psi."

Or as the Department of Energy itself declares to all consumers and manufacturers: "Federal regulations mandate that new showerhead flow rates can't exceed more than 2.5 gallons per minute (gpm) at a water pressure of 80 pounds per square inch (psi)."

As with all regulations, the restriction on how much water can pour over you at once while standing in a shower is ultimately enforced at the point of a gun.

Manufacturers must adhere to these regulations under penalty of law, and to be on the safe side, and adjust for high-water-pressure systems, they typically undershoot. If you try your showers right now, you will probably find that they dispense water at 2 gallons per minute or even less. Together with other regulations concerning water pressure, your shower could fall to as low as 1.5 gallons per minute!

This creates a rather serious problem for nearly everyone in the country. America is the land of the shower. Popular lore holds that Americans are some of the most showered people in the world, and this stands in contrast to, well, to lands of the less showered. (Not naming any names!)

As for Zoe Industries, they set out to address this strange problem that has made our showers less functional than they ought to be.

They are not water anarchists; we aren't talking about shower-reg secessionists here. But the company did insightfully observe that the restriction applies on a *per-shower-head basis.*

So Zoe sells full units that have three full heads per shower! What a solution—truly in the spirit of American enterprise in the best sense. These remarkable units are both brilliant and beautiful, and they comply with the letter of the law. The one that annoyed Bureaucrat Al is the Nautilus II Chrome—and what a piece of work it is!

If it turns out that the feds can't prove him in violation, Congress might have to go back to work. The regs might have to be changed to specify one head per shower space.

But then what can the government do about the length of showers? After all, there is no real way to regulate how much water we use (and pay for). Maybe the shower heads have to have timers on them. And maybe the feds need to put up little monitors in our showers to make sure that we have stopped and started them.

And what happens to shower offenders? One can see federal S.W.A.T. Teams screeching up to your house, black-clad men pouring out, securing the perimeter, and shouting through a bull horn: "Drop the soap and come out of the shower with your hands up!"

Most manufacturers adhere to the regulations. But savvy consumers know how to get around the problem.

Warning: The following section is for information purposes only; I am not advocating egregious violations of federal law as some trouble-making rebel might. Do not endanger your status as a law-abiding citizen who takes wimpy showers.

Many people now hack their showers—or *customize* them, if you prefer. You can take your shower head down, pull the washer out with a screwdriver, and remove the offending intrusion that is restricting water flow. It can be a tiny second washer or it can be a hard plastic piece. Just pop it out and replace the washer. Sometimes it is necessary to trim it out using a pen knife or even a drill.

Using such strategies, you can increase your water flow from 2 gallons per minute to 3 and even 4 gallons per minute. You can easily clock this using a stopwatch and a milk carton.

Using this method (just as an experiment for the sake of journalism—again, do not try this at home) I was easily able to expand my gallons per minute on each shower in my house to an average of 3.4 gpm, thereby recreating that childhood sense of gushes of water pouring down.

Now, that doesn't compare to the amazing 12.7 gallons per minute that BR Labs claims they were able to clock with the Nautilus II (wow wow wow!) but it still exceeds federal regulations.

Why would anyone want to do this? According to the head of Zoe Industries, people somehow have the sense that I described above. "Generally, they don't like the water savers," he says, "the flow of water is too weak and they feel as though they haven't gotten a shower."

The whole craziness here recalls the similar frenzy about toilet tank size that resulted from the same act of Congress. Eventually manufacturers figured out ways to make the toilets flush, but, even today, you never want a plunger to be too far from the toilet. Thus has it spawned an entire industry of designer plungers!

You might say that water needs to be conserved. Yes, and so does every other scarce good. The peaceful way to do this is through the price system. But because municipal water systems have created artificial shortages, other means become necessary. One regulation piles on top of another, and the next thing you know, you have shower commissars telling you what you can or cannot do in the most private spaces.

Has central planning ever been more ridiculous, intrusive, and self-defeating? The U.S. Geological Survey of the U.S. government reports that all domestic water use ("Common indoor uses include drinking, preparing food, bathing, washing clothes and dishes, and flushing toilets; the major outdoor uses are watering lawns and gardens") constitute less than one percent of the total water use. Whether our showers spray a lot or a little makes no notable difference at all. If we want pay slightly more to be clean and happy, we are so entitled.

If Zoe Industries is bankrupted by federal fines, who will stand up for our rights to take showers our own way and make our own judgments about how much water to use?

2

The Turn of the Screw

February 20, 2004

You may have had a sense lately that something is just not right in your domestic life, not calamitously bad but just bad enough to be annoying on a daily basis and in seemingly unpredictable ways.

You are not alone. In fact, a huge variety of personal and social problems trace to a single source.

First an inventory to establish what I mean:

- You have the vague sense that your bed linens are not so much comforting you as hemming you in, restricting you and just not breathing as they should;
- To clean your bathtub and kitchen sink requires an inordinate amount of cleanser and bleach;
- Whereas you remember showers that once refreshed you, they now leave you only feeling wet;
- It should be pleasure to put on a bright white crisp undershirt but instead it seems rather routine, dull, even uneventful;
- The mop has a dusky smell of an old rag and you keep having to replace it to get rid of the reappearing and never disappearing stink;
- Your dinner tonight reminds you of your dinner last night and that night before, and the flavors seem to be piling up into one big haze.

These are just six of the many dozens of typical symptoms of one of the most common household problems in American today. What is that problem? The simplicity of the answer might shock you: *your water heater is set at too low a temperature.*

Most people don't want to think about their water heaters. It is a subject we would rather avoid. It just sort of sits there like a steel totem pole in a dusty closet that is otherwise not used for much because there is not room for much else. The heater itself seems intimidating, plastered with strange insulating devices and warning stickers. It is something to be touched only by specialists. We even fear cleaning behind it, worrying that we will be zapped or scorched.

Sure, we know people who have had to "replace their water heaters" because their "water heater went out," but because this has never happened to us, we don't worry about it. Besides, what if it turns out that the water heater has some sort of scary blue flame and a clicking starter or something? Better to leave it alone so that it doesn't become volcanic.

All of these impulses are wrong. The water heater can be your friend. It can be your greatest friend in your struggle to create and maintain a happy domestic environment. It wants to be useful. There is nothing to be frightened of. There are no blue flames (they are mostly electric now.) A water heater is made to heat and hold water. It is begging you to do something that will change your life from grey to bright white: turn up the temperature!

Chances are that your water temperature is set at 120 degrees. This is the preferred temperature of the establishment. Water heaters are shipped this way and installed this way. The regulations on new home construction mandate it to be this way. Who thinks to change it?

But 120 degrees? Come on. By the time the water leaves the heater and travels through the pipes and hits the air before landing whenever it is supposed to land, chances are that it will fall to 118 degrees. In the dead of Winter, with pipes running under the house, it can be even lower.

Think about this: 118 degrees is the temperature at which yeast thrives. It is the temperature for proofing. What does that tell you? It tells you that things can grow at 118 degrees.

In other words, this is too cool! To know what 118 degrees feels like, imagine a bowl of water that you stick your hand in. It is warm, even quite warm, but you don't really have the drive to pull your hand out to keep yourself safe. You can adjust. You know what? Everything adjusts to 118 degrees: germs, viruses, bacteria, dirt, smudge, sludge, stink, dust, and every other damnable thing in the world. All of this lives, even thrives, at 118 degrees.

Revelation 3:16 has it right: "So then because thou art lukewarm, and neither cold nor hot, I will spew thee out of my mouth."

Who came up with the idea that the standard temperature should be 120 degrees? The usual bunch: governments that want to impose a variety of deprivations on you, anti-energy people who think the less technological consumption the better, environmentalists who want to stamp out all things bright and beautiful, litigious lawyers who have intimidated heater makers, and safety freaks of all sorts. A quick search shows all.

We know these people. They are the people who say we should eat our own garbage, invite bats to live in our attics, and refrain from killing mosquitoes in the marsh. They are the ones who gave us toilets that don't flush and shower heads that don't spray. They seem to think we should all go around dirty and dissatisfied, and that anything resembling clean, neat, and, well, civilized has to be stamped out.

These people are always worrying about the risks of life, but what about the health risks of living in squalor of *their* creation?

Defy them all in one fell swoop! Turn your temperature up to 130 degrees. How hot is this? Contrary to the claims, it will not scald you. Imagine again a bowl full of water. Put your hand into this temperature and you will say: "Yikes!" or "Ouch!" or "Yeow!" and pull it right out and shake your hand in the air. However, it leaves nothing red, no burns, nothing awful. It is just what used to be called hot water before the lukewarm crowd changed everything.

How does yeast respond to 130 degrees? It dies. Bread bakers know this. You know what else dies? All the icky things mentioned above. They all die mercifully quick deaths at this temperature. Clean clothes! Clean sinks! Satisfyingly hot showers! Comfortable sheets! Clean-smelling mops! Plates that come out of the dish washer without dinner build-up on them! All of this awaits your act of defiance.

A brief note on shoes. Have you ever bought a new pair because your old ones...stank? Of course they did. Your socks are not getting clean. They infect your shoes. Oh sure, try to keep it at bay with Dr. Scholl's. It won't work. A shoe stink sticks forever. You thought you had a physical disability, and embarrassing foot odor problem. Nope. It's your hot water heater.

How to fix all this? It will take less than a minute. If your temperature dial is in the open, good for you. Turn it to 130 degrees or higher. There is a reason these tanks go up to 170 degrees. I read a manual for a dishwasher that says it wants water of 145 degrees. When I was in the dish-washing business, you had to use heavy rubber gloves just to get near water. So be it.

If your dial is covered, ignore all stickers and scary warnings about scalded babies. Take off the steel plate that covers up the setting. Remove the Styrofoam. There you will find a tiny little dial. Use a dime or a screwdriver and give the dial a teeny tiny little turn over to 130 degrees. The benefits will start within hours. Within a day, you will experience the greatest increase in your standard of living since your gas grill and automated sprinkler system.

Your new life begins with a comfortable and happy sleep, a blasting hot and refreshing shower, a crisp T-shirt, and clean socks, followed by breakfast on a plate so clean it squeaks. Even cleaning up breakfast will be pure pleasure: the sink gleams, the floor has never been cleaner, and your mop will end up as fresh as the day you bought it.

Indeed, with a water heater set at 130 degrees, all is right with the world—at least that part of it that you can control. Even if the whole world is conspiring against civilization, you can preserve your part of it with the smallest turn of a screwdriver.

3

Rain, Rain, Go Away

February 26, 2008

Once again, for the umpteenth time this month, I arrive at work soaking wet. Just getting from the car to the front door of the Mises Institute is like going through the rinse cycle—and umbrellas just aren't my thing. What's striking is how this weather pattern follows a year of dire warnings from government officials about the deadly drought that is destroying the region, as you can easily see from the government's own U.S. Drought Assessment maps.

Actually, these are interesting maps. They give the impression that the whole of the nation is a parched land that vacillates between persistent drought and improving droughts. Nowhere is listed as "soaked" or "just the right amount of rain." And if you reflect on government announcements of these things, all places seem to fall into one of three categories: catastrophic flooding, catastrophic drought, or forgettable.

Some years ago, the head of the local bureaucracy in charge of the distribution of water was quoted in the newspaper along these lines: "If these conditions persist, rationing will certainly become necessary." If these conditions persist? That's quite the assumption. We could say during the next rainfall: "If these conditions persist, it will become necessary for everyone to build an ark." Conditions never persist. They change. Bureaucrats really hate that.

One suspects that these same people love droughts. Droughts give them power, not just over the aggregate use of water. They enjoy pressing people on the smallest details of life. They get to tell you that you must take short showers. They tell you that you must flush less. They impose a profound sense of guilt on your for watering the basil growing in your window box.

Droughts can turn the most innocent public employee into the moral equivalent of a Gestapo agent, issuing dictates and imposing fines, ferreting out the water thieves, all in the name of the public interest.

Droughts turn neighbor against neighbor, and force the whole of everyone into the criminal class, reduced to sneaking around at night to water tomato plants. Droughts make everyone feel dependent on the state. We must read their rules, such as, "Even-numbered houses may water their lawns from 4 A.M. to 6 A.M., Monday, Thursday, and Sunday."

So rain, rain, go away. That's their theme.

Bureaucrat International has a common feature: loathing of "consumerism." Whereas people want to have choice over how they spend their money, bureaucrats want us to suffer constantly, and be intensely aware of what we use, not trusting the price system to determine our consumption patterns but rather obeying regulations and strictures.

Note that no drought ever officially ends. The papers are packed with warnings of impending doom during the worst of it. But when the torrents of rain come—and they invariably do, eventually—there is no press release that says something along the lines of: "Praise Be to God, the drought is over. Use as much water as you are willing to pay for!"

Never, never, never. They never say this. They would rather that we carry with us some sense that the drought is never really over, since, after all, it *could* come again.

The core of the problem here has nothing to do with rain and changing weather patterns. The weather has in fact been changing since the dawn of time. What creates the problem is public ownership of the means of production and the utterly irrational system under which the price doesn't change regardless of availability. There is no real profitability here. Nor are there losses. So there is no economic calculation going on. Prices are determined by extra-market indicators.

Think of the difference with the market system. Every day we are enticed to consume every product you can imagine: cars, celery, computers, anything. There is constant calibrating of supply and demand. If anyone attempts to overprice a product and make profits, another entrepreneur sweeps in to offer the same for less and draw profits away. Innovation is everywhere, so that suppliers are required to adopt the latest thing in order to stay afloat. No profits are permanent. They are always and everywhere threatened. These days, this happens almost overnight.

Now think of the difference with public water markets, in which the theme is always: you are using too much. Interesting isn't it? Why is this? It's because the market is not being allowed to work. This has nothing to do with the product in question. If you doubt it, make a visit to your local grocery and the bottled water section in particular. There are vast numbers of choices, with each supplier begging you to consume. But in public water markets, they demand that you conserve. State ownership and management of the means of production are the key reason. Privatize—completely privatize—the supply of water and a change would emerge overnight.

People immediately respond that this is a crazy idea. Streams, lakes, reservoirs, and water towers can't be owned privately! But is that really so? There are many cases of partial privatization on record, though the mandates are extreme. No doubt that there are efficiency gains that come with contracting out and privatized but regulated markets. The best solution is the same one that applies to all of the areas of life that are considered public goods, from trash collection and disposal to schools and defense: the government should get out of the business entirely.

Talk about opposition. Labor unions go bonkers when presented with the idea. Bureaucrats do too. Even religious groups have gotten in on the act. See, for example, the growing movement of Nuns Against Bottled Water. Presbyterians for Restoring Creation are circulating pledges for people to sign that foreswear drinking bottled water. These people claim that we shouldn't have to pay for what should be a free gift from God. But, oddly, these same people don't seem to have a problem with people's paying of the government's water bill.

Look, it's not complicated: drought is another name for shortage. Government is capable of creating a shortage in any good through bureaucratic management. Prices do not respond to supply and demand, and a lack of innovation characterizes production. We see this in schooling, mails, defense, courts, and every other area in which government enjoys a monopoly. It shouldn't surprise us that the same is true in water provision. Instead of blaming Mother Nature and the consumer, the water commissioners should look closer to home to see why everyone is required to live in fear and is reduced to doing rain dances to keep the water gods happy.

4

The Relentless Misery of 1.6 Gallons

January 5, 2010

My order at my favorite Chinese takeout was taking too long. I stopped into the men's room. There I witnessed a common scene: the modern toilet disaster. An otherwise clean business had a restroom calamity on its hands, one so grim that I hesitate to describe it.

The conjectural history is not difficult to reconstruct. The toilet apparently had trouble flushing. There was a plunger by the toilet, of course, as we see everywhere today. The toilet was plunged to get rid of the obstruction, while the obstruction itself spilled all over the floor and stuck to the plunger too.

The customer probably left the ghastly scene in a rush. Management knew nothing. But now customers were coming and going into this bathroom, surely losing all inspiration to eat or order food.

It would be easy to blame the restaurant owners. What is with these people and why can't they at least have a clean restroom? But reacting this way would be unjust. The hidden hand behind this unsanitary calamity is the U.S. government. The true origin of the mess was not in the hour before I arrived but back in 1994, after Congress passed the Energy Policy Act (passed in 1992).

This act, passed during an environmentalist hysteria, mandated that all toilets sold in the United States use no more than 1.6 gallons of water per flush. This was a devastating setback in the progress of civilization. The conventional toilet in the U.S. ranges from 3.5 gallons to 5 gallons. The new law was enforced with fines and imprisonment.

For years, there was a vibrant black market for Canadian toilet tanks and a profitable smuggling operation in effect. This seems either to have subsided or to have gone so far underground that it doesn't make the news. I've searched the web in vain for evidence of any 3.5 or 5.0 gallon toilet tanks for sale through normal channels. I wonder what one of these fetches in the black market. This possible source has no prices and an uncertain locale.

The toilet manufacturers, meanwhile, are all touting their latest patented innovations as a reason for the reduced hysteria surrounding the toilet disaster. I suspect something different. We have all gotten used to a reduced standard of living—just as the people living in the Soviet Union became accustomed to cold apartments, long bread lines, and poor dental care. There is nothing about our standard of living that is intrinsic to our sense of how things ought to be. Let enough time pass and people forget things.

So let us remember way back when:

- Toilets did not need plungers next to them, and thank goodness. Used plungers are nasty, disease carrying, and filthy. It doesn't matter how cute the manufacturer tries to make them or in how many colors you can buy them. In the old days, you would never have one exposed for guests. It was kept out in the garage for the rare occasion when someone threw a ham or something stranger down the toilet.
- Toilet paper was super thick and getting thicker. None of this one-ply nonsense.
- You never had any doubt about the capacity of the toilet to flush completely, with only one pull of the handle. The toilet stayed clean thanks to five gallons of rushing water pouring through it after each flush.

These were great cultural and civilizational achievements. In a state of nature, the problem of human waste and what to do about it is persistent. Do the wrong thing and you spread disease and misery.

Indoor plumbing since the time of the ancient world has been a sign of prosperity and human well-being. Indoor toilets that flow into a sewer have been around since 1500 B.C., but every new settlement of people in a new area presents the problem anew. In rural America, indoor toilets weren't common until the 1930s. That today everyone assumes them to be part of life is a testament to the creative power of economic progress.

What we have in these regulations passed since the 1990s is therefore a step backwards from a central aspiration of mankind to dispose of human waste in the best possible way. We have here an instance of government having forced society into a lower stage of existence.

Government has reduced us as people to the point that we either have to enter the black market to get good sewage or come to terms with living amidst periodic spreading of human waste all over our domestic and commercial environment.

Again, this is wholly unnecessary. Capitalism achieved something spectacular in waste disposal. Government came along and took it away from us. That's the story in a nutshell.

Today, every toilet company touts its latest innovations to overcome the problem. There are high-pressure blasters that run off electricity, designed to force a paltry 1.6 gallons of water through fast enough to make the difference. They are shockingly loud and scary. There are new shapes of tanks and new flow mechanisms that are said to compensate for the calamity, but this works only some of the time.

Each of these innovations is patented—meaning that a successful project cannot be copied and improved by other companies. So even if these are improvements, their distribution is limited and the successful aspects of them are not extended by others, for fear of patent lawsuits. The entire market is hobbled.

The result is an entire society of poorly working toilets and a life of adjustment to the omnipresence of human feces, all in a short 15 years. Thanks so much, Congress!

Of course the environmentalists are in on the whole project. They started telling us back in the 1970s that our large tanks were sheer waste. We should put bricks in them to save and conserve. If you didn't have a brick in your toilet, you were considered irresponsible and a social misfit. Eventually of course the brick became, in effect, a mandate, and finally toilet tanks were reduced to one third of their previous size.

Back then, it was just assumed that toilet manufacturers cared nothing at all about wasting water. Surely there was no rationale at all for why they consumed five gallons per flush as opposed to 1.6 gallons. This is just capitalist excess and down with it!

Well, think again: there was wisdom in those old designs. The environmentalists didn't account for the present reality in which people typically flush twice, three times, or even four times during a single toilet event.

Whether this ends up using more or less in the long run is entirely an empirical question, but let us just suppose that the new microtanks do indeed save water. In the same way, letting people die of infections conserves antibiotics, not brushing teeth conserves toothpaste, and not using anesthesia during surgery conserves needles and syringes.

Here is the truth that environmentalists do not face: Sometimes conserving is not a good idea. There are some life activities that cry out for the expenditure of resources, even in the most generous possible way. I would count waste disposal as one of those.

It is also possible that some people just like to get their kicks out of spreading misery and making it impossible for us to enjoy a clean and prosperous life. Like Puritans of old, they see virtue in suffering and would like to see ever more of it. It sounds perverse, but such an ethos does exist. And clearly, government doesn't care in the slightest.

There are many tragedies associated with the toilet calamity. There are private embarrassments at guest houses and disgust at every turn. Many of the customers at that Chinese takeout probably blame the owners, who themselves are probably mystified as to why toilets in communist China probably worked just fine but in capitalist America are throwing filth all over their restaurant.

It's the hidden hand of government that has mandated this leap back to barbarism.

5

The Great Drain Debacle

September 26, 2006

In Purgatory, there probably aren't any garbage disposals. People there will have to scrape all food remains into the trash, and if so much as an onion bit gets into the drain, it will have to be carefully fished out before the water is turned on, lest the drain clog.

And also it will be as in many cities on the East and West coasts: the garbage will have to be separated into plastic, glass, cans, and food muck. So there will be no peace after dinner, no shoving all leftovers down a hole in the sink and flipping the switch to grind it up. No, we will have to think really hard about all our trash, let bottles soak to remove labels, put the foil from the potato in a separate bag from the potato itself.

But so long as we are on earth, the garbage disposal and the unified trash system seem perks of life itself. For years, I've reveled in it. They still don't have them in Europe, where things seem to have regressed since the Middle Ages when sewage systems became more common. Nowadays, the Euro-people commonly toss their trash in their own yards, and try to cover up for this primitive reality by calling it "composting." If you were a New Yorker before 1997, you were guilty of a crime if you used a garbage disposal. But the state finally relented and granted the freedom to grind.

When my last garbage disposal wore out, the search for a replacement was a joy. You can get a normal household disposal with ½ horsepower or you can step it up with a ¾ horsepower engine. Or you can dare to step into the future with X-treme disposals with 1 horsepower engines, capable of grinding up a whole pineapple or a sack of potatoes or set of glass tumblers you are tired of.

And so of course there was no choice for me. With my new unit, there was nothing that wouldn't go down. That crab leg dinner left piles and piles of orange crustaceans on plates, but in they went. Thanksgiving turkey remains: in goes the corpse! My double batch of muffins overcooked, but no problem: down the grinding machine go 24 muffins. Chickens, pork chop bones, and even the much-dreaded banana peel.

It all worked so well. Where's the downside? I couldn't see any. The next step of course is grease. Everyone knows, or so we are told: never ever put grease down the drain. But, hey, this the modern age! Why take household appliance advice from people who are still living in the 50s?

So it started with bacon grease. Zoom! Then I pushed the envelope further and further. In the most outrageous act of disposal extremism ever, I dumped a full gallon of hot grease straight into the sink and watched with pride as it slid lazily and effortlessly down. Again, where's the downside?

For a time, it seemed that I could get away with these "sink sins" forever. Then one day I noticed a certain bogginess. The disposal side didn't seem quite as robust. Water would back up sometimes before flowing out again. Then one day—and now it seemed inevitable—it stopped. A bit of plunging pushed it right through again, and I figured that all was well. But then the plunging became more frequent.

I must have slipped into some state of denial as my plunging became weekly, then daily, and then several times daily. I had to have the plunger very nearby if I was to work in the kitchen at all. My conscience was telling me the truth: all my abuse of the system was finally catching up to me. But I ignored that quiet inner voice, and figured I could live this way. I was living an illusion. My dream of grinding a mountain of trash came to an end.

Finally one day I gave in and called a plumber. He came and went, announcing that all was well. Fine, I thought: back to my old ways. But of course all was not well. Then it finally happened this past weekend: a stoppage that would not be broken. As if to confirm the persistence of natural law, it began following another bacon-grease dump. The water wouldn't move.

I plunged and plunged until my back muscles were sore. Sometimes if I put the plunger in the wrong spot, water would splash up and I would taste the muck, that combination of old garbage with the overriding smell of bacon, a tepid and thick gray-brown oily muck. The more it splashed in my face, the more I didn't care. The muck soared high in the air, dropping on countertops far and wide, landing in my hair, soaking my clothes. Sweat mixed with the bacon muck and dripped all over my face. Blisters began to appear on my hands. But the pain was not an issue: I had to beat this clog!

No progress.

It was time to break out the chemicals. Liquid Plumber Gel. Baking Soda. Lye. Boiling Water. Vinegar. Anything! Nothing worked.

Should I call a plumber? Heck, I thought, what does a plumber have but the right tools? So it was off to Wal-Mart to acquire them myself, and I ended up with a dazzling little addition to my do-it-yourself toolkit: a 15-foot drain snake. This would surely to it! I put that snake down, a free passage for 15 feet until I reached the end. No blockage. But still the sink did not drain.

Despair set in. I imagined the crews from the city arriving the next day, with city officials and even the city planner. They would have to dig up my yard with huge tractors. The sidewalks would be ripped up. Specialists would have to be brought it to assess the damage I had caused. There are probably 15 different agencies that oversee the water supply and they would all be allied against me.

I would be sitting there in my kitchen alone, vulnerable, guilty, and they would be writing citations, wagging their fingers at me, fining me—maybe even hauling me off to jail for failing to abide by sink regulations. My neighbors will hate me. My life will fall apart. I would sit in prison and rethink my life. This is the price I would pay for ignoring my conscience.

Another day passed, another day of tepid sink muck. And then something struck me. The left side of the sink works fine. Only the garbage disposal side is stuck. But both the garbage disposal and the other sink flow down the same tube, so how does this make any sense? And I've already snaked out the garbage disposal, so that can't be it.

Then, finally, a revelation. There are two tubes coming from the disposal unit. One goes to the main drainage and one goes to the dishwasher. I had snaked out the wrong one! But then another problem arose. I could not get the snake down the right one, because the entry point was hidden beneath the choppers on the disposal unit. How will I get in?

At long last, I opened the counter door. The pipes were plastic PVC. They all fit together nicely with large bolts that can be twisted by hand. I twisted the one that led from the disposal to the main pipe and gently moved it to the side.

And there was the offending glob. It was just sticking there, sort of lifelike. With a fork I removed it. It was an accumulation of six months of grindings. But tangled up at the very front of the glob was the most marvelous thing. It was a big piece of green plastic, something shaped sort of like a washer. It could have been from anything. No one had ever seen it before. It might have been there for years. It had evidently fallen down the sink, managed to slip through the grinding and then rammed into the pipes were it stayed lodged and began to accumulate muck. It might have been there for many years, for all I knew.

Once having removed this, I screwed the pipe back together, and voilà: everything worked perfectly again. Better than ever! Three days of hell were over, after an operation that took maybe 90 seconds. Unbelievable!

But here was the real triumph. This little green plastic thing had expiated my sins. It turned out that none of my supposedly bad habits had done anything to clog my disposal. In fact, to the extent that some of those bones and grease finally caused a choking, that was a good thing because it led me to the fundamental source of the problem. I was guilt free! I could again walk with an upright heart.

Every civic culture in human history has attempted to distort our moral sense. They want us to believe that right and wrong consist in obeying social and civic priorities. But there is no moral norm involved in such issues as whether we own disposal units or what we put in them. Those are merely issues of technology that change with the times; our only restriction is not to impose on others' person or property.

Morals do not come from the state and society. Morality deals with weightier matters that measure our thoughts, words, and deeds against universals that are true regardless of time and place. And in this time and this place, we can grind our garbage to our hearts' content.

6

Crush the Sprinkler Guild

May 9, 2006

I suspected as much! What the lady at Home Depot called the "sprinkler repair cult" is an emerging guild seeking privileges and regulations from the government. That means a supply restriction, high prices, or another do-it-yourself project. But there is a way around it.

I first began to smell a rat when the automatic irrigation system on my front yard needed work but I had unusual struggles in trying to find a repair guy.

The first place I called informed me that they could accept no more clients. Clients? I just wanted a new sprinkler thing, for goodness sake. I don't want to be a client; I want to be a customer. Is there no one who can put on a new sprayer or stick a screwdriver in there or whatever it needs?

Nope, all full.

The next call was not returned.

The next call ended with the person on the line fearfully saying that they do landscaping but will have nothing to do with sprinklers or "automated irrigation systems." Umm, ok.

The next call seemed more promising. The secretary said they had an opening on the schedule in three weeks. Three weeks? In that period of time, my yard will be the color of a brown paper bag.

The next call failed. And the next one. And the next. Finally I was back to the off-putting secretary. I made the appointment but the guy never came. Fortunately, in the meantime, a good rain came, and then at regular intervals for the whole season, and I was spared having to deal with this strangely maddening situation.

Why all the fuss? We aren't talking brain surgery here. These are sprinklers, little spray nozzles connected to tubes connected to a water supply. Why was everyone so touchy about the subject?

Why did all the power seem to be in their hands, and none in mine? Must I crawl and beg?

Above all, I wonder why, with most all lawns in new subdivisions sporting these little things, why oh why are the people who repair them in such sort supply?

Little did I know that I had stumbled onto the real existence of a most peculiar thing in our otherwise highly competitive economy: a guild.

It had all the earmarks. If you want your nails buffed, there are thousand people in town who stand ready. If you want someone to make you dinner, you can take your pick among a thousand restaurants. If you want to buy a beer, you can barely go a block without bumping into a merchant who is glad to sell you one. None of that is true with sprinkler repair.

What does a guild do? It attempts to restrict service. And why? To keep the price as high as possible. And how? By admitting only specialists, or supposed specialists, to the ranks of service providers, usually through the creation of some strange but largely artificial system of exams or payments or whatever.

Guilds don't last in a free market. No one can blame producers for trying to pull it off. But they must always deal with defectors. Even the prospects of defectors can cause people who might not otherwise defect, to turn and attempt to beat others to the punch.

There is just no keeping a producer clique together for long when profits are at stake.

There is also the problem that temporarily successful guilds face: high profits attract new entrants into the field. They must either join the guild or go their own way. This creates an economically unviable situation in a market setting that is always driving toward a market-clearing rate of return.

Further evidence of the existence of a sprinkler guild came from the checkout lady at the Home Depot. I was buying a sprinkler head and she said in passing that they didn't used to carry these things, and the decision of the manufacturer to supply them in retail got some people mighty upset. She spoke of the sprinkler repair people as a cult that should be smashed!

Now, does this guild really exist or is it an informal arrangement among a handful of local suppliers? As best I can tell, here is the guild's website (http://www.irrigation.org/default.aspx). The Irrigation Association is active in:

- Providing a voice for the industry on public policy issues related to standards, conservation and water-use on local, national and international levels
- Acting as a source of technical and public policy information within the industry
- Raising awareness of the benefits of professional irrigation services
- Offering professional training and certification
- Uniting irrigation professionals, including irrigation equipment manufacturers, distributors and dealers, irrigation system designers, contractors, educators, researchers, and technicians from the public and private sectors.

Catch that? Certification. Unity. Standards! Public policy. These are all dangerous words, that come down to the same result: high prices and bad service.

Why should anyone become certified? "Prestige and credibility among peers and customers"; "professional advancement opportunities"; "Enhances the professional image of the industry—your industry."

I thought I needed a sprinkler repairman but these people want me to hire a Certified Landscape Irrigation Manager, a CLIM. How do you become a CLIM? Well you have to send in $400 plus a résumé that includes an "overview summary of how you plan to meet program criteria:

Two examples of project development to include:

- System design objective
- System budget estimate
- Water source development
- System design drawings: hydraulic, electrical, detail drawings, pump station

Project specifications:

- General specification
- Installation specification
- Material specification
- Pump station

Two system audits or evaluations to include:

AUDIT

- System performance (uniformity)
- Base schedule
- Recommendations for improvement

EVALUATION

- System performance (uniformity)
- Hydraulic analysis
- Electrical analysis
- Grounding
- Water source
- Product performance
- Recommendations for improvement

Two construction and/or construction management projects:

- Site visit reports
- Drawing of record
- Final irrigation schedule
- Punch lists

Of course they are working with government, federal, state, and local. They want restrictions of every sort. They want their own Turf and Landscape Irrigation Best Management Practices or BMP to be the law of the land. You can read more about this here.

How hip-deep are these people in government? It's hard to say. But I'm guessing that local developers, landscapers, builders, and others are intimidated by all these and are reluctant to challenge their monopoly.

So thank goodness for hardware stores! They are working to bust up this vicious little guild, to the benefit of the consumer and everyone else. It means having to stick your fingers in mud and read instruction manuals and the like but sometimes the defense of liberty requires that you get your hands a little dirty.

7

The Key to a Happy Life

April 17, 2003

Ah, Spring, the time when the landscape appears as if it were painted by a great artist, when the birds make music of symphonic quality, and when the very air we breath feels air conditioned. That last point is particularly important, because it is only true so long as we are outside.

If we are inside, it is a different matter altogether.

Most of the year, indoor air is fabulously fresh, clean, and circulating at the right temperature, thanks to the greatest source for clean wonderful air: not the Clean Air Act but central air conditioning and heating. When people say, hey, turn on the air, it is literally true. We hardly open windows anymore, which (not being Mr. Outdoors) I think is fine in principle.

But in the Spring, the air goes off. It is no longer cold enough for heat but not yet warm enough for air conditioning. The thermostat tells the machine to stay put. You could turn on just the blower, but who thinks of doing that? So the air just sort of sits there, dormant and still. It is the right temperature, but it is not moving.

You might not notice this at first. But once you focus on it, you suddenly realize: I'm suffocating!

This is precisely the revelation that hit me two nights ago. For two weeks, nights had been oddly miserable. I wasn't too hot or too cold, just oddly and unidentifiably uncomfortable. I would wake somehow unrested. Am I sick? Am I getting old? Finally it hit me. The only circulation in this room comes from human breath!

This room needs a fan running! On it came, and with it, life itself. The night was suddenly glorious, clean, and happy. All dreams were dreamy. I awoke and there was once again music in the air, the feel of flowers, the sound of birds (metaphorically of course). The fan had brought the Spring indoors.

Then I began to notice something. This problem isn't limited to the bedroom. It afflicts virtually all indoor space. In the Spring, with neither heater nor air conditioner, indoor air begins to sink into a stultifying blechiness. If you are sitting in the same spot, you are breathing the same air again and again.

My office needed a fan too! I turned it on to the same effect: the flowers appeared, the birds sang, the air moved! Suddenly my day has become as glorious as my night, filled with rapturous, Spring-like freshness. The fan! God bless it.

At this point in a superficially trivial essay such as this, one is supposed to plunge into history and reveal all the details that one knows about the history of the fan, so that the reader won't walk away thinking: I can't believe this guy thinks that his personal fan experience is worthy of an article.

Or I could plunge into the economics of the fan, how it is the system of free enterprise that gives us such choice: ceiling fans, stand-up fans, desk fans, clip-on fans, hand-held fans, and more. Hence the system of delivery must be guarded against all encroachment by the state.

But thanks to the fan running in my office, I feel no burdens to defer to any model of writing that is so tediously conventional. In any case, the economic point is obvious enough in that fans are available everywhere. As for the history, it turns out that this isn't necessary. The history of the fan is already well documented at the website of the Fan Museum in London (http://www.fan-museum.org/history.htm).

Of course the history on this site, a bit pompous, deals with the inferior and primitive hand-held fan. For the serious stuff that we use in real life, you have to go to the site of the Fan Collectors Association (http://www.fancollectors.org/) in Andover, Kansas, which is appropriately hip to the magnificence of the electric fan. This site has an amazing array of pictures of its fans. You can also participate in the Fan Forum. You can attend an event, which, the site says, is "a great way to meet new friends, share fan stories, and buy, sell and trade fans."

Maybe so. What I do know is that a fan is the key to a happy sleep. It is the key to a happy, productive day. And because nights and days make up the whole of life, the fan is the key to a happy life. For a mere $9–20, you can bring the Spring indoors without the bugs, or pollen, or other natural menaces. Buy a fan and live a full life!

8

Municipalized Trash: It's Uncivilized

September 14, 2009

Driving in to work today, I saw garbage bins overflowing and city dumpsters spilling out with trash. It stinks. It's disgusting. It's uncivilized. It's probably dangerous to some extent.

It's a holiday, so of course the government workers charged with picking up this nasty refuse can't work, even though construction workers in private firms are busy bees taking advantage of the extra time.

It's true with house trash too: pickup is once per week—on schedule—and there is nothing you can do to make it more frequent. It's part of the master plan, don't you know, and if you make more trash than the once-per-week pickup can contain, that is your problem, not the city's.

The very fear that people have about private trash collection—that trash will pile up and no one will do anything about it—turns out to be a regular feature of government trash collection. But we look the other way. Why?

Before getting to this, let us first establish that garbage is a serious issue. William F. Buckley, his head full of schemes for threatening populations with nuclear annihilation, once chided libertarians for bothering with such petty concerns as trash collection.

"It is only because of the conservatives' disposition to sacrifice in order to withstand the enemy," wrote Buckley in 1961, "that [libertarians] are able to enjoy their monasticism, and pursue their busy little seminars on whether or not to demunicipalize the garbage collectors."

Ah yes, little seminars. Seminars about such things as the avoiding the plague. Humanity has some experience with the results of failing to dispose of trash properly, and that experience was deadly. Plagues swept the ancient world every 50 years or so, spread mainly through a lack of good sanitation. The Black Death in Europe might have been avoided with better sanitation and a decent system for disposing of trash rather than letting it pile up on the streets.

History's fight with the plague in the developed world came to an end at the time of the rise of capitalism in the late middle ages, and no surprise there. With the accumulation of capital came innovation in trash disposal, since living in sanitary conditions and staying alive turns out to be something of a priority for people. This is why the largest advances in garbage collection came about during the Industrial Revolution.

And yet here we are in 2009, with trash piled up on the streets and stinking to high heaven, bags full of raw animal parts (chickens, pigs, cows, fish), baby diapers stuffed with waste, rotting eggs mixed with sour cream dip from game-day parties, piles that are right now being scavenged by roaches and rats. This is in a town that prides itself on its tidiness.

And we put up with this for the same reason that we put up with lost mail, potholes in roads, dilapidated schools, depreciated money, and a clogged court system: because these services are monopolized by government.

Now you can make all the public-goods arguments you want to about roads and courts, but trash disposal is not rocket science and could be easily handled by the market. Everyone wants trash removed, and the sooner the better.

That means that there is a market demand for the service. There is money to be made. The only way to keep something like this at bay is to make it illegal.

If the market were in charge, pickup would surely be more than once per week. We wouldn't have to drag our trash bins out to the curb. In fact, we would be faced with several or many options for trash pickup.

If we made more trash than we "should," we wouldn't get angry notes from the city government. The private pickup companies would be thrilled. We might be paying by frequency of pickup or perhaps by the pound. That would be for the market to decide.

In fact, trash pickup services might actually be characterized by—perish the thought—innovation, just as they were in the early part of the 20th century, when trash collection was mostly private. Our houses might be directly connected to underground trash-transmission services that would whisk it all away in an instant. Our kitchens might have highly effective trash chutes that would zap away trash as we make it.

But because of this ghastly tradition of municipalizing trash pickup (or we might call it Sovietizing), the entire industry is stuck in the past, utterly impervious to improvement and modernization.

We get our news through fiber optics, walk around with tiny wireless phones that can instantly connect with anyone anywhere, and shop digitally with any vendor in the world. But when it comes to trash, we are still relying on once-per-week, strictly scheduled pickups by tax-funded workers driving monstrous, old-model trucks.

In my town, even the trashcans are paid for and owned by the government, as if the private sector has yet to figure out on its own initiative how to make a tub for holding things.

So why does this system persist? I asked a few people about this, and the answer usually came down to some system of graft. Powerful people make the trucks, manage the landfills, and dole out the contracts. Perhaps so, but why do we put up with it?

It seems like a preposterously unobjectionable plan: open this system to private ownership and competition, and thereby innovation.

I don't just mean contracting out. I mean abolishing city trash pickup and letting private enterprise completely take over. There is just no way that the existing muck would persist, for it offends every aesthetic sensibility and it may pose a ghastly health risk.

As for the old conservative claim that libertarians are insufficiently worried about the Soviet threat and too worried about garbage collection, note that the Soviet Union is gone and the garbage problem is still with us.

9

A Lesson in Mortality

January 19, 2005

A death in the family is always hard, but three in three weeks is especially difficult for children, even though it only involved pets.

First it was the green tree frog discovered at the local car repair shop and taken home to be cared for. "Sticky" lived two months, long enough for the kids to become very attached. One day we found him dead in his cage.

Then it was the two chickens brought home soon after being hatched at a friend's chicken coop. They lived only two days, and died so innocent, so young and vulnerable.

Below I reprint the grave-side homilies that I offered when they were buried. But first: a reflection on mortality, a fact of life even more inevitable than taxes that modernity still can't seem to come to terms with.

Death impresses upon us the limits of technology and ideology. It comes in time no matter what we do. Prosperity has lengthened life spans and science and entrepreneurship have made available amazing technologies that have forestalled and delayed it.

Yet, it must come.

As Mises puts it: "Man lives in the shadow of death. Whatever he may have achieved in the course of his pilgrimage, he must one day pass away and abandon all that he has built. Each instant can become his last. There is only one thing that is certain about the individual's future—death."

Modernity has a problem intellectually processing the reality of death because we are so unwilling to defer to the implacable constraints imposed on us within the material world. Whole ideologies have been concocted on the supposition that such constraints do not have to exist. That is the essence of socialism. It is the foundation of U.S. imperialism too, with its cocky supposition that there is nothing force cannot accomplish, that there are no limits to the uses of power.

To recognize the inevitability of death means confessing that there are limits to our power to manufacture a reality for ourselves. It is akin to admitting that certain fundamental facts of the world, like the ubiquity of scarcity, cannot be changed. Instead of attempting to change it, we must imagine social systems that come to terms with it. This is the core claim of economic science, and it is also the very reason so many refuse to acknowledge its legitimacy or intellectual binding power.

To discover the fountain of youth is a perpetual obsession, one that finds its fulfillment in the vitamin cults that promise immortality. We create government programs to pay for people to be kept alive forever on the assumption that death is always and everywhere unwarranted and ought to be stopped. There is no such thing as "natural death" anymore; the very notion strikes us as a cop out.

Thus do we insist on always knowing the "cause" of death, as if it only comes about through an exogenous intervention, like hurricanes, traffic accidents, shootings, and bombs. But even when a person dies of his own accord, we always want to know so that we have something to blame. Heart failure? Well, he or she might have done a bit more exercise. Let this be a lesson. Cancer? It's probably due to smoking, or perhaps second-hand smoke. Or maybe it was the carcinogens introduced by food manufacturers or factories. We don't want to admit that it was just time for a person to die.

The denial of death's inevitability is especially strange since life itself serves up constant reminders of our physical limits. Sleep serves as a kind of metaphor for death. We can stay awake working and having fun up to 18 hours, even 24 or 36, but eventually we must bow to our natures and collapse and sleep. We must fall unconscious so that we can be revived to continue on with our life.

Pills can delay the need for sleep but cannot obliterate it. There are no substitutes for sleep, no foods we can eat, no exercise we can undertake, no special words we can say. We can shake our fist in anger at our body's demand for sleep but we still must give in. Sleep wins out over our individual wills every day of our lives, just as death wins out over our will to live forever.

Our struggle against mortality can take productive forms of course, as when we seek to leave great legacies in the material world: wealth, art, children, literature, charity, changed lives. We do all this in part because we seek ways to make our brief lives take on meaning beyond themselves. To be high-minded means to care not only about our own times but also about those that follow. If we cannot live forever, we at least want our impact on this world to live longer than nature permits us to live.

All these impulses appear to be unique to the human person, a reflection of our unique rationality and (for theists) the presence of a soul. Animals are another matter entirely. They avoid death by instinct (yes, I realize the term explains nothing) but they do not seek immortality or strive to leave legacies or work to extend the life span of their species, or otherwise improve the lot of their fellows through innovation. They are what we would be if we lacked rationality and souls.

When a pet dies, all children ask the question: will my pet go to heaven? I suppose the answer must be: not in the way we will find heaven. And yet the children want hope that their pet will live again, and that they will see them living again. And because no Scripture seems to say that there cannot be, it is reasonable to say that animals can live eternally if God so desires it. There are many problems with this idea, of course, since orthodoxy says there is no flesh in heaven but if animals have no souls, how, precisely, would they go there?

In the moments following the death of a pet, such theological ramblings have no place. What the moment calls for is "closure," to use an overused buzz word.

And so we gather in silence and dig the hole in the ground, place the corpse in and say some words.

> We gather to bury and pay tribute to Sticky, a tree frog who has been a good friend to us all. Quiet and unassuming, he lived a good life, stirred our imaginations, and delighted us with his antics. We will miss you, Sticky. We are grateful for the life you lived. If there were ever a tree frog that deserved to enter the gates of heaven, it was surely Sticky.

Each child takes some dirt on the shovel and tosses it in the grave, and it is patted down. We stand in silence for a few moments, and walk away in the quiet evening.

A similar scene repeated itself with the tiny chicks.

> We gather to bury these two tiny chicks. Though they were so young, and lived such short lives, we still gave them names: One-Minute Egg, and Two-Minute Egg. We will always remember them. Let us remember that we too will die one day, and, when considering the whole length

> of eternity, our lives are not much longer than theirs. May our souls be as innocent as theirs when we breathe our last breath.

By this time, the children were rather bored with funeral drama. They quickly scampered off to live full lives in the sunshine of day, deciding right then to think about death only when they must, but otherwise to live and love every breath. And so it should be.

10

Truth in the Coin Shop

August 12, 2008

You are uptown in a shopping district of a small community, and you pass by the meat shop, the wine shop, the coffee shop, two churches side by side, a coin shop, an antique store … and hold it right there.

A coin shop? This is irresistible, because, as implausible as this may sound, all political truth can be found in a coin shop. And not just political truth: you find in here the story of the whole of modern life on exhibit, and learn more from looking than you find in a multivolume history.

There they are on display: coins from all lands. Why are they worth more than the coins in your pocket? Because they are old? That's part of it but not the essence of it. There are some new coins here that are also just as valuable as the old ones.

What is critical is that they are made of gold and silver. You can pick them up and tell the difference. They are heavy. Stack them and let them fall on each other, and they make a different sound from the coins that usually rattle around in your pocket.

It strikes everyone and anyone immediately. Somehow these coins are "real"; the coins we use today are not. But what does this really mean? And what does it imply?

The value of the coins amounts to far more than their marked value. Even dimes before a certain date sell for ten and fifteen times the face value. The larger coins can be quite expensive.

What is real here is their substance, not the printing on the outside. This is the opposite of modern coins, the substance of which is completely irrelevant; all that matters is what is printed on the outside.

So the use of the term "real" here parallels how we use this term in any other context. Reality TV is said to provide the unvarnished truth about what people really do. We say someone should "get real" if we suspect that their thought or behavior is a mask or a blindfold that is obscuring a more obvious truth.

So it is with coins. The new coins we use in transactions are not real. They are wearing a mask, a disguise, one put on by the state. More absurdly, the state tells us not to look at the reality but rather to trust God that all is right with the money in the realm.

The old coins, in contrast, are precisely what they say they are and therefore have nothing to hide. There are no invocations that require a leap of faith. The truth is found on the scale and is told in ounces.

The gold ones are of course the ones you really want to hold. Their value reflects the metal content. Melt them, restamp them, make them into jewelry, and they are still worth no less than the market value of the metal.

And who decides what the values of these old coins are? The coins might bear the likeness of a politician. They might bear the name of the nation-state. But these pictures and slogans are merely interlopers on the real point. What you hold is valuable not because some legislature, treasury department, or central bank says it is valuable. Its worth was and is dictated by the market, which is to say, the choices and values of human beings. No government can add to or take away this value except by physically manipulating the coin itself.

Not only that. If you dig deep enough in the coin shop, you might run across coins that were not minted by governments at all but by private manufacturers. In the early years of the Industrial Revolution, this was the way coins were made in Britain, not by the Royal Mint but by entrepreneurs no different from any other. George Selgin tells the whole story in his aptly named book *Good Money*.

It turns out that making money is a business like any other, not something that only governments do. In a free world, it would be something done entirely by private enterprise. The same is true of exchanging money. Some of the world's first great fortunes were made this way, profiting from the buy/sell spreads in coinage markets. Today the business is the same in some respects, and one can see the appeal of it all. Bless those who sustain it and believe in it.

So long as this good money is in your hands, it is your independent store of wealth. There are no taxes due, no withdrawals required, no forms to fill out. It is the physical embodiment of independence. It gives you freedom. It secures your rights. And because this coin is valued not by the nation-state, it rises above it and extends beyond it. Its value is recognized the world over, and not because the UN has proclaimed it but rather because it is something everyone on the planet agrees on.

Geographic mobility is only part of it. Look at the dates on the older coins: 1910, 1872, 1830, 1810, and carlicr and carlicr. Thcy arc still bcautiful because they are durable. Their value is not diminished over time, as with just about everything else we know about; rather, it increases over time. And by its very nature, gold protects your investment from the depredations of modern life.

How they inspire the imagination. What was the world like when such coins served as money? The economy wasn't managed by some central authority. It managed itself from within, by the buying and selling decisions of economic agents themselves. The coins were selected by the market to serve as the facilitator of exchange, the things by which we were permitted to rise above the limits of barter.

They made possible calculation between goods and services that were as widely diverse as the whole of the human project, and revealed what was profitable and what was not. So these coins made it possible to organize the world's resources into lines of production that served society in the most efficient way.

And how did the politicians figure into this mix? When they got their hands on these coins, they could do terrible things. But it was rather difficult for them to get them. They had to demand that the citizens fork over the coins *or else*, which is to say, they had to tax people. You have to have a pretty good reason to do this. Or the lie you tell has to be pretty darn compelling. You can only tell fibs so many times before people catch on.

If this is the only money that circulates, the aspiring leviathan state faces a serious limit on its capacity to expand—a limit imposed by physical reality and the unwillingness of most people to give up something for nothing.

This is why every state is so anxious to see money *substitutes* circulate widely, preferably in the form of paper that can be made at will. If that samc statc can get banks to cooperate in creating more paper than can be redeemed by gold and silver coins, it can begin to habituate the population to the idea of a "fiat" currency, that is, money that is invented out of whole cloth.

Even better for the state is a system that completely separates "paper money" from its historical roots in good money. Then there are no limits at all to how much money it can make to fund itself and pay its friends, even if that means that money in general becomes ever less valuable. (On this process, see Hayek's *Prices and Production.*)

And here we have the short history of how money came to be destroyed and how the modern world came to host the ghastly leviathans that dominate the world. Here is the basis of destructive and unnecessary wars that last and last, the character-shredding welfare state, and the swarms of bureaucrats who run our lives in every respect. It all comes down to the way money was destroyed.

You can tell from looking at the dates on coins that all of this happened surprisingly recently. The process began in the early 20th century with the cartelization of the banking system so that banks could loan money out of deposits they promised to pay on demand. The government's own debts would be paid no matter what. This helped with the war—taxes don't cut it when it comes to funding global war—and so the financial system was encouraged to set aside its usual concerns over stability since it was now guaranteed not to fail.

The process continued with the attack on gold during the New Deal under the influence of people like John Maynard Keynes, who believed that paper money would usher in a new utopia of a government-managed economy. So desperate was FDR to have people stop trading good money that he demanded it all be turned in; he said this was necessary to stop the Depression. Then the paper-money revolution was furthered by people like Milton Friedman, who 0believed that a pure paper money would somehow bring about a stable price level—through a formula that may have looked good on paper but failed to account for the realities of politics.

In the end, we ended up on the other side of the great divide between freedom and tyranny, all symbolized by the contrast between the coins of the past and the coins of the present. It is reality versus fiat, independence versus dependence, value that lasts versus value that is the whim of the transitory political class.

You discover all of this when you walk in the coin shop.

Have a conversation with the proprietor, who tends to be of a type: perhaps a bit crusty, but highly knowledgeable and independent-minded. At his office, he lives amidst this history. He is surrounded by the truth about money that most people never discover. He is daily faced with the beauty of what once was, and perhaps too he imagines the possibility that it could be again. He is not usually the despairing type either. He sees the difference between what is permanent and what is transitory. If you take the time, you can learn from him.

If you trade with him, you can enter into his world of knowledge and partake in the ancient truth about money, politics, and civilization. To own these coins helps grant some sense of independence to you too. You will possess a store of wealth that is not subject to wild bubbles, state-manufactured inflations, and political whims. It is a kind of privatized secession.

Is it any wonder that people who enter this world think differently from others? Their blinders are off. They see what is real and true. They no longer believe in the great modern lie that the state is our wise master, in whom we should trust our very lives. The owner of gold and silver coins is just a bit less attached to the state than others. And should a time of great crisis come, and you look among the survivors, you can be pretty sure that preeminent among them will be those who love the coin shop as much as I do.

11

Does Money Taint Everything?

May 08, 2008

Let's pull this sentence out of the civic pieties of our time and see what's wrong with it: "We should all volunteer our time in charitable causes and give back to the community in a labor of love."

We can't argue with the instruction here, or the sentiment behind it. There is nothing wrong with giving and sacrifice. My argument is with the choice of language. It contains a word and three phrases the common usage of which can be highly misleading.

Voluntary

This word "volunteer" is used to describe a person who does things in service of others, and we all know the intent of the term. We speak of volunteering all the time. The United States has what is called the *voluntary sector*, which is supposed to refer mostly to nonprofit organizations that elicit nonremunerative employment. But think of the literal meaning of *voluntary* or *volition*: the act of making a conscious and noncoerced choice to do something. The opposite is to be forced to do something. So prisoners are forced to sleep on mats; people in the army are forced to march here and there. Or you and I can volunteer to sleep on a mat or to march here and there.

It's true that people serving soup to the poor are not forced to be there. But in what sense does introducing wages or profit or money generally change the nature of choice? Are the paid administrators of homeless shelters any less volunteers? Not at all. They are making a conscious choice to serve the poor, just as the unpaid "volunteers" are making a conscious choice to be there. They are all free to do something else.

Let's expand this to the for-profit sector. No one who works in retail or software or any other industry in a free economy is being forced to do anything. They are all there by choice, a result of having evaluated a variety of options and chosen one option over every other possible option (the opportunity foregone here is what might be called the "cost" of that choice).

The doctor who administers medicine, the lawyer who writes a legal brief, the salesman who sells you a suit, the clerk who rings up the total—these are all volunteers. The investment banker is a volunteer. The introduction of money into exchanges (and all actions, charitable or profitable, are exchanges) doesn't change anything about the nature of the action. It doesn't switch it from voluntary to forced.

This is not merely a terminological dispute. There is an ideological import to the use of the term "voluntary" to describe nonremunerative activities. It evidences a bias against the cash economy, as if monetary exchange and profit is a tainted motive, whereas the removal of money makes an action pure and beyond reproach. This is *completely* wrong.

It's time we demystify the role of money in society. It serves a useful purpose. Under barter, goods and services are exchanged directly for each other. That works for primitive economies, but once complexity appears, barter has its limits. You can't exchange a cow for an egg or an auto plant for a hat, because these goods aren't divisible. You need money to serve as a proxy for goods and services to exchange later.

Money also serves the vital function of permitting economic calculation, so you can know if exchanges are profitable (nonwasteful and productive) or yield losses (wasteful and nonproductive). Thus is the institution of money not inherently corrupt or tainted; it is highly useful and necessary, and arises merely in response to the desire of people to cooperate.

Give Back to the Community

"Give back to the community" is a phrase used to implore people who have been successful in business to donate their time, talent, and treasure to some cause besides their business. There is no arguing with the injunction to serve others, but there is a problem with the phrase "give back." It implies that people with money have taken something from others. But presuming that the businessperson has been successful through enterprise, their wealth comes not from taking but from *cooperating* with willing buyers.

Let's see how this works: When you need milk in a hurry, you dash to the convenience store and pick up a carton. You put it on the counter and the clerk says what you owe. At that moment, there is a calculation made. The clerk determines that he (or the person who employs him) values $2.50 more than the milk. You, on the other hand, determine that you value the milk more than the $2.50 you have been ask to pay for it. You exchange, and *voilà*—you are both better off as a result.

You have done a service to the convenience store, and the convenience store has done a service for you. The store is richer in money, and you are richer in goods. What do the two parties to the exchange owe each other afterwards? Nothing. What does justice demand? That they keep the bargain, and nothing else. The milk can't be sour. The check can't bounce. Nothing else is required or asked. Now, if the store clerk is sick and needs help, or the customer is poor and needs shelter, that's another matter. But what is asked in this case is completely unconnected from the results of the economic exchange.

Expand this logic more broadly, and we can see that it applies to all people who make money, even vast amounts. Even the richest person, provided the riches comes from mutually beneficial exchange, does not need to give anything "back" to the community, because this person took nothing *out* of the community. Indeed, the reverse is true: Enterprises give to the community. Their owners take huge risks, and front the money for investment, precisely with the goal of serving others. Their riches are signs that they have achieved their aims.

Labor of Love

The phrase "labor of love" is used as a kind of euphemism for doing work without pay. It is an apt phrase if it means only that the person is so wild for his work that he is willing to do it even when there is no remuneration. But the phrase is also laden with the implication that if you are getting paid, it is not a labor of love.

Surely the most successful employees are those who love their work. That they receive salaries or wages in return for services offered only serves as a sign and a symbol of the value that the business owner attaches to that work. They are cooperating to their mutual satisfaction, which one might say is a form of showing love. In that way, all labor in a free market is a labor of love. Both parties are giving and receiving.

Another unfortunate way to use this phrase is to imply that if you refuse to work without wages, you are not showing love. It is an undeniable fact that the use of time means the use of the most valuable resource we own. If a worker gives up a day that he could otherwise use earning wages, he might be forgoing a few hundred dollars of income. This lost income is the cost; it is what he pays in order to pursue a "labor of love." So he is not merely foregoing income: there is a sense in which he is contributing what otherwise would have been his income to the cause he is serving instead. What if that money was meant to buy groceries or medicine for his children? In this case, doing a "labor of love" instead would be a cruel act.

It is even true of the wealthy businessperson. What if staying at work—even earning money—is the best way to serve the community? What if that person is a pharmacist or a doctor or a website worker who is helping to provide people vital information about religion or health or some other vital issue? Labor for wages is just as much a contribution to society as working somewhere else for free. What if a person is responsible for the well-being of thousands of employees? Is it not an act of love to stay on the job?

There is no point in claiming that love is involved only when donating your time at no pay. You can pay or be paid and still show love.

Again, this is not just about terminology. It is about the assumptions many people bring to the subject of economics as it affects ethics. People often take it for granted that the "cash nexus" is incompatible with clean living. We gain a clearer understanding of this issue by seeing that money and finance are merely instrumental institutions that serve the cause of human cooperation and human betterment.

Yes, we should volunteer in charitable causes, and give to the community, in labors of love. That may not mean serving soup in a homeless shelter. Indeed, it might mean pulling down a large salary as an investment banker for commercial real estate ventures. Once we understand that the market economy is not incompatible with social justice, but is rather a form in which authentic social justice is realized in the real world, we will be more careful with the language we use.

12

Are We a Self-Hating Commercial Society?

April 20, 2010

I'm on a Sunday walk and a nice boy tries to sell me lemonade. A budding entrepreneur! Still, I decline. So he strengthens his pitch:

"I'm donating the profits to stop child abuse."

Still I decline, and more easily now that he has linked his praiseworthy commercial venture with a big social pathology that a 12-year-old boy can't possibly solve — unless he is saving money to run away from home?

In one short day, it was about the tenth time that I'd been assaulted by social consciousness in the course of just going about my business. At the grocery store, I was assured that I would save the planet by purchasing this cereal and that bag of potato chips. If I bought this instead of that coffee, I would help poor peasants in some far-flung place achieve social justice. Some pennies from a sports drink were supposedly donated to cure muscular dystrophy. My coffee cup is so socially aware that it saves trees and thereby stabilizes the global temperature. If I use the following search engine, I help fund charities that are making the world a better place.

I have two reactions to all this static interference on what would otherwise be the clean lines of commercial society:

This proves that the traditional rap on capitalism is false. It is not only about private gain for the few. Business can be as enlightened as the individuals running them. Note that all this praiseworthy other-directedness is being accomplished within the matrix of exchange, which has wrongly been maligned as selfish. As we can see, there is no contradiction between doing good and doing well. All these innovations that merge the third sector of charity with the first sector of profiteering illustrate that capitalism can adapt itself to an age of broad-minded social concern.

Can we all please cut the sham and go back to plain old buying and selling?

Reaction No. 2 is dominating my thoughts here.

Very few of the claims of these enterprises really stand up to any serious scrutiny. Take the coffee-cup case as an example. If buying this cup saves trees, an even better way to save trees is not to buy coffee at all. And it's not clear that lowering the demand for paper is going to actually save trees at all, since a lower demand would eventually mean less reason to plant and renew the resource. And do we really need to save trees anyway? Does someone know the optimal number of trees that are supposed to be alive on the planet at any one time?

The case of socially just coffee is the one that really gets my goat. The coffee plantations that pay the highest wages and offer the most benefits to their workers are the largest, most established, and most well-connected plantations. The smaller, family-owned plantations can't afford all these things, but they are less likely to have access to the rating agencies and export companies. Why, precisely, are consumers supposed to favor the corporate big shots over the family farms, and do so in the name of enlightened social consciousness? The whole campaign for fair-trade coffee is one of the most bizarre and contradictory schemes that the dumb-dumb Left has ever dreamed up.

On the one hand, it is part of the genius of capitalism that it gives rise to a class of entrepreneurs that can use any fashionable culture shift to make a buck. Whether a cereal is called "Sugar Smacks" or "Earthen Honey Morsels" is neither here nor there to me, and if some marketing genius figures that the cereal company can make more money with one name over another, good for him and the company. Capitalism is so darn good at what it does that it can even bamboozle muddleheaded socialists to cough up money for its products; that's wonderful.

And yet, I'm pretty fed up with the duplicity of the whole scheme. Consider that kid who tried to sell me lemonade. It is an admirable thing to set up a lemonade stand. He used his energy and time. He has to keep the ice cold and provide cups and persuade people to buy. He has to choose a good corner of the subdivision to do this. He might have had to buy his own ingredients. Will he make a profit? Nothing is for sure in this world. Most likely he will not and he will have to be subsidized by mom and dad. But what if he does make a profit? Wouldn't that be wonderful? There would be nothing at all wrong with the world in which this kid, who gave up his Sunday to sell refreshment, could put $5 in a piggy bank as a result.

But no, we can't have that! Instead, he has learned from the social ethos that he must never, ever admit to making private gain. He has to manufacture some phony tale about how he will donate all proceeds to achieving some grand social vision of a world without child abuse. Isn't it enough that he gives a dozen people some Sunday refreshment and takes away a few bucks?

Let's review the oldest contribution of liberal thought: The market society uses private gain to achieve social good, via the mechanism of mutually beneficial exchange. I buy a jug of milk and the shopkeeper takes my money. We both say "thank you" to each other because we have both given each other a gift and we are both better off. The profits in the form of money, if there are any after expenses, are used to expand production so that there are ever more opportunities for trade. Multiply these little exchanges and investments by the world's population and you have an ever-more beautiful and fruitful garden of peace and prosperity.

In this scheme, what is the role of giving to charitable causes? This is provided for by the growth of capital and wealth. When there is enough left over after providing for basic survival needs, people turn their attention to widows, orphans, the sick, the symphonies, art galleries, saving salamanders, promoting religion, establishing quilt-weaving societies, and billions of other causes — all of which are evidence of rising prosperity.

The direction of causation here is important. First: markets. Second: investment and exchange. Third: prosperity. Fourth: a zillion social causes that fall into the category of charity, social justice, and the like. Why is it that we are so fearful of telling the truth about this step-by-step plan for building civilization? Why are we so anxious to blur the distinctions between the stages?

What's more, if I want to give to charity, I'm perfectly capable of doing this on my own and according to my own values. I do not need business enterprises to intervene to help me along and show me the path to true enlightenment. When someone comes along to dictate to me what my values should be, I tend to push back. I just want products and services; I'll take care of the rest on my own dime. What is so complicated about this?

During the Haitian crisis earlier this year, I could hardly move from place to place without someone's demanding that I cough up for Haiti. It didn't matter if I had given $1,000 at the last stop, the not-so-subtle push at the next stop was for me to demonstrate that I care yet again. At some point during this mania, the number of people collecting for Haiti seemed to outnumber the number of people giving to Haiti by two to one. It's like there is some special social status to the class of charity collector, and we are all required to honor that.

How to account for all this giving mania? Maybe it is all just a racket. Call it the "cause racket." There are more bucks to be made by spreading guilt and pity than by offering goods and services. Therefore, everyone gets in on the act.

That's one theory, but it only goes so far. My own theory is that the anticapitalistic mentality has taken a serious toll. It hasn't yet destroyed commercial society, but it has caused commercial society to no longer be proud of the magic and glory embedded within its structures and logic. Why is this? Because we no longer understand how it is that markets convert private interest to public good. The simplest lesson of economics, proven again and again and again for 500 years, is lost on people today.

By the way, when that kid told me that he was raising money to stop child abuse, I replied as follows: "I hope you keep some for yourself. You have to make a living somehow."

His mouth fell open in shock. I hope he remembers what I told him, and I hope his parents don't hunt me down to accuse me of child abuse.

13

The Glories of Change

September 15, 2008

The events on Wall Street, the collapse of Lehman Brothers and the selling off of Merrill Lynch are magnificent and inspiring events. What we see here are examples of sweeping and fundamental change taking place, a huge upheaval that affects the whole of society, and toward the better, since what we have going on here is a massive reallocation of resources away from failing uses toward more productive uses.

Hundreds and hundreds of billions of dollars are on the move, sweeping all before them. And yet take note: it is not war accomplishing this. It is not violence. It is not the result of a planning committee. No election is necessary. No terrorist act took place. There was no government edict.

The agent of change here is the composite of all the world's exchanges that relentlessly shove resources this way and that way, so that they will find their most economically valued uses in society.

No one person is in charge. Layers upon layers of decisions by millions and billions of people are the essential mechanism that makes the process move forward. All these decisions and choices and guesses come to be aggregated in a single number called the price, and that price can then be used in that simple calculation that indicates success or failure. Every instant of time all around the world that calculation is made, and it results in shifts and movement and progress.

But as wonderful as the daily shifts and movements are, what really inspires are the massive acts of creative destruction such as when old-line firms like Lehman and Merrill melt before our eyes, their good assets transferred to more competent hands and their bad liabilities banished from the face of the earth.

This is the kind of shock and awe we should all celebrate. It is contrary to the wish of all the principal players and it accords with the will of society as a whole and the dictate of the market that waste not last and last. No matter how large, how entrenched, how exalted the institution, it is always vulnerable to being blown away by market forces—no more or less so than the lemonade stand down the street.

Dramatic shifts are essential for progress. But adapting to changing conditions and becoming an agent of that change, staying with the curve and jumping out in front of it—this is the real challenge. Enacting change—any kind of change, but especially big and fundamental change—sometimes seems impossible in this world. We all desire it and know it is necessary. Seeking the reality of rebirth has an appeal. But finding the mechanism to make it happen is hugely difficult.

Try to change an institution from the inside and you will meet resistance around every corner. Bureaucracies are nearly impossible to change. Even firms in private enterprise are reluctant to adapt, and have to be pushed and nudged by the accounting ledger or no movement happens. Churches and other charitable organizations can whither and die without periodic and fundamental change and upheaval. Many institutions grow up around the principle of stability first. The organizational structure tends in the direction of the protective mode, with everyone burrowing in and resisting doing something different today and tomorrow from what he or she did yesterday and the day before. Inertia is the default.

How to break away from this problem is a great challenge. The theory of democracy was that we would have a voting mechanism to enact and force change, but the problem is that votes and personnel shifts bring a change in the look and feel of government but do not get below the surface. Wars and revolutions yield change but at too great a cost. The change wrought by markets goes to the very core of the issue. It makes and breaks whole institutions, sometimes overnight. And it does so in a beneficial way for the whole, without blood and without the risk of unanticipated calamity.

All the plans of big shots, all the desires of our governing masters, all the wishes and dreams of people who imagine themselves to be larger and more important than the rest of us, melt like snow on a sunny day.

In this sense, the market is the great leveler, the force in the universe that humbles all people and reminds them that they are no more important than anyone else and that their wishes must ultimately be shelved when faced with the overwhelming desire on the part of market traders that some other reality emerge.

For this reason, everyone should celebrate the end of Lehman and Merrill. Overnight, while we slept, the seemingly mighty were humbled, the first made last and the last made first. The greatest became the least, all without a shot being fired.

14

Cooperation: How a Free Market Benefits Everyone

June 27, 2008

The following attempts to explain the most important idea in the history of social analysis. The notion (actually, it's a description of reality that is all around us but rarely noticed) has been around for centuries. It was first observed by ancients. It was first described with rigor by late-medieval monks working in Spain. It was given scientific precision in the classical period. It is the basis of advances in social theory in the 20th century.

In fact, it is an essential part of the case for freedom. It was the basis of the belief of our ancestors that they could throw off tyrannical rule and still not have society descend into poverty and chaos. The failure to comprehend this idea is at the very root of the pervasive bias against liberty and free enterprise in our times, on the Left and the Right.

I speak of the division of labor, also known as the law of comparative advantage or the law of comparative cost, and also known as the law of association. Call it what you will, it is probably the single greatest contribution that economics has made to human understanding.

This law—a law like gravity, not a law like the speed limit—is a description of why people cooperate and the ubiquity of the conditions that lead to this cooperation. If you can take a few minutes to learn it, you will understand how it is that society functions and grows wealthy even *without* a visible hand directing its path. You will also see how the criticism that the market economy leads to the strong dominating the weak is actually a sham.

This law shows how it is that people can gain, materially and in every other way, by working together rather than working in isolation. They don't just gain the sense of satisfaction that comes with participation in solidarity with one's fellow man; they can actually gain in the real stuff of life, the goods and services that are available to us all.

What's more, they gain *more* than the sum of their parts. Through cooperation and exchange, we can produce more than if we work in isolation. This applies in the simplest economic settings as well as the most complex ones.

It helps to lay this out more rigorously so that you can observe the magic of the marketplace at work. (I owe the following exposition to Ludwig von Mises in *Human Action,* Murray Rothbard in "Freedom, Inequality, Primitivism and the Division of Labor" and, especially, Manuel Ayau's *Not a Zero-Sum Game*, which is available through Mises.org.)

Let's say you and I can both make bagels and pies. But there's a problem: you make both with incredible efficiency. In fact, you do a better job at making bagels and pies than anyone who has ever lived. You are the world-class, all-time champion.

Meanwhile, I'm not so hot at either. My bagels taste as good as yours, but they seem to take me an age to make. My pies are the same way. I struggle and struggle, but try as I might, I just can't seem to crank them out the way that you can.

What is likely to happen under these conditions? The intuitive answer, which you will hear in just about every sociology class in the country, is that you will make all bagels and pies. No one else will. You will lord it over the rest of us, and have massive market power. If anyone wants either, he or she must come to you and you alone. You are privileged, favored, rich, powerful, and the rest of us can only sit in awe and beg from you.

But in fact, that's *not* what happens at all. Let's back up a bit and see why.

Let's say you and I have never met, and we are both making bagels and pies. Here is what happens in a 24-hour period: You make 12 bagels in 12 hours, and 6 pies in the remaining 12 hours. I, on the other hand, only manage to make 6 bagels in the first 12 hours, and a mere 2 pies in the remaining 12 hours.

Production in Isolation:

	You	You	Me	Me
Hours	12	12	12	12
Production	12 bagels	6 pies	6 bagels	2 pies

If we both work at this pace, the total production is 18 bagels and 8 pies.

In each case, the cost of what you decide to do is the thing you give up. So for you the cost of each pie is 2 bagels, and, likewise, the cost of each bagel is 1/2 of a pie. For me, the opportunity cost of making a pie is 3 bagels, and the cost of making a bagel is 1/3 of a pie.

Just looking at this, you might observe that you have your act together, whereas I'm pretty shabby. What chance in life do I have?

Well, my hope is bound up with the reality that your time and resources are scarce and you want ever more of each. So you begin to think about exchange. Even though I'm not very good at either pies or bagels, you can still see that you can make more of one thing or the other by encouraging our cooperation, thereby freeing up your time to do what you do best.

If you specialize in making pies, you still need some bagels. So you plan to exchange pies for bagels from me. With this thought in mind, you increase pie production and reduce bagel production. I, on the other hand, stop pie production completely and devote myself to bagel production in hopes of fobbing them off on you.

Production with Cooperation:

	You	*You*	*Me*	*Me*
Hours	*8*	*16*	*24*	*0*
Production	*8 bagels*	*8 pies*	*12 bagels*	*0 pies*

So you now spend a mere 8 hours on bagel making, in which time you produce 8 bagels; in the remaining 16 hours of your day, you are able to bake 8 pies. Meanwhile, I can now devote all of my time to bagel-making, and I turn out 12 bagels in 24 hours.

Let's total up the production. Before cooperation: 18 bagels and 8 pies. After cooperation: 20 bagels and 8 pies.

So what is the gain here? Precisely two bagels. Can you believe it? Nothing else changed; there was no increase in our productive potential, no increase in technology, no change in consumer demand or the weather or the linearity of history itself. All that happened is that we agreed to produce in cooperative exchange rather than isolation, and voilà—two additional bagels.

You think there's a trick? Go back and check the numbers and the assumptions. I'm just as shabby as ever, and you are just as fabulous. And yet there's a role for both of us.

Let's say we now exchange the goods we make. You might give me 2 of the pies you made in exchange for 5 bagels that I made. That leaves you with 13 bagels and 6 pies, while I now have 7 bagels and 2 pies.

After Our Exchange:

	You	You	Me	Me
Results	*13 bagels*	*6 pies*	*7 bagels*	*2 pies*

This would be reasonable, since those bagels you buy from me would have cost you 5 hours of production time. True, it took me 10 hours to make them, but what do I get if I exchange? I get 2 pies, which would have taken me 12 hours to make. So there is a sense in which I, by specializing, have saved 2 hours. And how many hours have you saved by encouraging me to make bagels? Five hours, during which time you made pies.

And what is the cost of exchange in material goods for each of us? You have given up 2 pies. I have given up 5 bagels. If our time is measured in terms of goods, you have given up the time equivalent of 4 bagels for 5 bagels, and thereby gained 1. I have given up 5 bagels but gained the time equivalent of 6 bagels, since my pie-to-bagel ratio is 3 to 1.

So who gained the most? In terms of bagels, we gain the same: one. In terms of time, I have gained more. In terms of pies, you have saved more. Who is the winner? Both of us. Again, what made us gain? Cooperation and exchange. Nothing more.

Now, you might say that this is absurd. No one sits around drawing exchange matrixes to see how we might benefit by dividing up the production. But in fact, we do this all the time. I might be a wonderful musician and web programmer. But my advantage is web programming, so I leave the music production to other people, even if they do it less effectively.

It's true in the business world: the boss might do an amazing job at accounting, clean-up, marketing, and customer support. He or she might do these things more efficiently than anyone else, but the cost of doing one thing is another thing given up. It makes sense to depend on others so that we can all specialize.

Consider the great 19th-century pianist Franz Liszt. He was the best and mostly highly paid musician in Europe. Let's say he was also a great piano tuner. Would it make sense for him to give up practice time for a concert that would pay him $20,000 in order to tune his own piano? Not at all. He would rather pay someone $200 to do that. The opportunity cost of piano tuning for Liszt was very high, but for the tuner, it was very low. They exchange, and both benefit.

It is the same with doctors and nurses. The doctor might be great at prepping patients, but in doing so the doctor is giving up performing another surgery that would earn him many thousands of dollars.

Note that this makes sense even if one person has an absolute advantage in every area. What matters for the real world is not absolute advantage but *comparative* advantage. That is where the law of association comes into being. It is true for two people, two hundred people, two thousand people, or all people all over the world. Herein we have the case for international trade, for it changes nothing about people's mutual advantage that they reside in different lands.

This is why it makes sense for both poor and rich countries to trade, as noted by Bartolomé de Albornoz as early as the 16th century:

> If it were not for these contracts, some would lack the goods that others have in abundance, and they would not be able to share the goods that they have in excess with those countries where they are scarce.

Note that these gains come not from design but merely from the freedom to associate, which Pope Leo XIII called a human right in his encyclical *Rerum Novarum*:

> If [the state] forbids its citizens to form associations, it contradicts the very principle of its own existence; for both they and it exist in virtue of the same principle, namely, the natural propensity of man to live in society.

Both the moral and practical advantages were reiterated by Pope John Paul II in *Centesimus Annus*:

> It is becoming clearer how a person's work is naturally interrelated with the work of others. More than ever, work is *work with others* and *work for others*: it is a matter of doing something for someone else. Work becomes ever more fruitful and productive to the extent that people become more knowledgeable of the productive potentialities of the earth and more profoundly cognizant of the needs of those for whom their work is done.

The law was formalized by David Ricardo in England, and further emphasized by economists ever since. The significance is impossible to exaggerate: It means that it is not necessary that all people of the world have the same talents in order to benefit from cooperation. In fact, it is the very *diversity* of the human population that makes it advantageous for them to work together and trade to their mutual benefit.

What this means is that isolation and self-sufficiency lead to poverty. Cooperation and the division of labor are the path to wealth. Understand that, and you can refute libraries full of nonsense from both the Left and the Right.

15

How to Handle Getting Fired

July 30, 2007

Wired Magazine this month offers a few pointers on how to disguise on your resume the fact that you have been fired. The main point is to come up with a negotiated settlement that has you resigning from your job. Many employers will go along with these because they fear litigation. There will be no "wrongful termination" lawsuits if you are on record as having left voluntarily.

I don't dispute this advice. It seems fine enough. But it doesn't deal with the much more important matter of how to handle being fired from a psychological and sociological point of view. The truth is that getting fired is one of the best things that can ever happen to you, if you look at it the right way. There is no reason to consider it the end of the world. It can be the beginning of great things.

The key to understanding this is to zoom in on the nature of a labor contract. It is an agreement based on the expectation of mutual cooperation that betters the lot of both the employer and thc cmployee. In a world without scarcity, the employer would rather do all work alone and not have to hire anyone. This would save in resources, and, in any case, most employers figure that they can do a better job than anyone that they can hire, and, often, they are right.

The very existence of institutions that are larger than sole proprietorships grows out of the need to divide the labor. Even if the employer is the best sweeper, web developer, accountant, and marketing expert in the world, it is to his advantage to specialize in one area while farming out the other tasks, even if these tasks will not be done as well by others. Every employer, then, regards the hiring decision with a combination of dread (no one wants to waste money!) and relief (finally I can get something done around here!).

It is critically important for the employee to understand that he is doing no favors to the employer by working there, nor is the employer to be regarded as a generous distributor of funds, much less someone who is under some positive moral obligation to dish out. The employee is there because the nature of the world and the ubiquity of the scarcity of time and resources make it necessary. In order for there to be peace amidst this arrangement, there must be mutual benefit, always.

When that mutual benefit ceases to exist, it is in the interest of both parties to dissolve the relationship. The employee can leave for greener pastures. In the same way, the boss can stop paying the employee in exchange for services that he no longer believes are a benefit to the company. To be fired only means that the employer takes the initiative in ceasing to fund further engagement. Both or either side of this exchange could be wrong, of course, but all human decision-making is speculative, and we can only act on the information we have.

Why would anyone want to hang around at a dinner party at which he is not wanted? It's the same way with a labor contract. If you aren't wanted, you should walk away and consider yourself better off as a result. No lawsuits, no complaints, no bitterness, no acts of vengeance. Just a clean and happy break.

Doesn't the reason you are fired matter? Not really. The employer doesn't always know the reason. He just knows it is not working out from his point of view, and he is perfectly within his rights to terminate the prior agreement.

Let me tell a quick story from my own work history. When I was in clothing sales, I was one of the top-ranked salesmen on the floor, but I didn't always see eye to eye with the owner-boss. One Christmas season, he told all the salespeople that all alterations had to be promised out three weeks from the date they were sold. That struck me as outrageous.

Sure enough, within the next hour, I had a customer come in and buy seven pricey suits, on the condition that all alterations were to be done within the week. Now, I should have gone to the boss and asked him. He would have said no, I'm quite sure. So I didn't: I went ahead and promised the suits out. At closing time, the boss found the tickets and threw all seven suits at me and demanded to know "who is going to alter these?"

I said, "I will," and I promptly hit the sewing machines and began to sew. I had them all finished by 9P.M. that evening. I brought them in to him and said that I would deliver them to the customer personally in the morning. My boss said, that's great, and added: "after that, I won't need your services anymore."

Was he wrong or right? He was wrong that firing me was good for his business. But he was right that he could not countenance an insubordinate employee, and just as a tip to the worker: there is no surer way to make yourself unwelcome than to be insubordinate. Even from a business point of view, he needed a staff that would follow his orders, right or wrong. Hey, it's not my style but it was his clothing store, for goodness sake. (I ended up as a manager in another store and we outcompeted his store in every season that followed.)

Being fired does not mean that your time with the company was a waste. In the time you were there, both you and your boss benefited in some way. Because conditions change doesn't negate that reality. The boss gained a worker. And you gained valuable experience—and one of the most valuable experiences is the shock of being fired. Sometimes it is the best way to get a person's attention. We all need improvement, and experiencing outright rejection provides a poignant reminder of this fact, and an impetus to change.

You might feel anger and even hatred. You might want to curse out your boss. You might plan a lawsuit (which seems to be everyone's first reaction). Instead, you need to do something completely counterintuitive. You need to thank your boss for having had confidence in you and for giving you the opportunity to work there. You need to say this as sincerely as you can. And when you see your boss at the grocery store or sports event in the future, you should bound up to him as if he were an old friend and thank him again.

If you do this, there might come a time in the future—in fact, there certainly will—when this person will be in a position to recommend you for a job. He is far more likely to do so. In fact, he might be so impressed at your magnanimity that he will offer you your job back. You can politely turn him down, if you so wish. The point is that there is nothing productive about resentment or hate, any more than you should hate the convenience store from which you no longer buy milk. You once benefited from exchange and you no longer perceive the advantage in doing so. Big deal.

If it makes it any easier, let us remember that you were most likely paid more than you contributed to the firm. Wages work this way. I can recall that

I worked with some jerk who refused to straighten inventory in the back room. "For minimum wage, I won't do this." But the truth is that he was paid far more than he gave back. An employer often pays wages in advance of productivity, hoping that he is making some kind of investment in the future. It is only later that you become productive enough to make it worth it for him, at which point he has to raise your wage in the anticipation of future productivity. So there is a sense in which everyone is indebted to the employer.

The worst fate to befall the American labor market came after World War II when employees began to think of all jobs as lifetime jobs—the way they are in economically backward and decaying Europe today. In a free market, we would hop from job to job without any problem. Employers would freely hire and fire, trying people out the way we try on shoes, and employees would be the same way. In this way, we are most likely to find the right fit, and our places of work would become less contentious—places of happiness and peace.

Nothing is more absurd than the attempt to restrict the right to fire. Voluntarism goes both ways. The employee can leave, and the employer can fire. Any other system, such as one that would restrict either action, is an act of coercion that diminishes the well-being of both sides.

Thinking of our kids here and their job experiences, we should hope that they get fired from at least one job or several in their early work years. Being fired reminds us of our obligations, the contractual nature of work, and the need for agreement and voluntarism in all social relations. The act of getting fired underscores the existence of the freedom of association, which is the key to social peace and a foundation of a growing economy. Do your part and take it well.

16

The Trouble With Child-Labor Laws

February 11, 2008

Let's say you want your computer fixed or your software explained. You can shell out big bucks to the Geek Squad, or you can ask—but you can't hire—a typical teenager, or even a preteen. Their experience with computers and the online world is vastly superior to that of most people over the age of 30. From the point of view of online technology, it is the young who rule. And yet they are professionally powerless: they are forbidden by law from earning wages from their expertise.

Might these folks have something to offer the workplace? And might the young benefit from a bit of early work experience, too? Perhaps—but we'll never know, thanks to antiquated federal, state, and local laws that make it a crime to hire a kid.

Pop culture accepts these laws as a normal part of national life, a means to forestall a Dickensian nightmare of sweat shops and the capitalist exploitation of children. It's time we rid ourselves of images of children tied to rug looms in the developing world. The kids I'm talking about are one of the most courted of all consumer sectors. Society wants them to consume, but law forbids them to produce.

You might be surprised to know that the laws against "child labor" do not date from the 18th century. Indeed, the national law against child labor didn't pass until the Great Depression—in 1938, with the Fair Labor Standards Act. It was the same law that gave us a minimum wage and defined what constitutes full-time and part-time work. It was a handy way to raise wages and lower the unemployment rate: simply define whole sectors of the potential workforce as unemployable.

By the time this legislation passed, however, it was mostly a symbol, a classic case of Washington chasing a trend in order to take credit for it. Youth labor was expected in the 17th and 18th centuries—even welcome, since remunerative work opportunities were newly present. But as prosperity grew with the advance of commerce, more kids left the workforce. By 1930, only 6.4 percent of kids between the ages of 10 and 15 were actually employed, and three out of four of those were in agriculture.

In wealthier, urban, industrialized areas, child labor was largely gone, as more and more kids were being schooled. Cultural factors were important here, but the most important consideration was economic. More developed economies permit parents to "purchase" their children's education out of the family's surplus income—if only by foregoing what would otherwise be their earnings.

The law itself, then, forestalled no nightmare, nor did it impose one. In those days, there was rising confidence that education was the key to saving the youth of America. Stay in school, get a degree or two, and you would be fixed up for life. Of course, that was before academic standards slipped further and further, and schools themselves began to function as a national child-sitting service. Today, we are far more likely to recognize the contribution that disciplined work makes to the formation of character.

And yet we are stuck with these laws, which are incredibly complicated once you factor in all state and local variations. Kids under the age of 16 are forbidden to earn income in remunerative employment outside a family business. If dad is a blacksmith, you can learn to pound iron with the best of 'em. But if dad works for a law firm, you are out of luck.

From the outset, federal law made exceptions for kid movie stars and performers. Why? It probably has something to do with how Shirley Temple led box-office receipts from 1934–1938. She was one of the highest-earning stars of the period.

If you are 14 or 15, you can ask your public school for a waiver and work a limited number of hours when school is not in session. And if you are in private school or home school, you must go ask your local Social Service Agency—not exactly the most welcoming bunch. The public school itself is also permitted to run work programs.

This point about approved labor is an interesting one, if you think about it. The government doesn't seem to mind so much if a kid spends all non-school hours away from the home, family, and church, but it forbids them from engaging in private-sector work during the time when they would otherwise be in public schools drinking from the well of civic culture.

A legal exemption is also made for delivering newspapers, as if bicycles rather than cars were still the norm for this activity.

Here is another strange exemption: "youth working at home in the making of wreaths composed of natural holly, pine, cedar, or other evergreens (including the harvesting of the evergreens)." Perhaps the wreath lobby was more powerful during the Great Depression than in our own time?

Oh, and there is one final exemption, as incredible as this may be: federal law allows states to allow kids to work for a state or local government at *any* age, and there are no hourly restrictions. Virginia, for example, allows this.

The exceptions cut against the dominant theory of the laws that it is somehow evil to "commodify" the labor of kids. If it is wonderful to be a child movie star, congressional page, or home-based wreath maker, why is it wrong to be a teenage software fixer, a grocery bagger, or ice-cream scooper? It makes no sense.

Once you get past the exceptions, the bottom line is clear: full-time work in the private sector, for hours of their own choosing, is permitted only to those "children" who are 18 and older—by which time a child has already passed the age when he can be influenced toward a solid work ethic.

What is lost in the bargain? Kids no longer have the choice to work for money. Parents who believe that their children would benefit from the experience are at a loss. Consumers who would today benefit from our teens' technological know-how have no commercial way to do so. Kids have been forcibly excluded from the matrix of exchange.

There is a social-cultural point, too. Employers will tell you that most kids coming out of college are radically unprepared for a regular job. It's not so much that they lack skills or that they can't be trained; it's that they don't understand what it means to serve others in a workplace setting. They resent being told what to do, tend not to follow through, and work by the clock instead of the task. In other words, they are not socialized into how the labor market works. Indeed, if we perceive a culture of sloth, irresponsibility, and entitlement among today's young, perhaps we ought to look here for a contributing factor.

The law is rarely questioned today. But it is a fact that child-labor laws didn't come about easily. It took more than a hundred years of wrangling. The first advocates of keeping kids out of factories were women's labor unions, who didn't appreciate the low-wage competition. And true to form, labor unions have been reliable exclusionists ever since. Opposition did not consist of mining companies looking for cheap labor, but rather parents and clergy alarmed that a law against child labor would be a blow against freedom. They predicted that it would amount to the nationalization of children, which is to say that the government rather than the parents or the child would emerge as the final authority and locus of decision-making.

To give you a flavor of the opposition, consider this funny "Beatitude" read by Congressman Fritz G. Lanham of Texas on the U.S. House floor in 1924, as a point of opposition to a child-labor ban then being considered:

> Consider the Federal agent in the field; he toils not, nor does he spin; and yet I say unto you that even Solomon in all his populous household was not arrayed with powers like one of these.
>
> Children, obey your agents from Washington, for this is right.
>
> Honor thy father and thy mother, for the Government has created them but a little lower than the Federal agent. Love, honor, and disobey them.
>
> Whatsoever thy hand findeth to do, tell it to thy father and mother and let them do it.
>
> Six days shalt thou do all thy rest, and on the seventh day thy parents shall rest with thee.
>
> Go to the bureau officer, thou sluggard; consider his ways and be idle.
>
> Toil, thou farmer's wife; thou shalt have no servant in thy house, nor let thy children help thee.
>
> And all thy children shall be taught of the Federal agent, and great shall be the peace of thy children.
>
> Thy children shall rise up and call the Federal agent blessed.

In every way, the opponents were right. Child-labor laws were and are a blow against the freedom to work and a boost in government authority over the family. The political class thinks nothing of legislating on behalf of "the children," as if they are the first owners of all kids. Child-labor laws were the first big step in this direction, and the rest follows. If the state can dictate to parents and kids the terms under which teens can be paid, there is essentially nothing they cannot control. There is no sense in arguing about the details of the law. The critical question concerns the locus of decision-making: family or state? Private markets or the public sector?

In so many ways, child-labor laws are an anachronism. There is no sense speaking of exploitation, as if this were the early years of the industrial revolution. Kids as young as 10 can surely contribute their labor in some tasks in ways that would help them come to grips with the relationship between work and reward. They will better learn to respect private forms of social authority outside the home. They will come to understand that some things are expected of them in life. And after they finish college and enter the workforce, it won't come as such a shock the first time they are asked to do something that may not be their first choice.

We know the glorious lessons that are imparted from productive work. What lesson do we impart with child-labor laws? We establish early on who is in charge: not individuals, not parents, but the state. We tell the youth that they are better off being mall rats than fruitful workers. We tell them that they have nothing to offer society until they are 18 or so. We convey the impression that work is a form of exploitation from which they must be protected. We drive a huge social wedge between parents and children and lead kids to believe that they have nothing to learn from their parents' experience. We rob them of what might otherwise be the most valuable early experiences of their young adulthood.

In the end, the most compelling case for getting rid of child-labor laws comes down to one central issue: the freedom to make a choice. Those who think young teens should do nothing but languish in classrooms in the day and play Wii at night will be no worse off. But those who see that remunerative work is great experience for everyone will cheer to see this antique regulation toppled. Maybe then the kids of America can put their computer skills to use doing more than playing *World of Warcraft*.

17

Generation Sloth

September 7, 2009

It's Labor Day, but there's nothing to celebrate.

On July 24 this year, the government raised the minimum wage to $7.25, which is another way of saying that unemployment is mandatory for anyone who is otherwise willing to work for less. You have no freedom to negotiate or lower the price for your service. You are either already valuable at this rate or you are out of the game.

Here is how it works. I've never been good at shaping pizza dough by hand, throwing it up in the air the way those guys do, so it would certainly cost more for any pizza joint to hire me at that high rate than I could bring them in revenue. I would be a sure money loser. As a result, the government has made it effectively illegal for me to attempt this kind of work.

This is done to help me, so they say.

This predicament is no longer isolated to a small sliver of the population that no one cares about, namely people who dabble in second careers (such as the pizza example) and the poorest of the poor. Now the problem is culture-wide, so perhaps someone will start to get interested in its causes and consequences.

August data show that more than a quarter of teenagers looking for work cannot find employment at the existing wage floor. Many have just stopped trying. The teen unemployment rate is nearly three times the national rate and it is four times the rate of skilled and experienced workers over the age of 55.

This is the highest rate ever recorded in the United States. The data have only been kept since 1948, but we can be quite sure that never in U.S. history have so many teens been so alienated from gainful employment and work experience.

These are the years in which young people learn valuable skills and ethics that they will carry with them until they die. At work, they meet a great variety of people and have to learn to deal cooperatively with different temperaments and personalities. They learn how to do things they do not really want to do and they also discover the relationship between work and reward. They gain their first experience with independent use of money—acquiring and spending—and how to calibrate the relationship between the two.

These are skills people draw on forever. They are far more important to their future than is the main activity taking up their time: sitting at school desks.

This portends terrible things for the future of the American workforce. People dumped on the labor market after college will be even more worthless than they are already.

And when I read that the "stimulus package" includes funding for job training for teens as a way of addressing this problem, I couldn't stop laughing: government-funded job training has a long record of being a full-employment program for tax-funded job trainers but otherwise amounting to a big nothing.

Interestingly, there is a corresponding trend affecting those who are getting their first jobs out of college. It turns out that half of college graduates under the age of 25 are working in jobs that require no college education at all. Think of Starbucks, the Gap, Target, and the like. Not that there is anything wrong with these jobs. But here's the thing: these positions used to be held by young people before they finished college (which is in turn devoting itself to remedial education on the basics).

Do you see what is happening here? The minimum wage, subsidized college loans, child work laws, and other interventions are conspiring to prolong adolescence as long as possible—to the point that these young adults are seeing as much as a full decade of life experience pretty well stolen from them.

And there are no signs that this will change once the recession ends; after the last recession, youth unemployment never recovered its losses.

Why are we not seeing the Million Teen March on Washington? Not everyone understands what is happening or why. I doubt that 1 in 100 teens would consider that the minimum wage is what is keeping them unemployed. And the college grads themselves are pretty well befuddled as to why the great promise of future riches if they "stay in school" is not panning out. Rather than be angry at government, most of these kids are merely cynical and dependent on periodic parental bailouts.

College students themselves lack work experience so they don't have a realistic understanding of what the work world requires of them. They major in "management" and imagine that, with this fabulous degree, they will possess the right to earn big bucks by bossing people around. A degree in "communications" will get them on Fox News. An "urban planning" degree will provide the opportunity—nay, the right—to build cities and highway systems.

Then the day of graduation comes and reality hits hard. There is no one who wants what they know, and, in fact, they know very little that makes them useful. Their resumes are barren, without a single professional reference or anything that is connected to the real world. All they really know is how to vegetate in class and socialize with peers on nights and weekends.

For example, I've been personally shocked at the lack of basic software skills that college grads have. There is hardly any professional position anywhere that doesn't require some facility with software and technology. Is this not common knowledge? I guess not: people are continuing to graduate today with no more technical skills than it takes to manage a Facebook page.

As for work ethics and the ability to add value to an enterprise (versus merely serving their own interests), forget it: generation sloth knows nothing about this.

It's probably not their fault.

Aside from the economic costs, the biggest cost is to the human character. It encourages the worst possible value system during the critical years in which character is shaped. Our country is caging people up for a quarter of their lives in government holding tanks and then dumping them on a cold, cruel world for which they are not prepared.

It's true that this trend began back in the 1930s, when FDR decided that he could help the unemployment problem by making it illegal for young teens to work (unless, of course, they are child actors like Shirley Temple). That's like losing weight by rigging the scale to lie to you. Ever since, federal law has tightened and tightened to the point that nearly the entire teenage population is being barred from the division of labor and otherwise told nothing about what it requires to be part of it down the line.

I end on an optimistic note, and not merely because it is customary. The digital age is providing ever more opportunities for people to make their own way in this world, outside the old definition of formalized work. The government closes doors. The market, incredibly and fortuitously, keeps opening them.

18

How Free Is the "Free Market"?

January 21, 2008

See if you can spot anything wrong with the following claim, a version of which seems to appear in a book, magazine, or newspaper every few weeks for as long as I've been reading public commentary on economic matters:

> The dominant idea guiding economic policy in the United States and much of the globe has been that the market is unfailingly wise....
>
> But lately, a striking unease with market forces has entered the conversation. The world confronts problems of staggering complexity and consequence, from a shortage of credit following the mortgage meltdown, to the threat of global warming. Regulation ... is suddenly being demanded from unexpected places.

Now, a paragraph like this one printed in the *New York Times* opinion section on December 30, 2007—in an article called "The Free Market: A False Idol After All?"—makes anyone versed in economic history crazy with frustration. Just about every word is misleading in several ways, and yet some version of this scenario appears as the basis of vast amounts of punditry.

The argument goes like this:

Until now we've lived in a world of laissez-faire capitalism, with government and policy intellectuals convinced that the market should rule no matter what. Recent events, however, have underscored the limitations of this dog-eat-dog system, and reveal that simplistic ideology is no match for a complex world. Therefore, government, responding to public demand that something be done, has cautiously decided to reign in greed and force us all to grow up and see the need for a mixed economy.

All three claims are wrong. We live in the 100th year of a heavily regulated economy; and even 50 years before that, the government was strongly involved in regulating trade.

The planning apparatus established for World War I set wages and prices, monopolized monetary policy in the Federal Reserve, presumed first ownership over all earnings through the income tax, presumed to know how vertically and horizontally integrated businesses ought to be, and prohibited the creation of intergenerational dynasties through the death tax.

That planning apparatus did not disappear but lay dormant temporarily, awaiting FDR, who turned that machinery to all-around planning during the 1930s, the upshot of which was to delay recovery from the 1929 crash until after the war.

Just how draconian the intervention is ebbs and flows from decade to decade, but the reality of the long-term trend is undeniable: more taxes, more regulation, more bureaucracies, more regimentation, more public ownership, and ever less autonomy for private decision-making. The federal budget is nearly $3 trillion per year, which is three times what it was in Reagan's second term. Just since Bush has been in office, federal intervention in every area of our lives has exploded, from the nationalization of airline security to the heavy regulation of the medical sector to the centralized control of education.

With "free markets" like this, who needs socialism?

So, the first assumption, that we live in a free-market world, is simply not true. In fact, it is sheer *fantasy*. How is it that journalists can continually get away with asserting that the fantasy is true? How can informed writers continue to fob off on us the idea that we live in a laissez-faire world that can only be improved by just a bit of public tinkering?

The reason is that most of our daily experience in life is not with the Department of Labor or Interior or Education or Justice. It is with Home Depot, McDonald's, Kroger, and Pizza Hut. Our lives are spent dealing with the commercial sector mostly, because it is visible and accessible, whereas the depredations of the state are mostly abstract, and its destructive effects mostly unseen. We don't see the inventions left on the shelf, the products not imported due to quotas, the people not working because of minimum wage laws, etc.

Because of this, we are tempted to believe the unbelievable, namely that government serves the function only of a night watchman. And only by believing in such a fantasy can we possibly believe the second assumption, which is that the problems of our society are due the to the market economy, not to the government that has *intervened* in the market economy.

Consider the housing crisis. The money machine called the Federal Reserve cranks out the credit as a subsidy to the banking business, the bond dealers, and the big-spending politicians who would rather borrow than tax. It is this alchemic temple that distorts the reality that credit must be rationed in a way that accords with economic reality.

The Federal Reserve embarked on a wild credit ride in the late 1990s that has dumped some $4 trillion in new money via the credit markets, making expansion of the loan sector both inevitable and unsustainable. At the same time, the federal bureaus that manage and guarantee the bulk of mortgages have ballooned beyond belief. The popularity of subprime mortgages is the tip of a massive but buried debt mountain—all in the name of achieving the "American dream" of home ownership through massive government intervention.

Say what you want to about this system, but it is *not* the free market at work. Indeed, the very existence of central banking is contrary to the capitalist ideal, in which money would be no different from any other good: produced and supplied by the market in accord with the moral law against theft and fraud. For the government to authorize a counterfeiter-in-chief is a direct attack on the sound money system of a market economy.

Let's move to the third assumption, that government intervention can solve social and economic problems, with global warming at the top of the heap. Let's say that we remain agnostic on the question of whether there is global warming and what the cause really is (there is no settled answer to either issue, despite what you hear). The very idea of putting the government in charge of changing the weather of the next 100 years is another notion from fantasy land.

The point about complexity counts *against* government intervention, not for it. The major contribution of F.A. Hayek to social theory is to point out that the social order—which extends to the whole of the world—is far too complicated to be managed by bureaus, but rather depends on the decentralized knowledge and decisions of billions of market actors. In other words, he gave new credibility to the insight of the classical liberals that the social order is self-managing and can only be distorted by attempts to centrally plan. Planning, ironically, leads to social chaos.

You don't have to be a social scientist to understand this. Anyone who has experience with public-sector bureaucracies knows that they cannot do anything as well as markets, and however imperfect free markets are, they are vastly more efficient and humane in the long run than the public sector. That is because free markets trust the idea of freedom generally, whereas other systems imagine that the men in charge are as omniscient as gods.

In one respect, the *New York Times* is right: there is always a demand for economic intervention. The government never minds having more power, and is always prepared to paper over the problems it creates. An economy not bludgeoned by powerful elites is the ideal we should seek, even if it has a name that is wildly unpopular: capitalism.

19

The Other Side of the Transaction

November 12, 2007

The cashier overlooked the milk in my shopping cart, so there had to be a separate transaction to process it. I paid for it with American Express, and it suddenly occurred to me to apologize.

"I'm so sorry for that. Your fees on that card will probably exceed your profit."

She looked at me as if I were speaking an unintelligible language.

"My fees?" she asked.

"Yes, American Express is the most expensive card on the market. You guys have to pay per charge and also a percentage of the transaction. This was only a couple of bucks spent here, so these fees can really eat into your profit margin."

"I don't pay any fees," she said.

It was at this point that I realized that we were on two different planets. She works for the company as a worker. The store makes a contract with her to show up and do certain things. She does them. She gets paid for this. That's the beginning and end of her economic role in the matrix of exchange. She is unaware that she is a consumer too, of the employment services offered by the store; these services must be paid for out of revenue generated by sales.

From this revenue, the business pays the clerk. The business pays the credit card company. The business pays tax. The business pays rent. The business pays for shelving and machinery. The business must acquire—usually *purchase*—the goods it sells before it sells them. In doing all of this, it is taking a risk because the profit is that last stage of the transaction; the expenses are paid earlier in the production process.

Here is the other side of the coin that the worker doesn't have to think about at all. Neither does the consumer. We walk into stores and think, "Wow, great stuff." Or, "What a bunch of junk." We examine the place to see if there is anything that would be valuable enough for us to acquire in exchange for the marked amount of money that the store wants from us. The deal is there for the taking. It is up to us to decide if we want to take it. No one forces us. If we walk away, there is no penalty for us.

We don't have to think about the strange reality that these retail and grocery stores carry millions in inventory. Tens of millions, all of it gathered together in one spot in the hope that we will like it and be willing to give our money in exchange for it.

I was in a sporting goods store the other day that seemed to have everything one can imagine. How much inventory? $10 million? $100 million? It was all beyond belief, and trying to run the numbers in my head boggled my mind. And here I was buying a $2 pair of socks. That's a tiny chink out of the inventory. They might clear 25 cents on that transaction after all the expenses are paid. And yet they did it all for me and others like me: consumers who are free to buy or not buy.

And then what does the store do with its profit after wages, expenses, and inventory? Why, it has to replace those socks that I just bought so that someone else can buy another pair. It has to expand more to compete with the new sporting-goods store that just opened up down the street, so it has to acquire ever more great stuff and sell it at the lowest price possible. There is no final victory in this battle. All profits are yesterday. All losses could be tomorrow.

To call enterprise a risk is really to understate the problem. Entrepreneurs have a special capacity to discern the uncertain future but they possess no power to actually create that future. It could be that tomorrow morning, no one will show up at the grocery store. That could persist through the afternoon, and so on through the evening. The same could happen the next day and the next, until the company goes bankrupt. And how long will that take? It depends on how much money the owners are willing to lose in the course of betting on a profitable future.

This crazy uncertainty of the future—a factor which we cannot overcome, no matter how much data we accumulate or how many fortune tellers we call upon—is a universal condition, always maddening and infuriating but completely unsolvable. It doesn't change for rich or poor. The largest corporation and the smallest lemonade stand face this trial in precisely the same way. Neither knows what the future truly does hold. The difference between the rich and the poor is how much money a person can afford to lose when he turns out to be wrong.

To possess a consciousness about the two sides of enterprise is a burden in some ways. It destabilizes you, and actually makes you wonder how the system can work at all.

How can a store hold on to millions in inventory and pay for it 25 cents at a time while being required by competitive pressure to expand ever more?

More questions:

How can a business employ hundreds, thousands, tens of thousands of people to produce goods long before they know with certainty that anyone will buy them?

Why are there such people as entrepreneurs who are willing to take all this on?

Why are they so unlike the masses of people who would rather act solely as consumers of all the glories that the free enterprise system dishes out?

These thoughts are the ones economic understanding gives rise to, and they are not exactly comforting. The old-style classical liberals reveled in the fact that all these "impersonal forces" worked without anyone really being aware of them, or having to understand them. The checkout lady at the store just shows up, pushes buttons, gets paid, and stays or leaves based on her assessment of her own well-being. Everyone else does the same. The pursuit of self-interest generates this amazing global matrix that benefits everyone.

The old liberals reveled in the fact that no one had to understand it, but then the system itself came under attack, and needed defense. It had to be understood to be explained, and explained in order to be preserved.

This is why Ludwig von Mises set out to revise liberal doctrine. It is not enough that people participate unknowingly in the market economy. They must understand it, and see how, and precisely how, their smallest and selfish contribution leads to the general good, and, moreover, they must desire that general good.

All of which is to say that in an enlightened world, it would be a good thing for that cashier to understand economics from the point of view of those who pay her. It would be good for striking workers to understand how they are harming not only their bosses but also themselves. It would be good for voters to see how supporting government benefits for themselves harms society at large.

An economically literate public is the foundation for keeping that amazing and wild machine called the market working and functioning for the benefit of the whole of humanity.

20

Lounge Lizards, Weak Wastrels, & Forgetters

May 17, 2002

Pity the businessman who hires someone just out of school! Most graduating seniors have lived a lush life in college, after living a lazy life in high school, and a goof-off life before that.

Graduating seniors know all about credit cards, popular culture, web surfing, internet chat, and PC politics, but next to nothing about what used to be called the work ethic. In short, they are worse than useless to the world of commerce.

What follows is a primer in 500 words, easy rules for how new workers can go from worthless to super valuable with nothing other than a change of attitude.

The current job market is tight, which makes it look very much like most job markets in human history: *workers are paid in proportion to what they contribute to the overall productivity of the firm.*

It doesn't seem possible, but this is the number-one fact about work that new hires do not seem to understand. So let me repeat it: People are not paid because they finished school. They are not paid because they got through the job application process. They are not paid simply because they now enjoy a new job title. They are not paid so that the firm can enjoy the privilege of their presence.

People are not paid for any of these reasons, or at least they are not paid for any of these reasons *for very long*. They are paid for only one reason: to make the firm more productive than it would be in their absence.

Moreover, if workers hope to keep their position and improve it, their contribution to the productivity of the firm must exceed the resources that the firm is putting into them.

I recall once when I was working in retail at the age of 16, the manager came by and told me and another employee to straighten up the some messy products on a shelf. After the manager walked on, my coworker turned to me and said: "I don't straighten shelves for minimum wage."

A few weeks later, of course, he wasn't getting minimum wage to do anything because he was tossed out on his ear. New workers need to understand that they are mostly overpaid, even vastly overpaid. The employer is making an investment in hopes that you will become more valuable over time. The point is that you must always strive to be worth more to the firm than you are paid to be.

Beyond understanding this elementary point, there are only five simple rules for getting by in the world of work. If you adhere to them, you will be an immense success in life, now and until the day you die. If you do not, you had better hope for a job in the government, join a union, or aspire to fulfill a quota.

Here they are:

1. Listen carefully to instructions and never expect to be told anything a second time.
2. Do a complete job, and do it better than your supervisor expects you to do it.
3. Work diligently to the point of discomfort, and without interruption or complaint.
4. Complete all tasks in a timely manner, meaning as soon as possible.
5. If you run out of assigned tasks, look for other jobs to do that help others and the firm.

That's it: five rules to a happy, productive job, to a happy, productive life. Do these sound absurdly commonplace? Perhaps. Why, then, are most all new workers, and many old workers, unable to understand them, or unable to follow through with them? It seems that people can pass their 22nd birthday these days without ever having encountered a setting where these things are expected of them.

There are a few more "don'ts" too. Don't get involved in office politics. Don't overstep the bounds of your authority. Don't envy the pay or working conditions of others. Don't be a smart-aleck. But these are just the finer points. The main point is to learn to be valuable to others by listening and following through. It's on this simple point where so many fail.

I know a wise man who says there are three types of losers in the world: The Lounge Lizard, the Weak Wastrel, and the Forgetter. Adhere to the five great rules of work, and you will be none of these. You will be immensely valuable to a business and therefore to the world. You will be constantly on the march toward better and better jobs. You will be happy. You will be financially successful. You will be loved, appreciated, and admired.

In any case, you won't be a loser. If you turn out to be, blame no one but yourself.

21

What Are Just Prices?

June 6, 2008

> "The kingdom of heaven is like a treasure hidden in the field, which a man found and hid again; and from joy over it he goes and sells all that he has and buys that field."
> — Matthew 13:44

We all have strange and contradictory wishes concerning what prices should be. We are outraged at what is happening to the price of gas and food. We don't think they should go up. In real terms, we want them to fall, and they *have* fallen in the last decade and a half. That's a good thing, right? That's how the world should work.

But housing? Now, that's a different matter. When the prices fall, people freak out. It's like the end of the world. How is it possible that my own home would fall in price?! That's not the way the world should work. Everyone knows that house prices are suppose to go up up up, all the time, without fail, until the end of time.

Same with stocks. We want to open the webpage that lists our portfolios and see the prices higher and higher all the time. When they fall, we flip out and demand justice.

But let's stop and think about how peculiar this is. What kind of theory of the world insists that houses and stocks always go up in price, whereas gas and grain prices always go down? That doesn't really make sense. A price is not set by natural law, nor are price movements intended to follow a preset pattern like the movements of stars. Prices are nothing but exchange ratios—points of agreement between buyer and seller. They reflect many factors, none of them fixed parts of the universe.

So why do we expect some to rise and some to fall? It all depends on whether you are in the position of a producer or a consumer. As homeowners, we are in fact "producers" of our homes; that is to say, we are holding them with the expectation of someday offering them for sale. The same is true of our stocks. We already own them, so of course we want the price to go up. Then we can sell them at a profit.

On the other hand, on things we intend to buy, things like gas and grain, we want the price to be as low as possible. We want their prices to fall. That way we save resources.

So what's at work here is self-interest. Think of the same situation from the point of view of someone who is a first-time homebuyer. Does this person want high prices or low prices? Of course the answer is obvious. This person wants the lowest price possible, so for this person this "housing bust" is not a bust at all. It is a boon. But once this person becomes a homeowner, matters change. Now he wants prices to rise.

Now think of the gas station owner. If it didn't affect how much he sold, would this person want prices to rise or fall? Of course, he wants the highest prices possible.

I recall once dickering with one of those insufferable car salesmen. I had my eye on some car and I said I couldn't afford it. He asked me how much I wanted to pay for this car. I said $0. He looked at me like I was crazy, but I was only telling the truth. I added that I know how much he wanted me to pay: a trillion dollars. And he reluctantly agreed. So how do the person who wants to pay $0 and the person who wants to get a trillion come to agreement? You find some meeting point in between, the point at which the car is worth more to me than the money I will give for it, and the money I will give for the car is worth more to him than the car. The resulting terms are called the price.

It's the same in all markets. We can see that it is perfectly absurd to attempt to fashion national policy around the interests of only one party to an exchange. To try to keep house prices high and rising cheats the first-time buyer. To keep them low cheats the current owner. To keep grain prices high helps grain producers but hurts grain consumers. Some gas companies might like high gas prices, but consumers hate them. On the other hand, gas prices forced lower by dictate might thrill consumers but producers might end up hurting so much that they shut down. That helps no one.

The only real answer here is to let the free market rule, which is another way of saying that people should be free to come to their own agreements about the prices they are willing to pay or accept for this and that. Those points of agreement should be as flexible as human valuation itself. That is to say, we should be free to change our minds, with each exchange taken as an end in itself, with no bearing on future points of agreement.

This is not only fitting with the needs of freedom—any attempt to force prices to do this or that does in fact impinge on our freedom to negotiate—but it is also essential to a well-functioning economy. That's because the price is heavily influenced by factors such as resource availability, the subjective valuations of consumers, and the profitability of the undertaking in light of accounting costs. In the end, the books have to be in the black. The prices that are accepted in the market must sustain this state of affairs. Even in mega-industries like oil, the difference between revenue and expenses can be surprisingly thin. Even small regulatory and tax changes can drive companies of all sizes to bankruptcy.

Prices are crucial to the wise apportioning of resources in a world with unlimited wants and limited resources. Prices affect the way in which we use things, whether conserving them or throwing them away. You will note that higher gas prices change the way you make judgments about going places and doing things. This is a good thing. Higher prices signal the need to conserve—and without unworkable mandates from government. And from a producer's point of view, prevailing prices provide crucial information concerning the forecasting of future profits, and hence today's investment decisions.

Now we must address the matter of justice. We think we know what a just price is. But do we really, and what actually constitutes justice in prices? What comes first to my own mind is the Parable of the Treasure in the Field. An unknowing land owner is just living day to day with no knowledge that there is a treasure in the backyard. Some other guy, however, has knowledge of the treasure, so he sells everything he has, knocks on the owner's door and nonchalantly says, you know, I would be glad to buy your property. The owner sells.

But let's be clear here: the owner did not know that there was a treasure back there. Nor did the buyer say a word about it, lest the price he had to pay go sky high. Today, people might say that the owner got ripped off. But Jesus doesn't say this. He holds up the buyer as wise and moral. Interesting, isn't it? Is there justice in this exchange? Most certainly. And why? Because they agreed voluntarily. That's all there is to it.

There is no way to observe an existing price and declare it just or unjust. As St. Bernardino—a shrewd observer of economic affairs—said,

> Water is usually cheap where it is abundant. But it can happen that on a mountain or in another place, water is scarce, not abundant. It may well happen that water is more highly esteemed than gold, because gold is more abundant in this place than water.

The Late Scholastics, followers of St. Thomas Aquinas, all agreed that the just price has no fixed position. It all depends on the common estimation of traders. Luis de Molina summed up the point:

> A price is considered just or unjust not because of the nature of the things themselves—this would lead us to value them according to their nobility or perfection—but due to their ability to serve human utility. But this is the way in which they are appreciated by men, they therefore command a price in the market and in exchanges.

(For more on the views of the Schoolmen on prices, see *Faith and Liberty: The Economic Thought of the Late Scholastics*, by Alejandro Chafuen.)

Now, there are ways for a price to become a matter of injustice. It can mask fraud. The prices can result from or be influenced by some act of force, such as price controls or taxation or restrictions on supply and demand. Behind each of these, we find coercion, a body of people who are mandating or restricting in a way that is incompatible with free choice. Arguably, this is not just.

We can conclude, then, that to the extent we complain about unjust gasoline prices, we need to look at the restrictions on refineries or exploration or drilling, or examine the role that high gas taxes have in pushing up prices beyond what they would be under conditions of free exchange.

And as for those who believe that all prices should move in ways that benefit their own particular economic interests at the expense of everyone else, don't confuse your agenda with a matter of justice. Prevailing prices in a business-based economy are a reflection of cooperative arrangements involving people with free will.

by imposing the costs of promotion and distribution entirely on the producer, while the choice to buy or not buy lies solely with the consumer.

But why must it be tacky and unbearable to so many of us? Well, let's be blunt: business is trying to reach the masses. Mises explains:

> "Business propaganda must be obtrusive and blatant. It is its aim to attract the attention of slow people, to rouse latent wishes, to entice men to substitute innovation for inert clinging to traditional routine. In order to succeed, advertising must be adjusted to the mentality of the people courted. It must suit their tastes and speak their idiom. Advertising is shrill, noisy, coarse, puffing, because the public does not react to dignified allusions. It is the bad taste of the public that forces the advertisers to display bad taste in their publicity campaigns. The art of advertising has evolved into a branch of applied psychology, a sister discipline of pedagogy.
>
> Like all things designed to suit the taste of the masses, advertising is repellent to people of delicate feeling."

A sister discipline of pedagogy? Yes indeed it is, and it is also art, and those with "delicate feeling" need to learn to appreciate it for what it is. They don't have to believe a word of it. Decline to drink the potion to make you thin. Refuse the breakfast that will make you concentrate. Eschew the hand cream that will restore moisture. Be as skeptical as you want and, instead, save every penny. Turn off the television if you hate it and sit in your perfect environment and listen to Gregorian chant.

But don't push for a system that would deny producers the right to persuade others, and don't deny others the right to make a choice for themselves.

22

The Economics of Here to There

January 17, 2007

Not being a television watcher, I was amazed to discover, from watching an hour or two of commercials this weekend, that there is a little pill you can take that will turn your body from portly and weak to thin and strong in a matter of months, if not weeks.

And how much better will be the eventual results if you acquire this thing called The Bean, which looks like a blow-up pool toy but is really the key to flattening your belly and giving you abs of extraordinary beauty?

Also, there is this cream that will *triple* the amount of moisture in your hands, and there is a gel that will stop hair loss, and, also, it turns out that I would have a greater ability to concentrate if I ate a good breakfast that includes Frosted Mini-Wheats, each of which talks and has a charming personality. And there's this nose spray that will help me breath better and play trumpet like a pro, which will thereby earn my son's admiration, just like on TV.

Such are the claims we encounter minute by minute on the tube, advertisements on which millions and billions are spent, just so that we will buy this instead of that. And the socialist says: what a ghastly waste it all is! They ask: what is wrong with the economic system as it exists that vast sums of wealth are consumed to get us to believe the improbable when, at the same time, whole populations around the world suffer without access to clean water and enough food to feed children? And so they propose a global regime to expropriate the capitalist class.

And yet it is not as if the capitalists welcome the chance to spend vast sums on television advertising. How great it would be if all a capitalist had to do was to create something, and that alone would cause the multitudes to flock to the warehouse and buy! Alas, that is not the way the world works. There are multiple competing ends for how we spend our money. The first step that is required to persuade those resources to be used in one way as versus another is to have the knowledge that a particular product exists. The second step is to persuade the potential buyer to make a choice in favor of a particular product. It is the necessity of human choice in a world in which information is scarce that makes advertising a feature of our world.

If they knew in advance that the millions they spend this way would be for naught, they would use the resources in other ways. The boss could increase his own salary, the company might lower its prices to undercut the competition, or attract better workers through higher pay. The resources it requires to promote your product are some of the most painful ways to spend a buck. It is pure speculation as to whether there will be a payoff. Even a temporary payoff says nothing about the future.

What the entire critique of advertising misses is the crucial and even decisive economic issue that is solved by the principle of marketing. How does a product or a service go from being a good idea or even a physical possibility to being available for people and available for consumption? Here is the major issue that has never been solved by any other system but capitalism. And capitalism solves it in a way that is wealth-generating and leads to constant improvements.

Thanks to the advent of mass blogging, many more people are acquainted with this issue than ever before. Let's say you take what is for most people a big and exciting step of creating a blog. There are so many sites now that make it easy. You sign up, you fiddle around with the look and feel, you add links, and the all-important "about me" page. You are ready to go.

You write your first post, thoughts you find funny, profound, insightful, or otherwise compelling in some way. Submit. And voilà! You are published in a medium that is accessible to the entire world. Who can believe it?

The thrill doesn't last long because you suddenly realize something that had not yet presented itself. Only your family is reading this. Maybe. It's true that anyone in the world can access it but why should anyone want to? How are people even going to find out about it? How can you be sure that people are going to come back again and again?

This is a striking problem mainly because it is something that hadn't actually occurred to you before. You created a beautiful product. You could create a profound post. But you must then persuade people to read it.

You might have read somewhere that the key to blogging is to do it often. So you blog and blog. You post three times, or even 10 times, per day. You keep this up for weeks, even months. Exhausted, you check your stats. They show no increase in readership. Still only your family is reading—or at least they claim to be reading.

You then turn to other means. You link, you beg for links, you turn on trackbacks. You try boosting your search-engine ranking. Finally, you take the step: you buy a spot on Google ads. Then things begin to happen. And then you marvel at how much time you have spent on this project. It seems that you have spent 10 times as much time promoting as you ever spent writing your blog. And yet what is the point of writing if you have no readers?

In this way, average people are beginning to see the great hidden cost of capitalist production: getting from here to there. And take note that with blogging, the problem of distribution is already solved. The final product is delivered via a click.

Imagine if you had a book or a tire or an air conditioner part to sell. That presents all sorts of new problems. You must produce something physical. How many? You must have a warehouse. How big? You must be prepared to process credit cards, do the accounts, meet a payroll. And you must do all of this, not after you have the revenue, but before! It all seems like a wild act of faith. It is indeed.

And keep in mind that the costs of distribution are not only a problem that faces the capitalist class. It also confronts the charity worker. What i I made a massive dinner and set it on the table and proclaimed that it wa reserved for the poor of the world. Well, there are a few steps missing, aren' there? No matter what your ideology, the reality that you must do somethin to get the food to those who need it is inescapable. The costs of promotio and distribution are far more vast than the costs of production alone.

In order to be willing to undertake such a thing and bear such hig costs, you must really believe in your product, or at least believe that yo have entered into some kind of sustainable undertaking. The prospect o bankruptcy looms large and relentlessly.

Am I saying that the inventor of The Bean really believes that it can giv you fabulous abs? Most certainly. And if used correctly, it probably doe The same goes for the hand-cream company, the mini-wheats makers, an the stop-hair-loss capitalist. These people are indeed believers. There ar such things as hoaxes, to be sure, but capitalism tends to discourage the

23

The Pope and the Cause of Freedom

October 24, 2001

Ten years ago, Pope John Paul II released Centesimus Annus, an encyclical, at once subtle and sweeping, that addressed the future of the post-communist countries of Europe and the general subjects of freedom, society, and faith. The document represented the fullest embrace that the Catholic Church has given in the modern period to classical liberal ideas, particularly as they apply in the economic sphere.

In *Centesimus*, the Pope argues that socialism failed, not just because it was bad economics, but mainly because it rejected the "truth about the human person." The state under socialism treats the individual, not with dignity, but as "a molecule within the social organism, so that the good of the individual is completely subordinated to the functioning of the socio-economic mechanism." As an alternative, the Pope recommends the "business economy" and the "free market" as "the most efficient instrument for utilizing resources and effectively responding to needs."

These observations are the conclusions of an in-depth discourse on the structure of society itself, with reflections on the place of intermediating institutions, private property, the price system, the division of labor, the family, and how all of them relate to the role of faith in sustaining a social commitment to liberty.

Pope John Paul II draws attention to the ways in which the commercial sector, rooted in voluntarism and cooperative work, sustains "solidarity," which comes not through coercion but through cooperation and exchange. *Centesimus* revives the idea of "subsidiarity": the view that problems are best solved by those people and institutions closest to them, and that outside interventions should take place only when necessary and only on a temporary basis. The coupling of these two ideas of "solidarity" and "subsidiarity" draws attention to the unlimited possibilities for human cooperation under freedom and the severe limits that must always be enforced against the power of the state.

The Pope is blunt on the nature of the total state:

> In the totalitarian and authoritarian regimes, the principle that force predominates over reason was carried to the extreme. Man was compelled to submit to a conception of reality imposed on him by coercion, and not reached by virtue of his own reason and the exercise of his own freedom. This principle must be overturned and total recognition must be given to *the rights of the human conscience,* which is bound only to the truth, both natural and revealed. The recognition of these rights represents the primary foundation of every authentically free political order.

He offers severe criticisms of the democratic state:

> Authentic democracy is possible only in a State ruled by law, and on the basis of a correct conception of the human person ... if there is no ultimate truth to guide and direct political activity, then ideas and convictions can easily be manipulated for reasons of power. As history demonstrates, a democracy without values easily turns into open or thinly disguised totalitarianism.

And of the welfare state:

> By intervening directly and depriving society of its responsibility, the Social Assistance State leads to a loss of human energies and an inordinate increase of public agencies, which are dominated more by bureaucratic ways of thinking than by concern for serving their clients, and which are accompanied by an enormous increase in spending.

The document is just as severe in its attack on the warfare state:

> I myself, on the occasion of the recent tragic war in the Persian Gulf, repeated the cry: "Never again war!" No, never again war, which destroys the lives of innocent people, teaches how to kill, throws into upheaval even the lives of those who do the killing and leaves behind a trail of resentment and hatred, thus making it all the more difficult to find a just solution of the very problems which provoked the war.

The Church is not a policy think-tank, nor an international planning agency like the IMF or World Bank, and thus warns that it "has no models to present." Civil society must develop organically from a healthy culture.

> Models that are real and truly effective can only arise within the framework of different historical situations, through the efforts of all those who responsibly confront concrete problems in all their social, economic, political and cultural aspects, as these interact with one another. For such a task the Church offers her social teaching as an indispensable and ideal orientation.

As versus the imposition of a particular political and economic structure, the Church echoes classical liberalism's claim that free societies, when circumscribed by individual moral conviction, are essentially self-ordering:

> Not only is it wrong from the ethical point of view to disregard human nature, which is made for freedom, but in practice it is impossible to do so. Where society is so organized as to reduce arbitrarily or even suppress the sphere in which freedom is legitimately exercised, the result is that the life of society becomes progressively disorganized and goes into decline.

Among the self-ordering systems in society is the commercial sector, which is based on private property, profit ("When a firm makes a profit, this means that productive factors have been properly employed and corresponding human needs have been duly satisfied"), the division of labor, entrepreneurship, and the business firm.

There's another reason the Catholic Church isn't proposing a political blueprint: even in its social teaching, the Pope is focused on the central mission of the Church, which is not building the kingdom of God on earth but evangelizing souls. The entire approach is oriented toward guarding human dignity and creating the social conditions that best enable man to work out salvation.

If Woodrow Wilson wanted to make the world safe for democracy, and George W. Bush wants to make the world safe from evil, John Paul II has an agenda that is more politically modest but more spiritually challenging: he wants to make societies safe for the spread of the gospel. He concludes that the best approach is a "society of free work, of enterprise and of participation."

It's no wonder that, on its release, *Centesimus Annus* was something of a new phenomenon. It was front-page news in the *New York Times*, and over the decade, the debates and discussions of the encyclical have filled many volumes. Its lessons and intellectual orientation are still being discussed and discovered, as are its intellectual antecedents (which include the Austrian School of economics).

Lacking in most of the discussion has been a reiteration of a basic tool for understanding the structure of social teaching itself. What is its status, and to what extent is it regarded as authoritative and binding? There are three general categories of argument in *Centesimus*: principles, historical observations, and applications. Only the principles are said to be binding on the conscience because these "involve the exercise of her teaching authority." As for analysis of history and the "new requirements for evangelization," they do "not fall *per se* within the Magisterium's specific domain."

Among the *principles*: dignity and rights of the human person, solidarity through human cooperation, subsidiarity and limits of state power, the advancement of the common good, the moral imperative of freedom and peace, the obligation to justice and charity, the universality of truth.

Among the *observations*: the failure of socialism, the success of the business economy, the advances in economic sciences, the problems inherent in democracy unhinged from morality.

Among the *applications*: the rule of law, the productivity of individual initiative, dangers of bureaucratization, the centrality of intermediating institutions.

Breaking the document down in this way (the lists could be much longer) helps to account for how the Catholic Church can at once claim that its statements are not contingent on time and place, and, on the other hand, only recently have given such a full embrace to certain free-market ideals. It's true that past statements on economics have stumbled, and even *Centesimus Annus* errs in its recommendation of a minimum wage, for example. These are applications that fall outside the teaching authority of the Church and are thus subject to change.

To fully appreciate the role of this encyclical in the history of our time, consider two points: 1) the Pope played a direct role in undermining the legitimacy of the communist states and thus bringing about their collapse, and 2) so surprised were Western intellectuals by the collapse that precious little work had been done to prepare for a transition to a post-communist era. When this Pope spoke on the matter, it created shockwaves that are still being felt today.

It is sometimes observed that ministers and priests face a special temptation to despair—and the same could be said of great scholars and intellectuals because they are forever preaching principles that people themselves will never live up to. Certainly, neither the U.S. nor the post-communist societies come close to embracing the full vision presented here. But it is the role of ideals to keep us on the right path and warn of the dangers along the way. It is here where *Centesimus Annus* succeeds the most.

24

Authors: Beware of Copyright

January 21, 2009

When an author signs a publication contract, insofar as it contains strict and traditional copyright notices, he is pretty much signing his life away. It used to be that the publisher would maintain control only so long as the book is in print. Today, with digital printing, this means forever: your lifetime plus 70 years.

During this time, you can't even quote significant portions of your own writing without permission from the publisher, and you could find yourself paying the publisher for the rights. You can't read your own book aloud and sell the results. You certainly can't give a journal a chapter.

You could try to be sneaky and change the text a bit, right? Wrong. They've thought of that. You will own and control new matter but the old matter is still the private possession of The Man.

What if the publisher isn't marketing your book? You can yell and scream but they don't have to answer. In fact, most publishers have a system for dealings with authors. It's called voice mail. Emails go unanswered.

You are done for. You sold your soul and you can't get it back. Not within your lifetime. Your creation, which copyright is designed to protect, is now the possession of someone else. This follows the trajectory as laid out in Michele Boldrin and David Levine's smashing new book *Against Intellectual Monopoly*.

As they explain, this racket began in the 17th century when government instituted the idea of ownership of ideas, precisely so that the government could crush ideas it didn't like. Only approved authors got the stamp of approval. Same with art. But then the authors and creators rose up and demand their rights in the 18th century, and the copyright idea was transferred from government to private parties, who were then in a position to crush competitors. In the 20th century, this changed again, when the right was transferred from individuals to corporations.

In the digital age that exists simultaneous to the most tyrannical copyright laws ever, this is creating an intolerable situation that amounts to a form of involuntary servitude. Creators write and paint and watch corporate interlopers doom their work to obscurity. The creator hoped to make a dent in the universe but only sees his material land in the recycle bin of history.

Yes, it is done by contract—contract backed by the power of the state. So why do authors put up with it? Mostly because it is a convention, and they haven't known about alternatives. Also, they are bribed by the ego-exploiting promise of royalties which never arrive.

The practical effects can be devastating. There is, for example, a book on Austrian business cycles that was published some years ago, and it is in print from an academic house, but in print only in the most technical sense. It is essentially unaffordable for anyone but a state-funded library with an inelastic demand curve.

The Mises Institute wants to bring it back in paperback and make it affordable. Nope, can't happen. The publisher says that it will do it for us, at a very high price with virtually no discount. They are in their legal rights to do this.

Of course it makes the whole project completely unviable. No deal. The authors are cornered. There is nothing they can do. There is nothing we can do. A great Austrian book, written over the course of ten years, is consigned to the dusty shelves of a handful of libraries, for at least another 70 years.

This is only one case of a hundred that I've seen. It is even worse when the author is dead. The publisher may or may not have handed back the rights to the manuscript. Those rights may or may not have been transferred. They may or may not have been handed on in the will or perhaps they are in probate.

Yes, a potential new publisher can hunt this down to find out who among six billion potential owners actually controls rights to this manuscript. A lawyer is always glad to spend vast amounts of your money doing research. He may or may not come up with an answer you can trust. Meanwhile, you have spent the equivalent of a first print run.

Most potential publishers will say: to heck with it. Again, you have failed to be immortalized by your work. This goes for art and musical compositions and even recordings of your band or voice. Thanks to federal law since the 1980s, all this material is bound up in a thicket of law, and this thicket will not evaporate for more than one hundred years.

This is what the "intellectual property" of copyright has wrought.

So I say to all authors: please look at your contracts. Don't sign your life away. Publish on the condition of Creative Commons. Claim your rights back as a creator and an author.

How does this work? You have to copyright your work, if only to prevent others from claiming copyright and thereby binding all other living persons, including you, from publishing it. Once you claim copyright, add that it is published under the Creative Commons License 3.0. This rids your manuscript or song or painting of copyright's provision of doom: the requirement that only one institution can control it.

In other words, it makes your creation part of the free market. It can be posted, recorded, shown, photographed, celebrated by one and all forever. Isn't this why you create in the first place? Isn't this what drives you to write, paint, photograph, sing, or whatever? You want to make a difference. You want credit for your work. This permits this.

Old-fashioned copyright is nothing but a form of modern tyranny in the digital age. It has no future. Bail out of this wicked institution and make sure that your work has a future too.

25

If You Believe in IP, How Do You Teach Others?

November 16, 2009

Some Harvard professors are taking very seriously their "intellectual property rights" and have claimed copyright to the ideas that they spread in their classrooms. What prompted this was a website in which students posted their notes to help other students.

The professors have cracked down. It might have been enough to legislate against this behavior in particular. Instead, they wrapped their objection in the great fallacy of our age: the professor owns his ideas and they may not be spread without his permission.

This action has opened up a can of worms, and now other universities have taken up the puzzling question: how do you at once enforce intellectual property and uphold the ideal of a university, which is, after all, about teaching and spreading ideas to others?

The problem is a serious one that highlights the absurdity of the notion that an idea—infinitely reproducible and thereby not scarce, and also taught with the overt purpose of gaining adherents among students—can be somehow contained and restrained once it is unleashed. The only way to retain exclusive possession of an idea is never to share it with anyone. But of course that not only cuts against the grain of teaching; it is contrary to the human impulse for bouncing ideas off others and still claiming some credit for innovation.

There are two possible ways out of this problem in a digital age: open source or IP. The open-source model has been adopted by MIT, which has made its entire curriculum open source and freely available online. This is a fairly straightforward approach, which finally gets down to the reality that what MIT is charging for is not so much the education but the degree itself. Clarity at last.

Another approach is the one taken by Harvard and, most explicitly, by the University of Texas, which has suggested that professors make the following contract with students:

> My lectures are protected by state common law and federal copyright law. They are my own original expression and I record them at the same time that I deliver them in order to secure protection. Whereas you are authorized to take notes in class thereby creating a derivative work from my lecture, the authorization extends only to making one set of notes for your own personal use and no other use. You are not authorized to record my lectures, to provide your notes to anyone else or to make any commercial use of them without express prior permission from me.

You can make "no other use" of what you learn? Really? That sort of smashes the whole point of education, doesn't it?

The goal of the university is to spread knowledge, not to grant a one-time use for what you learn in the classroom. The aim of an individual student is to gain knowledge that is used in every possible way for a lifetime—and to pass the ideas on to others.

In fact, what the contract requires is impossible. It is not as if our bodies are equipped with hard drives that can be wiped clean after the semester is over. In any case, even if we were so equipped, that would defeat the whole point of taking classes and paying universities for offering them.

I don't find this struggle ridiculous in the slightest. Once you posit the ownership of ideas already made public, this problem becomes inevitable. Of course the institution of teaching has been around since the ancient world, and yet this issue has never really presented itself before. But since the publishing mercantilists first asserted that property rights could be applied to ideas, the problem of what to do about teaching has been waiting in the wings. The advent of digital media forces the issue, because ideas, once stated, can spread globally in an instant.

I'm further struck by this problem in light of a fantastic new book on Ayn Rand called *Goddess of the Market*, by Jennifer Burns. The author isn't quite zeroed in on this issue as such, but she provides enough information to document the fact that for Rand the issue of her intellectual property became increasingly important throughout her life. She documents how

Rand's royalties from her work *Night of January 16th* gave her the first taste of financial independence, and how she later came to believe that she had not received enough. With each successive negotiation for book royalties and film rights, her terms became ever higher and ever more strict.

Now, in a free market, there is nothing wrong with an upfront payment for first-run rights to a book or movie. It is by being first past the post that profits are made. This was how artists were paid in the Renaissance: not through royalties, as if the artists owns the image or work, but through a payment that comes with granting some third party the opportunity to be the first to reveal the work. In the 19th century, for example, British authors would sell their manuscripts to American publishers, who could not copyright the work (there was no such thing as international copyright in those days). It turned out that the authors made more money through this means of payment than through royalties in their own country.

So on this score, Rand had perfectly sound instincts (a person should charge as much as he or she can for first run) but Rand's rationale was rooted in this modern notion of intellectual property, a theory, shared by nearly all her contemporaries, on which she was never once challenged. In fact, to a great extent, her philosophy exalted the role and rights of the creator more than any, probably, in the history of ideas. This is a great contribution, but she took the notion too far—for Rand, intellectual rights trumped real rights.

This comes through not only in her writings (*The Fountainhead* can be given a property-rights spin but ultimately it is about intellectual rights) but also in her personal relationships. Here, property in her ideas became a source of conflict with friends such as Isabel Paterson, with whom Rand was friends for many years. Tensions entered into the friendship when Rand accused Paterson of taking her ideas in the writing of *God of the Machine.* Paterson responded that Rand's contribution to the ideas in this book was minimal. They wrote back and forth and argued over specific instances of who said what to whom. They sorted through events in their associations, attempting to reconstruct them and divvy the ideas.

In truth, what had happened to Rand and Paterson is called a "conversation." One person says something, and another elaborates, which prompts new thoughts, new directions, new comments—a consensus—which then gets interrupted by new thoughts, points of departure, new elaborations, a new consensus, and so on. And if you know how Rand was, staying up all night in these detailed discussions of theory, you know that it would be simply impossible to sort out who owned what.

You can try this yourself with a friend. Talk for 15 minutes and then attempt to draw an ownership map of ideas. See if you can come to a consensus. Then see what the attempt does to your friendship.

Reading through the history of Rand's relationships with people, we find that this dynamic was pervasive—again, I'm not saying this as accusation but merely observing that it as an extension of her theory concerning the ownership of ideas.

This is particularly a problem for a theory of life that exalts independent thinking and creativity. What if the idea that one should be independent and creative itself actually came from someone else? One must constantly acknowledge one's debts. And, moreover, one should be cautious about remixing the ideas, lest the property right in the idea of being creative be stained and marred.

Marrying the idea of intellectual property to the notion of being independent generates extreme dependence and mandatory intellectual compliance.

The famed role of Nathaniel Branden in the Rand circle was to be not only a teacher of her theories but also an enforcer of Rand's intellectual property rights, which involved excluding people as much as it did including people. He was caught on the horns of a dilemma in many ways. On the one hand, he was seeking followers for Rand's ideas. On the other hand, he wanted to protect her ideas from being stolen (he probably wanted to maintain his own monopolistic possession of them).

What kind of person, then, are you willing to tolerate as part of the inner circle? It would have to be a person who would repeat the ideas of Rand exactly, without alteration, and constantly cite Rand for her innovation—and assert her right to the idea. Taken far enough, one can imagine the result: a drone army of people who footnoted nearly every phrase coming out of their mouths.

It was in the pursuit of intellectual property that Nathaniel intervened in Objectivist clubs to prevent them from using the word Objectivist, to prevent them from using quotes from John Galt, to prevent them even from advertising lectures on the topic by students of her ideas. As Burns demonstrates—but without clarity of causal explanation—the movement for Rand's ideas only really took off after Nathaniel Branden had been cast out of the inner circle. The monopoly on her ideas could no longer be maintained. They were set free (not fully open source, but at least far less restricted), and so they flourished.

Rand was not entirely happy about this transition. Her impression was not entirely invalid that people were "robbing" her of her thoughts: Rand was having a huge influence. Like the professors discussed above, however, she turned away from an open-source model and towards IP enforcement. Of the Libertarian Party, for example, she wrote, "it's a bad sign for an allegedly pro-capitalist party to start by stealing ideas." But this raises the question, *Would it have been better had the libertarians not been influenced by Rand?* From her perspective, yes: it was even worse when ideas were stolen and then mixed with ideas with which she disagreed.

The rest of the story played out as we might expect. She ended up feeling robbed and looted by everyone who was influenced by her. My own reading of her biography is that her belief that her ideas were property, led to her experiencing unnecessary grief. After all, it didn't have to be this way. She might have been proud of her role as one of the most influential intellectual forces in the second half of the 20th century.

Lacking a university position and a professorship, she actually managed to make the whole of the English-speaking world her classroom. But rather than be thrilled at what she had done, she had the opposite reaction, which is exactly what one might expect from a deeply flawed conception of intellectual property.

What Rand went through is precisely what these Harvard professors are going through: deep ambiguity concerning the application of property rights to their thoughts. Eventually, they will have to come to terms with it: it is the MIT model, or retirement from teaching, or a lifetime of bitterness. The MIT model is the model of the ancient world and every university environment ever since, and it is the only way to deal with a digital society in which every thought becomes globalized upon utterance.

26

Is Intellectual Property the Key to Success?

July 5, 2007

One of the greatest tragedies of intellectual property law is how it generates intellectual confusion among successful businesspeople. Many are under the impression, even when it is not true, that they owe their wealth to copyrights, trademarks, and patents, and not necessarily to their business savvy.

For this reason, they defend intellectual property as if it were the very lifeblood of their business operations. They fail to give primary credit where it is due: to their own ingenuity, willingness to take a risk, and their market-based activities generally. This is often an empirically incorrect judgment on their part, and it carries with it the tragedy of crediting the state for the accomplishments that are actually due to their own entrepreneurial activities.

Certainly there is no shortage of narratives ready to back up this misimpression. Countless business histories of the U.S. observe how profits come in the wake of patents, and thereby assume a causal relationship. Under this assumption, the history of American enterprise is less a story of heroic risk and reward and more a story of the decisions of patent clerks and copyright attorneys.

As a result, many people think that the reason the United States grew so quickly in the 19th century was due to its intellectual property protection, and they assume that protecting ideas is no different from protecting real property (which, in fact, is completely different).

A clue to the copyright fallacy should be obvious from wandering through a typical bookstore chain. You will see racks and racks of classic books, presented with beautiful covers, fancy bindings, and in a variety of sizes and shapes. The texts therein are "public domain," which isn't a legal category as such: it only means the absence of copyright protection.

But they sell. They sell well. And no, the authors are not misidentified on them. The Brontë sisters are still the authors of *Jane Eyre* and *Wuthering Heights*. Victor Hugo still wrote *Les Miserables*. Mark Twain wrote *Tom Sawyer*. The much-predicted disaster of an anti-IP world is nowhere in evidence: there are still profits, gains from trade, and credit is given where credit is due.

Why is this? Quite simply, the bookstore has gone to the trouble of bringing the book to market. It paid the producer for the book and made an entrepreneurial decision to take a risk that people will buy it. Sure, anyone could have done it, but the fact is that not everyone has: the company made the good available in a manner that suits consumer tastes. In other words, with enterprise comes success. It is no more or less simple than that. IP has nothing to do with it.

So it would be in a completely free market, which is to say, a world without IP. But sometimes businessmen themselves get confused.

Let's consider the case of an ice-cream entrepreneur with a hypothetical brand name Georgia Cream. The company enjoys some degree of success and then decides to trademark its brand name, meaning that it now enjoys the monopoly on the use of the name Georgia Cream. And let's say that the company creates a flavor called Peach Pizzazz, which is a great success, so it copyrights the recipe such so that no one can publish it without the company's permission. It then realizes that the special quality of its ice cream is due to its mixing technique, so it applies for and recieves a patent on that.

So this company now has three monopolies all sewn up. Is that enough to ensure success? Of course not. It must do good business, meaning that it must economize, innovate, distribute, and advertise. The company does all these things and then goes from success to success.

If you suggest to the founder and CEO that we should get rid of intellectual property law, you will elicit a sense of panic. "That would completely destroy my business!" How so? "Anyone could just come along and claim to be Georgia Cream, steal our recipe for Peach Pizzazz, duplicate our mixing technique, and then we'd be sunk."

Do you see what is happening here? A small change that would not threaten the very life of the business is indirectly being credited, by implication, for being the very life of the business. If that were true, then it would not be business prowess that made this company, but government privilege, and that is emphatically not true in this case. The repeal of intellectual property legislation would do nothing to remove from the business its capacity to create, innovate, advertise, market, and distribute.

The repeal of IP might create for it an additional cost of doing business, namely efforts to ensure that consumers are aware of the difference between the genuine product and impersonators. This is a cost of business that every enterprise has to bear. Patents and trademarks have done nothing to keep Gucci and Prada and Rolex impersonators at bay. But neither have the impersonators killed the main business. If anything, they might have helped, since imitation is the best form of flattery.

In any case, the cost associated with keeping an eye on imitators exists whether IP is legally protected or not. To be sure, some businesses owe their existing profits to patents, which they then use to beat their competitors over the head. But there are costs involved in this process as well, such as millions in legal fees.

Big companies spend millions building up war chests of patents that they use to fight off or forestall lawsuits from other companies, then agree to back down and cross-license to each other after spending millions on attorneys. And no surprise, just as with minimum wage or pro-union legislation, the IP laws don't really hurt the larger companies but rather the smaller businesses, who can't afford million-dollar patent suit defenses.

The Internet age has taught that it is ultimately impossible to enforce IP. It is akin to the attempt to ban alcohol or tobacco. It can't work. It only succeeds in creating criminality where none really need exist. By granting exclusive rights to the first firm to jump through the hoops, it ends up harming rather than promoting competition.

But some may object that protecting IP is no different from protecting regular property. That is not so. Real property is scarce. The subjects of IP are not scarce, as Stephan Kinsella explains. Images, ideas, sounds, arrangements of letters on a page: these can be reproduced infinitely. For that reason, they can't be considered to be owned.

Merchants are free to attempt to create artificial scarcity, and that is what happens when a company keeps it codes private or photographers put watermarks on their images online. Proprietary and "open-source" products can live and prosper side-by-side, as we learn from any drug store that offers both branded and generic goods inches apart on the shelves.

But what you are not permitted to do in a free market is use violence in the attempt to create an artificial scarcity, which is all that IP legislation really does. Benjamin Tucker said in the 19th century that if you want your invention to yourself, the only way is to keep it off the market. That remains true today.

So consider a world without trademark, copyright, or patents. It would still be a world with innovation—perhaps far more of it. And yes, there would still be profits due to those who are entrepreneurial. Perhaps there would be a bit less profit for litigators and IP lawyers—but is this a bad thing?

27

Books, Online and Off

March 22, 2004

Many people find themselves mystified as to why the Mises Institute puts books online for free that it is also trying to sell. For example, here is Llewellyn H. Rockwell, Jr.'s *Speaking of Liberty*. Here is Hans-Hermann Hoppe's *The Myth of National Defense* (which you can also purchase). And the most accessed of all: Ludwig von Mises's *Human Action*, in many different formats with an interactive index, even as the offline Scholar's Edition remains a bestseller on Mises.org.

Below is a detailed account of how we arrived at the policy that as many books as possible should be made available online and offline—and why we think it would be a good idea for all publishers to do the same. Of course Amazon.com has slowly come to this policy as well, and no one watches the relationship between information and sales as closely. At this point, they are limited only by a publisher's reluctance to let go. And here we are speaking of new books and issues of marketing and sales. The case for making older volumes fully available for purposes of education is even more obvious.

The point is to expand the market and not assume a fixed number of consumers. Books online and offline reinforce the viability of each other, just as movies in theaters boost movies in rental, and free radio helps the market for CDs for purchase. It takes some thought and entrepreneurial judgement to understand why, but the history of technological development informs the case. As one commentator put it on the Mises blog: "Nor did ideas written down in scrolls or illuminated manuscripts undermine the teacher/guru. Nor did knowledge in mass-printed books undermine schools/colleges."

The topic comes up because two weeks ago the Mises Institute released *Man, Economy, and State, with Power and Market*—by far our most time-consuming and expensive publication project in our 22-year history. At

$50, this hardbound, 1,550-page treatise on economics is an incredible bargain, but still expensive for any book. At the same time, the Mises Institute released a page with the full text of the book and Table of Contents in PDF to accomplish the step-by-step development of the full text in HTML. A number of readers commented that they believed this policy was generous but essentially nuts, and helpfully advised us that if we knew what was good for sales, we would take down this page immediately!!

Rather than take it down, it is our hope that people will put it in their favorites list and forward it far and wide. As a nonprofit dedicated to getting the word out about Austrian economics, and serving many people in the world who are interested in learning, it only makes sense that we pursue every viable means of doing so. To have the means of providing something as powerful as this book for free and not do so would amount to deliberately withholding the product pending payment from people who may or may not have the means of paying.

That prospect of withholding ideas when it would be easy to make them available has to make every nonprofit that cares about its mission somewhat squeamish. There is nothing wrong with making a profit but if that were the sole purpose and if doing so was financially viable, there would be no point in the non-profit structure that has existed since the ancient world. (For more on nonprofits as market institutions, see Rothbard's "The Myth of Neutral Taxation"). We gladly offer these texts at no charge simply because we believe that this is part of our core mission.

If that sounds implausibly high-minded, there are other considerations at work. There was much confusion in the early days of the web about whether online viewing would displace books. It didn't happen. In fact, the broad development of the web as a vehicle for commercial search and delivery has actually led to a boom in books sales, both new and used.

Also, experience suggests that online and offline books are different goods that serve different purposes (quick reference versus deep reading; quote checking versus extended study; etc.). What's more, these different purposes are complementary. On and offline books are complements (like bacon and eggs) not substitutes (like bacon and sausage).

All of this means that one does not necessarily cut into one's sales by offering the book online for free. By showing people what is inside the book, it is possible to increase sales of the offline book. The very existence of the online version means that the offline version becomes more valuable because now one can copy and paste quotations, easily refer back to the passage even when the book is not in hand, or send URLs around to friends or post them on the blog to make points. These days, if a book is not online, it faces an additional hurdle that it otherwise would not face (not substitutes or complements but tied goods, like piano strings and keys).

Here is a case in point. For some years, Misesians have worried about the status of Mises's wonderful book *Omnipotent Government* (1944). It was the first and still remains the most masterful study of the economics and politics of German National Socialism, perhaps the most anti-Nazi book published in its time. It demonstrates that the Nazi ideology was a species of orthodox socialist theory, and thereby corrects one of the most pervasive political errors of our time (that Nazism and Communism represent opposite ends of an ideological continuum.).

In any case, the point is that the book has long deserved far more attention than it has received. When it first appeared in 1944, from Yale University Press, reviewers saw it as a classic and expected it to have a huge impact. But many on the left and right had every reason to make sure Mises's book did not achieve a wider readership. For years, we've wanted to do something to correct for this.

Meanwhile, however, the current publisher would not allow the text to be put online through the Mises Institute. Many of Mises's books have been online and, as a result, were being referred to and quoted and discussed (and purchased) as never before. But not *Omnipotent Government*. It was not getting the attention it deserved, and, indeed, faced the prospect of forever living in the shadows of those books that are online.

After three years of letters, emails, and phone calls, we finally persuaded the publisher to let us go ahead, but we could only do so on the condition that we compensate the publisher in advance for all the lost sales they were sure that they would absorb. Their attitude is somewhat understandable. They figured: why would anyone buy the book now that it is being given away for free? They demanded an upfront payment. And so we paid, essentially leasing the book from the publisher. And, after lots of formatting and proofing work, we put it online here.

What happened was precisely the reverse of what the publisher expected. Instead of lost sales, the sales of the book shot up. In the few weeks since the text went online, more copies of this book left our warehouse than during the whole of the last decade. *Omnipotent Government* is now a top seller in the Mises.org catalog. The publisher not only obtained the leasing fee from our offices but suddenly enjoyed a flood of new orders for the book from us.

Most gratifying is how quickly ideas are disseminated in these times. Already commentators and bloggers have noted the parallel between the modern protectionist argument about outsourcing and the same arguments made by Nazi protectionists in the 1930s—citing Mises's study in particular. In only two weeks of being made available, the book and its arguments went from being invisible to being part of the circulating body of ideas that animate public debate. This experience illustrates the point very nicely that those who cling to copyright as a way of denying people knowledge are just wrong.

The same events repeated themselves with Mises's book *Bureaucracy*. Here is a book that offers a tremendously revealing analytical framework for understanding the public sector. Mises explains why government is inefficient, why it never seems to have enough money, why budget cuts seem arbitrary, and why there is no real way to know whether government is doing anything socially valuable or not. His analysis applies whether the bureaucrats in question are public-spirited or not. It is a very powerful work and yet it has long been obscured by the public-choice school's insights on the public sector—which, however valid, are not as foundational as Mises's.

In any case, the book no longer lives in obscurity. It can again be part of the living debate of our times. Why isn't the case for making these texts available more obvious? Part of the error at work here is having an unnecessarily restricted view of the potential market for these books. If you believe that they are bought only by a small group of libertarians or Misesians whom you have known from various conferences in the past, or you believe that the number of Misesians will always be restricted to a tiny remnant, you might believe that you must configure offerings in a way that somehow traps these people into purchasing a product.

But when you realize that the market for libertarian/Misesian books has been vastly underestimated and artificially restricted due to technological considerations, it is easy to see that an online text does great good on its own as an educational tool. The market for Misesian theory, delivered via whatever means one can conjure up, is not fixed but rather potentially enormous: it is just a matter of getting the word out.

We are hard at work doing this to other Mises texts as well, and putting up as many books as we can manage on a daily and weekly basis: Ludwig von Mises, Murray N. Rothbard, Frank Fetter, Fritz Machlup, Frank Chodorov, George Reisman, Hans-Hermann Hoppe, David Gordon, among many others. When possible, we like to offer full text, and a searchable and copyable PDF (which means more than just pumping the text through a scanner). Of course time and resources constrain us; making a searchable PDF is not a snap. A quality HTML, driven by a database, takes even more time—and money to pay for server space.

In any case, we try to make texts available whether the book was published yesterday or whether it is long out of print, and insofar as rights holders cooperate. This strategy makes sense to us both in terms of our educational obligations as well as our fiduciary responsibilities: doing good and doing well (or at least not going broke tomorrow). As with all exchanges undertaken on a voluntary basis, everyone wins.

28

Mises.org in the Context of Publishing History

October 26, 2009

[This speech was given on October 24, 2009, at the Birthplace of Economic Theory conference in Salamanca, Spain.]

Standup comedian Louis C.K. has a routine called "everything's amazing, nobody's happy." The gag has people on an airplane, sitting on comfy chairs and flying through clouds. They are complaining that the wireless connection is too slow.

There is truth here. Capitalism has made everything amazing, and yet everyone these days seems to hate capitalism.

Let's leave aside the problem that it takes economic understanding to see cause and effect. There is a more general tendency to take whatever material goods surround us as something granted by fate, our own personal state of nature, and a human right that is ours by a grant of justice. We fail to see our current wealth for what it is: a historical contingency that came about through the sweat and toil of generations that preceded us.

Its permanence is presumed. The goods are ours to redistribute by force if necessary. The services and the tools they require belong not to individuals but to all, so they can be taxed at will. Nothing can harm them or reduce their number.

I fear that the same is true with publishing. For only 500 years have books been copied by machines, after several millennia in which handwork was the only way to spread the written word. For only 150 years have books been available to all classes of society. Every innovation in publishing has meant greater distribution at ever-lower prices, culminating in today's print-on-demand methods and universal access. Digital methods have set the written word free as never before.

Kids today ask their parents, Were you born before the internet? They are vaguely aware that there was life before the web, but they conglomerate it with the days before automobiles and running water. There is something to this. The advent of digital media has meant a complete revolution in publishing, which makes Johannes Gutenberg's movable type appear as a mere stage of progress.

And yet, do we appreciate what this means for us? I don't think we do, not fully. And I worry that, failing to appreciate this, liberals in the Misesian tradition will not fully comprehend what it means to push the literature of our tradition into digital form.

If we could understand this meaning, we would be far more optimistic about the future, provided only that we believe in the power of ideas. So I would like to take a step back and have a look at the role of digital media in the history of publication generally.

Looking at the sweep of publishing history, the goal of all innovation has been the same:

- Lower the cost
- Widen the distribution
- Make the result permanent

There is no success for anyone who attempts to resist these three motivating forces.

There were sometimes tradeoffs between the goals. For example, the early scribes chose parchment over papyrus. Papyrus was less expensive, but parchment was seen as more durable and therefore the scribes' work would be preserved.

The work of a scribe was largely unchanged from the beginning of recorded history to the middle of the 15th century. The scribe in a monastery such as Salamanca would work every day for up to 8 hours, breaking for Psalm singing and Mass, and working with a whole team of other specialists in graphics and ink to produce perhaps one book per year.

Until this point in history, it might have been easy to believe that the book and all that it represents fell within the economic classification of a scarce good. This is to say that by its nature, a book cannot satisfy existing demand, must be rationed by price, and is radically finite, capable of being duplicated only with time and sweat.

It might have been easy to conflate the work that went into making the book, and the physical properties of the book, with the message and the signs in the book itself. In fact, these are really two different things, and all of the progress since has worked to delineate the difference between what is scarce by its nature (paper, binding, time) versus what is potentially capable of infinite duplication (the ideas and formulations in the book itself).

It was out of the institution of the scribe that the invention of printing came; not all at once, but over the hundred years preceding movable type, using leather and wood cuts and a variety of other techniques. The innovations began in monasteries. But with commercial printing came the most remarkable thing of all, a phenomenon that took books out of their scarce state toward their potential of being a completely nonscarce good. That phenomenon is known as the mechanized copy.

We can understand this by reference to the parable of the loaves and fishes. An apostle attending a sermon by Jesus had brought only enough food for himself. When the crowd became hungry, Jesus was able to copy his lunch infinitely and feed the entire multitude. The Gospels are careful to add that there was still more left over at the end.

This is precisely what printing made possible. The work on the ideas and the preparation of the first manuscript required time and labor on a scale few of us can even imagine today. But once the tools for printing were in place, an approximate copy of the original could be made.

Aside from paper and machines, there was nothing that limited the number of copies that could be made. The text itself was a nonscarce thing. To realize the unlimited potential of print became the dream of anyone with an idea to spread, whether it was in philosophy, music, law, or theology.

When movable-type printing appeared with the Mainz Psalter in 1457, it seemed that the institution of the scribe would be no more, and monks all over Europe debated what to do. On the one hand, the religious communities had the strongest interest in printing advances. On the other hand, the class of professional scribes associated with monasteries of course opposed the advance, in order to protect the high status of their specialized services.

After the development of printing, and then movable type, German abbot Johannes Trithemius exhorted his monks to continue to copy books. He claimed that printing had a shorter life, and that the automated printing technique denied monks the discipline associated with hand scribing. He worried too that the monks would have idle hands if printing became more fashionable.

But this concern didn't last longer than a few decades. By the late 15th century, the printing houses were working almost exclusively for monasteries, and monasteries themselves had established printing houses. Far from having taken away work for the monks, it became obvious that the new tool made their work more efficient. Their work could be made ever more valuable. The works of Trithemius himself, on a variety of topics, would eventually be printed in many editions.

Movable type made possible an unprecedented explosion in literary works. Michael Clapham says in his three-volume work on the history of printing technology,

> A man born in 1453, the year of the fall of Constantinople, could look back from his fiftieth year on a lifetime in which about eight million books had been printed, more perhaps than all the scribes of Europe had produced since Constantine founded his city in A.D. 336.

Other experts suggest that Gutenberg's commercial innovations led to an increase of book production by a factor of a thousand. About 115 books are attributed to the early movable-type printers. About 30,000 editions are attributed to the later half of the 15th century.

This increase is astonishing by the standards of the time but it is a blip on the screen in ours. After all, looking at Mises.org data, we can estimate to have sent some 100 million editions of our articles and books flying around the world. And keep in mind that this measures only the work of our servers, and doesn't include the thousands of servers around the world that host versions of our content.

Since we are in Spain, I would like to say a few words about the printing entrepreneurs from this country's 16th century. Their role in pushing history forward is not noted often enough.

Lambert Palmart (1440–1493) was the first printer in Spain. He worked from Valencia, the headquarters of commerce. He printed some 15 books in his career, which was an incredible accomplishment, the first in 1475. In Saragossa, there was also Matthew of Flanders, who printed four additional books. Seville was the third most prominent city for the expansion of printing in Spain. Here lived Antonio Martinez, Alonso del Puerto, and Bartolomme Segura, all of whom printed throughout the 1480s.

Tortosa was home to what became a vibrant and organized printing firm, which printed fully 28 books by 1500. Burgos was host to the firm of Frederick of Basel who was in business with Michael Wenssler, and they made 35 books. Another addition to the list of Spanish printing heroes is Arnaldo Guillen de Brocar, one of many so-called wandering printers who set up shop at Logrono, Alcala, and Valladolid. He, like the others, printed mainly Bibles and theological works.

Finally, our list would not be complete without mention of John and Jacob Kromberger, who set up shop in Seville with some partners and local workers and eventually came to print some 239 books of theology, law, medicine, and music. It was this firm that printed missionary tracts in Spanish to be sent to the New World, and Mexico in particular. They did even more than that: in 1539, they put together a full printing outfit and sent it directly to Mexico, where it printed eight books. This was the first printing press to appear in the New World.

So on behalf of the New World, I say thank you to Spain not only for the economic thought that made free enterprise thrive in the Western hemisphere but also for the first printing press to ever come to our shores.

For anyone in love with free markets, the 16th and 17th centuries was a time to witness that wonderful beauty of ordered production. New capital combined with new skills to bring the world more of what it needed and wanted. The rush into the book market by printers of all shapes and sizes, and in all countries of Europe, was a wonderful thing to behold.

But there was a threat on the horizon: mercantilism, the theory that producers needed special protection by government in order to remain healthy in an atmosphere of extreme competitive pressure. Producers were beginning to discover then what every business knows today: namely, that one aspect of free enterprise is that it denies long-run profits to producers.

The market process is always driving profits to zero, as profitable companies are imitated by innovative upstarts using cheaper and more efficient methods. Society benefits from this process, but in order for an established firm to stay on top, it can never stop innovating and striving for excellence.

The answer to this reality in many trades was to seek government protection from competition abroad and to ask favors from the prince to be the only and favored producer. This served both as a guarantee that people would continue to be provided with the goods and services they needed, and as a guarantee that the producer would be protected against the distraction of competitive pressure from others. That's the theory and practice of mercantilism, and it's a perfect recipe for hobbling progress.

Just as the printers had driven the scribes out of business, the printers were facing extreme competition by the 18th century. They sought protection from more efficient upstarts, often called pirates, who were making life hard for this very profitable industry.

These pirate firms were publishing older works and distributing them very cheaply and widely. The dominant firms claimed that this practice was undermining their ability to fund new works and was thus inhibiting innovation.

The established printers tapped into the mercantilist spirit, but with a special twist. They claimed that words on the page constituted a special form of property. When they were copied by a firm other than the current publisher, they claimed, their property rights were being invaded. Their "intellectual property" was being stolen.

Now, on its face, this is a preposterous claim. Once ideas are known by others, they are copied. They cannot be owned in the conventional sense. Another way of putting this is that the ownership of the ideas becomes multiplied without end. The only way to possess an idea as exclusive property is to never share it with another person. Once shared, the idea takes flight.

What's more, the entire industry had been born in the world of copying, not in making original work. Most famously, the most profitable text to publish was the Bible itself and its most ancient transcriptions and translations. In fact, this had been the driving motivation of the invention of the press in the beginning, just as it had been the driving motivation of the scribes.

For this reason, it is crucial to understand the appearance of copyright as nothing other than an aspect of the mercantilist principle. The claims about "intellectual property" were nothing but a ruse offered up by printers as a way of seeking legal protection from competition.

On the Continent, no one bought into this gibberish, seeing it for exactly what it was: a sop to producers, which would have inhibited the whole engine of publishing from the ancient world to the present. They saw that copyright does the opposite of the long-established goals. It raises costs. It limits distribution. And it dooms works to a short life, given the uncertainties of the industry.

This was a terrible direction to go, and in only one place in the world did it take hold: England, which was undergoing a terrible religious struggle. Copyright became useful to the crown in order to suppress works incompatible with the official religion, whatever it happened to be at the time. And so in the 18th century, there were endless fights in England over this matter.

Meanwhile, on the Continent, publishing remained competitive and free for the hundred years after the first copyright statute was imposed on England. Even given England's laws, copyright statutes were largely ineffective at hobbling the market process until the imposition of international copyright law in the late 19th century. Laws have grown tighter and tighter in the 20th century, until we have reached the point of absurdity since 1995 in the United States, with laws that have pretty well doomed a half century of scholarship to ruin.

If you leave the state and state-protected industries in charge long enough, they will strangle progress to the point that civilization completely stagnates. In the publishing industry, digital media couldn't have come at a better time. It is saving what the state and the dominant publishers are trying to kill.

The web and digital media are to the establishment what the printers were to the scribes, and what the pamphleteers were to the established book makers. Digital media threatens what they believe to be the core of their existence right now—namely the restriction of what should be completely free, and the imposition of scarcities on what should really should be nonscarce.

Let us return now to the three principles that drive progress in publishing: low costs, wide distribution, permanent results. The web has achieved all three in the most spectacular way. The marginal cost of downloads is approaching zero. The access is approaching universal. The capacity for copying is infinite. And the results are everlasting.

As you know, the Mises Institute is furiously posting as many works in the Austroliberal tradition as we can scan, and we are working at a pace and with a discipline that is on the order of the older scribes. Our entire literature archive is completely open-source, meaning that anyone in the world is free to simultaneously host our results. These editions are like fire. A spark can create a roaring blaze stretching hundreds of miles. This is the power of digital media. It has achieved the dream of every publishing innovation in all of human history.

When a new edition goes up on Mises.org, even before it is publicly linked, it is sent out via torrent to servers worldwide and immediately achieves immortality. It is archived on the site, and thus available to researchers and students all over the world. We have thousands of works available and the number grows daily. We are limited right now by copyright restrictions, but these are being chipped away steadily, and we push the envelope as far as we can.

One of the works that had been copied for hundreds of years, both before and after the printing press, was the *Etymologiae*, by the 7th-century, Spanish archbishop St. Isidore of Seville. The book summarized all knowledge up to the time it was written, including that of the ancient philosophers, and it somehow still had great notoriety in the 15th century.

Many of the Spanish printers of the 15th and 16th centuries busily printed Isidore of Seville's works. He not only was a brilliant intellectual; he had a passion for two great tasks: the preservation of knowledge through writing and the spreading of knowledge through copying and distribution. It is for this reason that St. Isidore was proposed as the patron saint of the Internet.

I think too of Mises himself, who labored for the six years between 1934 and 1940 to write *Human Action*, only to have it published in German in Geneva and have it vanish down a memory hole in the midst of ghastly war and global upheaval. He emigrated to the United States, where he started over again with an English translation, which was published in 1949 after much internal debate at Yale University Press.

After we became conscious of the power of the web, *Human Action* was our first giant project. Now we have it out in epub format, in which it can be downloaded an infinite number of times and fly around the planet at the speed of light. Seventy years ago, this work had a very unpromising start. It is now immortal. May we someday say the same of human liberty itself. With Mises.org and its supporters around the world, I do think that day will eventually come.

29

The Myth of the Cell-Phone Addiction

June 17, 2005

Pundits and bloggers are addicted to decrying the supposed cell-phone addiction of Americans. Calls for government to do something about it can't be far behind, especially considering the other claims that cell phones give us tumors, gut our memories, and jackhammer our brains. There are even reports of second-hand damage from others' cell phone use.

These articles go beyond merely claiming that cell phones are annoying—and truly people could learn some manners here, as in many other aspects of life. As regards this supposed "addiction," this is a word attached to any habitual behaviors of others we do not like.

What's interesting here are those who offer something like a Marxian-style critique of cell-phone use. We are alienated from society, we are told, and obviously tormented by loneliness, and thereby seek solidarity and community. But rather than seek out genuine connection to others, we reach for technology, the very thing that alienated us to begin with. We grow ever more dependent on our gizmos but they ultimately disappoint because they only cause addiction to machines and thereby increase alienation.

Also, we the oppressed long for empowerment and the ego-boost generated by the sense of importance granted by the idea of receiving and sending cell-phone calls. We can't stop using our cell-phones and yet they only further entangle us in an artificial world of machines created via the money matrix.

Oh just look at the cell-phone people everywhere! Surely this is the final stage of capitalism in which we ignore our brothers and sisters walking next to us but instead talk through electronic means to some distant party. And talk about what? About nothing: "It's, like, so cool to be on the phone!"

You can make this sort of critique up about anything, pepper the essay with references to Freud, Marx, Nietzsche, Kierkegaard, and, to stay in good with conservatives, the insufferable T.S. Eliot, finish it off with a hymn to primitivism—even a wish to return to the Garden of Eden without the taint of technological sin—and you have a winning piece of commentary.

It's all nonsense.

There is plenty wrong with this genre of criticism, as Tibor Machan points out (he found someone who regretted the invention of the mirror!). But let us address the cell phone in particular, because many people seem to have bought into the idea that it represents some sort of grave danger to the culture and an ominous sign of something or other.

Of course property owners are free to ban them or not. Burger King wouldn't, but a five-star restaurant probably would. Whatever is profitable. Private property solves whatever "problems" arise, but these are not any different from other problems of what dress, speech, and behavior is right for the time and place. Certainly there is no reason to ban cell phones on flights, as the FCC is considering; leave it up to enterprise itself to decide.

The critics, however, are not satisfied. They say cell phone addiction is a broader concern. To be sure, it's easy to defend the cell phone on grounds of its emergency services. With cell phones, people have never felt more safe and secure when driving or being out and about in potentially dangerous places. The critics will concede that. What drives them nuts is casual use, the whole middle-class casual culture of the cell phone, which seems to them wholly disgusting.

And yet it is the casual use of technology that makes its emergency use ever more economically viable. It is the demand for gab that has driven up the number of providers, driven down the prices, and made amazing technologies available to all, which then provides the spill-over benefit of making the emergency use of the same technology affordable and ubiquitous. A market of emergency-only cell service would not have become the mass phenom that it is today.

The appearance of addiction reflects a change in the use of public space made possibly by a new technology that was born into the marketplace only in 1994. Ten years ago, talking on the phone was a behavior that was tied to place, namely the home or the work station. Or there was the now-anachronistic phone booth.

In retrospect, it is obvious that a vast amount of productivity was being wasted by the requirement that we be strapped to a chair, or a room in our homes, or in a glass booth, in order to keep up with work duties, friends, and family.

Suddenly and almost like magic that changed. The cell phone made it possible to speak to anyone anywhere from any place. Think of it: what a dramatic transformation. For the first time in the history of everything, anyone can have direct personal contact with anyone anytime.

No more hiding out in the home, whiling away the hours with friends, or at the office, which used to be all about the phone but which is now all about email and instant messaging. Professional and personal uses of phone calls can take place anywhere. We can bluetooth our way through all informal life settings and get the most out of every minute.

Not only that: it seems obvious in retrospect that audio communications are an individual and not a community affair. When the telephone first came along, you had to walk to the post office or town market to use it. What a pain. Then there were lines shared by several homes. How tedious! Then there was one phone per household—owned and maintained by the government. Please!

The ability to completely privatize audible communication had been possessed by the private sector since at least 1947, but the government hogged too much of the radio spectrum to make it possible. It wasn't until 1994 that the government deigned to provide private enterprise what it needed to create a revolution in communication.

For this reason it is useful to think of the cell phone as a freedom technology along the lines of the world wide web. Both were developed by the private sector for the private sector. Both represent institutional revolts against the state's presumption to own and control the "command posts" of society. Cells and the web are the mode and means of liberation that the state will forever resent.

But back to the supposed addiction we all have. We are only making the best use of our time. What better time to talk on the phone than when other tasks are prohibited to us? You can turn driving into a multitasked operation. Same with walking to and from places. So too with shopping at the mall. These are the very times to pull out the cell phone, not as an addiction but as a means of making the most productive use of a period of time. It is a simple matter of economizing, that is, directing resources toward their highest-valued use.

But because our eyes see something new, something we haven't been socialized to expect, and because the market is expanding and democratizing so rapidly, it creates the illusion of something having gone oddly wrong. Instead of seeking to understand it, the temptation is to reach into pop culture's bag of ideological bromides and decry it as some sort of pathology.

The oddity of public phone use first dawned on the academic class several years ago when they would walk through campus and see throngs of students yammering away on the phone. Cell-phone addiction! Can these kids unplug themselves even for a minute to enjoy the scenery or talk to real people? Why should they be so very interested in their pathetic little materialist existence even after all the assigned readings from Veblen, Marx, and Derrida?

We need to realize something: these kids are walking to and from classes in which they must sit and listen and take notes for an hour or two. They are headed to another class where they will do the same. Or they might be headed to a library study session. Or they might be headed to the pool to meet friends.

In any of these cases, a phone call is not possible or desirable. But traveling from one spot to another? Shopping? Driving? It's just the time to call, even if only to leave a message.

Now, you might respond that these kids are not actually saying anything useful. They are engaged in conversational junk, punctuated by grunts of nothing. Well, productivity is a subjective concept. Meeting social obligations, making another person feel connected, letting someone know you care—these are all productive activities as understood by the individual speaking. Who are we to say what constitutes valuable or valueless conversations?

The pundit class has a penchant for judging the culture of freedom harshly. If, ten years ago, these same critics had walked up and down the block peering into people's windows, they might have spied people on the phone in every home. They might have decried this as a phone addiction but nobody would have taken them seriously. In fact, the response would have been readily at hand: mind your own business, bud, and get a life.

Actually that's not a bad response to most everything that comes out of the carping class of intellectuals who try to make us feel guilty and oppressed for using products that improve our lot in life. Modern technology has us all talking to each other again. That can't be a bad thing.

30

Another Central Plan Fails

December 31, 2002

For at least two decades, the conservative wing of education experts has touted one magic bullet (apart from vouchers): high-stakes testing. The idea is to subject students (and teachers too) to a standardized test that would create incentives to learn the basics, compel curriculum committees to toss out the fluff, yield reliable data for assessing performance, and inspire students and teachers to keep their noses to the grindstone.

In state after state for the last ten years, these tests have become the leading avenue for education reform. The trend began in Texas and spread. Now millions of students begin their first day of classes with a profound awareness of the impending make-or-break tests, to be taken at regular intervals from the first to the twelfth grade. On the face of it, it seemed to work. Curriculum committees threw up their arms in despair, teachers started teaching math and stopped teaching so much fluff, and everyone had a sudden sense of accountability.

A conservative victory? The Bush administration thinks so, which is why it is working toward the supposed dream of a national testing system. New data, officials say, can be generated that allow for a comparison between states, build proof of success, and otherwise allow for a better national system of education. The "No Child Left Behind" legislation uses carrots and sticks to impose high-stakes testing on states that do not currently use the system.

While the plan seemed sound on the face of it, the reformers forgot one thing: we are dealing with public school, which lacks any real means of operating in a sound economic (which is to say resourceful and rational) manner. Think of it this way. Let's say that Soviet grain production had been down for 3 years straight and some clique came up with the idea that the workers and managers needed clearer rules for daily operations. The plan may look good on paper, but in the end it doesn't address the underlying problem: the fact of central planning itself.

Central planning has several universal features. It is coercive. It bypasses the needs of the consumers for the sake of politics. It relies on edicts which may or may not reflect reality. It does not take advantage of the price system, profit, or loss. It is impervious to change. It ignores local conditions. It does not permit flexibility according to circumstance. It robs those who know the most of the ability of make decisions and innovate. It creates incentives to obey the plan but diverts attention from the real goal, whatever it may be (and it may be the wrong goal). It ends up overutilizing material resources, underutilizing human ones, and not generating the intended results.

All of these features have doomed the testing movement, at least if you take seriously the results of a new study from Arizona State University (http://www.asu.edu/educ/epsl/EPRU/epru_2002_Research_Writing.htm), the first to examine the issue nationally. The researchers have found an inverse relationship between the ability to pass the tests and the scores on independent assessment tools like the SAT and ACT. The latter come up with a measure of the student's mastery of the ability to think and solve problems. The school exams, on the other hand, only measure whether students have mastered the material on the tests, which are not thought-based but curriculum based.

It turns out that even as students have shown consistent improvement on state tests, the opposite is true with regard to performance on outside tests. After adopting these exams, twice as many states slipped against the national average on the SAT and ACT as gained on it. This turns out to be true across the board, even on math scores (with the exception of middle-school math). And the trend on Advanced Placement tests was also worse in states that had adopted tests.

What's the story? Well, the tests themselves have become the curriculum. That's all that teachers focus on, and they do so at the expense of teaching valuable learning and thinking skills. The one goal of passing the tests has replaced the goal of producing good thinkers, students, learners. The students are being trained narrowly (the school tests measure that) but not broadly (as is shown by SAT/ACT data) and hence the whole point of education is being lost.

Just as strikingly, the study also found an increase in drop-out rates. In fact, it is likely that the study underestimates drop-out rates because it relied exclusively on reported data, while most everyone agrees that there are more drop outs than are typically reported. Now, the conservative response to this bit of news might be: good! If a student isn't there to learn, better that he leave the classroom and cease to hold back those who do want to learn. And, in some way, there's a valid point here.

Yet, I think back to the story once told to me by former Soviet economist Yuri Maltsev. When the Soviet government became alarmed at the high death rate in hospitals, an edict was issued from Moscow that gave a quota on the number of people who could die under official care. The result was hospitals hurling people on their deathbeds out the front door and down the steps to die. They complied with the plan but missed the larger point.

Something similar may be happening with the high dropout rates. Teachers and administrators are probably encouraging failing students to leave school rather than drag down the aggregate numbers. One public school teacher revealed to me her tactic for dealing with the mandatory 90 percent pass rate. When she enters a class of 30, she identifies the three students she can ignore and otherwise write off as obvious failures. Now, this is not a cruel woman, just a person who knows what's necessary to survive in the new environment. She said all her colleagues do the same.

So while the results seem at first counterintuitive—how can testing lead to lower scores and more failures?—when you think about it, the results make perfect sense. Students are being run through a cruel gauntlet of narrow examinations produced by the politicians, while teachers are robbed of the ability to deal with the students as individual learners. This system might appear fine for the average student but the data can be deceptive. High-end and low-end learners are being neglected and those who ostensibly benefit are only given the tools necessary to master exams.

How do conservatives respond? They first point out that a lead researcher in the study, David Berliner, is a critic of school vouchers, and that the study was underwritten by an affiliate of the National Education Association, which opposes do-or-die tests. In other words, they are saying the people opposing this central plan are partisans of another central plan.

Granted. But what about the substance of the results? Chester Finn, an education official under Reagan, had this to say to the *New York Times*: "You almost never have a pure cause-and-effect relationship. Yes, you're introducing high-stakes tests, but maybe you're also changing the way you license teachers, or extending the school day, or changing textbooks. There's always a lot of things going on concurrently, so you really cannot peg everything to the high-stakes tests."

Aside from observing that his critique applies to all social-science research, which always and everywhere involves human volition and infinite variables, Finn's argument misses the point. The case for the tests was in part driven by the desire to be able to measure results in precisely the way the Arizona study has done. If you live by the data sword, you have to be willing to die by it too, and it is hard to argue against the reality that the new data has produced some very deep cuts.

Most compelling about the study is how it comports with anecdotal evidence. Teachers and students these days are obsessed with the tests, way beyond anything that anyone over the age of 30 knows anything about. The basics—reading, writing, math, science—are hammered home like never before. Preparation for tests has become the sum total of all public-school education. Advanced students are bored out of their minds, while weak students are relentlessly frustrated. Teachers wonder why they spent so much time learning how to teach, when all they end up doing is drilling for exams.

This new system is unsustainable, especially now that it turns out that the results produce the opposite of what it intended. Now, that is not to say that the alternative of left-liberal education policies—with no tests and no focus on basics or accountability—is the answer. The problem with education is more fundamental: it is run according to a central plan, so it has all the classic failures of central planning, including vast expense, vast waste of material and human resources, and results that are always disappointing.

The whole subject of education and the institutions that support it needs to be rethought, away from the still-surviving Deweyite-Progressivist model and toward the ancient tradition of private tutoring now being revived in homeschools across America. All schools can learn from the experience of homeschools, with their attention to individual needs, the flexibility that allows students to develop in unique ways, their privately run and funded character, their employment of localized knowledge and resources. These are the elements that make for good institutions of all sorts, whether it is commercial businesses, charities, civic institutions, or schools.

In short, the answer is not to adopt yet another central plan. It is to disempower the planners altogether, and restore decision-making power back to the parents, the teachers they employ, and the students. Testing and better data will not save education in America. A wholesale repudiation of all educational centralized planning will.

31

Department of Computer Security? It's a Joke

January 20, 2006

If you want to make a geek laugh derisively, suggest that responsibility for computer security be turned over to the government. This reaction is guaranteed, regardless of ideology. Everyone knows that this is not possible, but rarely are the implications for political economy noted.

Now, keep in mind that geeks know that producing fabulous looking and acting things for the web is only part of the job. These are people who spend a fantastic amount of time dealing with security issues, which change every season, day, hour, and even minute.

People know about viruses. Spyware and adware, meanwhile, are incredible threats to people's home computers. A new computer can be slowed to a crawl in a few days of quick browsing without good security against hijackings. And a huge industry has sprung up promising solutions, some good and some almost as dangerous as the thing they allegedly stop. Some of these are free, and some quite expensive, and the typical geek must work to discover what's what.

Other threats are less well known, such as the possibility that your own computer can be hijacked and controlled by other people who want to use it to store files or scan for other hijackable ports. This is mainly a threat faced by servers running large websites—huge magnets for hijackings and hacks—but it even affects home computers.

For example: I was recently talking to a technical administrator of a prestigious host of thousands of servers. He was amazed by the number of root-level compromises that had been taking place in recent months. The possible holes in people's systems are without limit. Software must be constantly upgraded. Even one small mistake can lead to data loss and disaster.

He tried a little experiment. He installed a new operating system on a new laptop, and disabled the firewall. He then hooked it up to a non-secure wireless network in an urban area. The first attack came in six minutes. In 12 minutes, the computer had already been hacked and was under the control of somebody or something else. All data on the computer was rendered vulnerable, available for looting or selling. In a few minutes more, it would have become a work station for more port scanning, denial-of-service attacks, or some other menacing behavior, and been added to the empire of servers being controlled by some of the world's smartest criminal minds.

Not that a good firewall and secure connection are infallible solutions. There is always a way in for someone with high-level skills and the will to take the risk. To keep threats away involves the technical equivalent of street fights between hackers and security professionals.

The fighters have similar skills; it's just that one group wears the black hats and one wears white hats. Some are criminals, some are saviors. The battle never stops. And yes, some of them change hats depending on their career prospects. The fight involves deploying skills that are far beyond what most any normal person could conceive of possessing. They can run circles around most computer science professors and even run-of-the-mill webmasters.

Some will rant and rave against the security holes in proprietary products such as those offered by Microsoft. And users of Internet Explorer would be likely to agree. The thing hasn't been properly updated in many years. It has not kept pace with the times, and so attracts web-based evil like a landfill attracts flies. Other products, however, are different. Server-level software is constantly monitored for holes, with updates sent out automatically and often (though not always as often as the people might like).

Still, open-source advocates say that this proprietary stuff is expensive and dangerous. The companies don't respond soon enough to threats, and no one but company employees can view the underlying code. That means that improvements come more slowly. With open source, the world community of programmers have access and work constantly to improve the product. To be sure, hackers too have access to the same code. So here too you have a battle between good and evil.

Among the good guys, there is a debate: should software holes be announced publicly (full disclosure) in the hope that the firms that work on open source will fix it before the hackers find out? But between the announcement and the fix, there is a gap that hackers can exploit. Perhaps, then, the hole should only be revealed to the firm or individuals who manage the open-source product (limited disclosure). The downside here is that the people responsible will lack the frantic sense of urgency that generates a quick hot-fix. Geeks thrive in emergencies, while non-emergencies fail to inspire.

So the debate over security rages furiously: open source or proprietary code, public security announcements or quiet revelations, development or risk? At any one time, all solutions are being used, with bulletin boards filling up thousands and thousands of pages of debate based on experience. Ideology can play a part here but, in the end, it comes down to what works best. And all the while, the war continues, pushed onward by the relentless pace of development and progress towards better living standards.

We haven't even touched on the war between the virus makers and the virus killers. The competition here is also intense. When a new virus is unleashed, the first firm to produce the fix wins new levels of consumer devotion and attention. A nothing company can become the next big thing by producing a fix for two or three viruses in a row, and doing it before the established firms get there. An established firm can lose its market edge in a month by failing to update its virus definitions in time. The difference between winners and losers in this struggle comes down to minutes, not days or weeks.

In this never-ending struggle, there are always tradeoffs between the pace of development and its security risks. No software is perfect. They all have bugs. But people demand development. The market never rests. We must all take some risk. How much is acceptable?

Competition prevails here too. A bad choice in favor of security over development can leave a company eating other companies' dust. A bad choice in favor of development over security can lead to bankruptcy in the face of a high-stakes security compromise. Geek personalities reflect this trade-off: some develop on live servers and deploy every beta the hour it appears, while others test and test and prefer only the tried and true.

All these fascinating details aside, keep in mind that the terrain on which these wars rage is wholly market based. The idea that any public bureaucracy could oversee the process is unthinkable. So let us ask the question again, so that the reader may join in the derisive laughter: in a world populated by black hats, should the government be the sole wearer of the white hat?

Actually, is there any point at all in giving a white hat to the state? It has no incentive to join the struggle. It lacks the calculational means to assess the trade-off between security and development. It lacks the entrepreneurial drive to produce either. The nature of the bureaucratic organization is to stay put, protect itself, and only move when kicked good and hard by political bosses.

As for the power to do good, how can anyone guarantee that it won't quickly become the power to do evil? If experience is our guide, the government in a position of authority is more likely to be creating viruses and spyware rather than stopping them. As for the impact of the law, I vaguely seem to recall some legislation passed a few years ago that made spam illegal.

Government can't produce software that can outsmart every hacker. Not now, not ever. But the government can violate liberty and waste vast resources in the attempt.

As important as computers have become, there are interesting implications here. On a day-by-day basis the security of these machines is a far bigger matter than the threat of terrorism. Whether we like it or not, and regardless of ideology, we all depend on market competition to bring us not only innovation but also to protect us in our dealings with information technology. It is not a perfect solution. It can be messy and fallible. But the market is the strongest and best hope for security, and the alternative is unthinkable.

How interesting that we have been told for, oh, some 400 years that government is the agency we need to give us the security that markets cannot give us. There are a thousand rationales why intellectuals have believed this, but none of them seem very robust by comparison to the experience of our times.

32

Society in Jail

April 10, 2006

"What are you in for?" the inmate of Lee County jail asked the new prisoner. "Rolling through a stop sign in my subdivision," answered the new inmate, to gales of laughter from others languishing in the same cell.

As they laugh, crumbs from their hard, dry sandwiches—distributed by the wardens twice per day—flew from their mouths to add to the debris of filth on the floor that was ground up by the cracked plastic sleeping mats and absorbed by the old, thin blankets inmates use to keep warm in this cold and wet eight-by-eight room.

The new inmate today joined 500 other prisoners, among whom were some of the most violent threats to society—but also people who, like Inmate 501, are no threat to anyone.

He had been trying to make his one phone call, to which you are supposedly entitled when you land in the big house. The phone would only call collect, even for local calls. That meant that it couldn't call cell phones. Most local services don't even have collect-call options anymore. So you dial and dial but the phone might as well be a prop on the wall. There is no way out.

There is also no way for you to be called, by anyone. You have no cell phone. No laptop. No book. No watch, and there is no clock on the wall. No one knows what time it is. No one who does know will tell you. Not even a single scrap of paper are you allowed to take into the cell after your arrest. You can only stand there in your paper-thin prison clothes and plastic sandals.

"Man, this is jail," someone screamed as the new inmate tried to dial for the tenth time. "Jail! Phones don't work in JAIL!"

So Inmate 501 stood for an unknown number of hours, hoping that he would be bailed out by his wife and kids, who had seen him handcuffed and dragged away from home after Sunday brunch. He also hoped that this would happen before he needed to use the toilet, which was filthy and frontally exposed to everyone, including the women coming and going.

The saga began last October, when he rolled through the same stop sign in front of a private swimming pool that he and fifty others roll through several times per day. He thought he had paid the ticket but he hadn't, and the court date came and went. He received no other notices.

But something interesting was brewing in local politics after he received the ticket. The local newspapers ran a series that claimed to unearth ticket-fixing going on in the Auburn city government. It seems that some friends of powerful people were getting their tickets dismissed. Auburn was already known for its lax enforcement but this had the whiff of corruption.

The papers lacked details but there were hints that the whole story was a result of a dispute between an elected official and an appointed city manager. The city manager later resigned or was kicked out.

The suggestion of corruption was enough to attract the attention of the FBI, which made some inquiries. The combination of the media pressure and FBI curiosity was enough to force a change in city policy. The new policy in Auburn would be total crackdown on ticket violators, particularly those that didn't pay and didn't show up to their court dates.

Now, usually people who don't show up for court dates for petty issues such as this are just contacted and eventually pay. But technically, they can also be arrested, just as this person was. When the city government is under pressure to show that it is not corrupt but good and clean and tough on crime, the result is that the fine print becomes a license for just about anything.

So in the last several months, the city has been busy issuing warrants for people who have outstanding tickets of any sort. Cops have been tracking down people in their workplaces, homes, on the streets or anywhere, and treating them all like violent offenders.

The new prisoner, for example, who had never been arrested in his life, still had discolored marks on his wrists where the handcuffs had been slapped on.

We tend to think of the law as some sort of oiled machine that works according to the regulations. The truth is that the law is administered by people with a great deal of discretion over how others are treated. The wardens and correctional officials can choose to humiliate a person in whatever way they want. They can put you in prison clothes that fit or in some that are way too tight. They can tell you the time or not. Leave you to languish or make a call for you. They can insult you and lie about your status or be kind.

The only sure way to elicit something approaching humane behavior from them is to crawl and beg like a dog. You are worse than a slave, because you have nothing of value to offer your new owners. You are worse than an animal in a zoo because you are of no value to your captors. They really don't care if you live or die. Those who do care cannot help.

No one has more discretion than the judge, who holds your life in his hands. You are dependent on his mood of the moment. If he lets you off easy, he considers himself benevolent. If he sentences you to 10 years or a life in prison, he is only doing his job. It's always your fault for not having been sufficiently subservient at the outset.

The dramatic change in Inmate 501's life occurred in the course of minutes. All it took was a knock on the door. It mattered not at all that the supposed crime was completely innocuous. Once you are on the wrong side of the law, your life is officially worth nothing to anyone but those who can do little or nothing to help you.

People talk of government compassion. But there is no compassion in jail, which is where anyone who resists the state—even in the smallest way—ultimately ends up. People talk of social justice but to implement it means requiring everyone to make a choice: obey or face humiliation and servitude.

Yes, people can "file grievances" or "sue," and that is always the first thought of anyone who finds himself in the hands of captors. But to whom do you appeal? Whom do you sue? You are here again appealing to the same class of people, the same group of coercive agents, who have robbed you of your freedom. Your rights extend only as far as your masters allow them to extend.

People who criticize government as nothing but beating, killing, and hanging—to use Mises's phrase—are sometime accused of using exaggerated and hyperbolic language. Surely government is more than that and is not always that. Something as simple as a stop sign doesn't beat you or kill you!

And yet, what the critics of government mean is that all law, even that which appears to be a mere guideline and a help, must ultimately be enforced at the point of a gun. It represents a threat to obey or lose all freedom.

This insight applies to all law, whether it results from a constitution, or from legislation, or appears out of nothing more than a regulatory body. Every regulation, no matter how small, is enforced at the point of the gun. Every tax can result in handcuffing and jailing and even killing those who fail to fork over. Hidden behind each mandate is an armed tough in jackboots and a bulletproof vest who is prepared to beat and kill to serve the state and its laws.

As legislation extends, so does the coercive arm of the state, its police powers, its jails, and its reach over society. It is like a poisonous fog that descends and grows by the day, seeping into every nook and cranny of life: schools, businesses, homes, churches. Nowhere is exempt. The sound of the jailer's key rattling grows louder and more ear-piercing. The culture of the jail, where people are treated worse than animals, proliferates. You can't move without risking life or limb.

At some point in his day, Inmate 501 heard someone holler out his name. The electronic click on the bars sounded and the door opened. He had been bailed out, $500 in cash having been extracted from his bank account and forked over to the city police. He was now free—pending payment of the ticket and another court date.

He left behind 500 others who are not so fortunate. Some of them are hardened criminals. Others are in jail for smoking pot. Others were in the same boat as he: a minor traffic violation gone wrong. None have rights. All are captive, like citizens in a city under military occupation where there is only violence and no law.

But how free is he really? He lives in a society where nothing takes place outside the purview of the state, which is to say that he will always live one step away from the prison cell that was his home for a day. One or two wrong moves and he has lost it all. All of society is not yet a jail such as you find in totalitarian societies or a society under occupation due to military conquest, but with every expansion of the state, the jailers get that much more power over all of us.

Their power is not always overt but it always lies in wait. This was triggered by a zealous cop looking to fill a ticket quota, and an attempt to clean up government from corruption—prompted by a media-driven non-scandal that attracted the attention of the Feds. It resulted in personal catastrophe. We really don't get all the government we pay for, and thank goodness. Lord protect us on the day that we do.

33

Victims on Trial: The Everyday Business of Courts

December 17, 2007

It is inherently implausible, if you think about it, that the state could be an effective administrator of justice, for which there is a supply and demand like any other good. Shortages, inefficiencies, arbitrariness, and high costs will be main features of such a system. And because we are dealing here with the meting out of coercion, we can add the presence of inhumane treatment and outright cruelty.

Even so, nothing had prepared me for what I witnessed in the courtroom the other day. Like a fool, I thought I might be able to beat a traffic ticket I received a block from my home. The policeman says I slowed almost to a stop rather than completely stopping at a three-way stop where there were no cars in any case. So my prize was a ticket.

The officer assures me that I'm not declaring guilt, but I have to sign this form anyway. I can challenge it on my court date. So, again foolishly, I decide not to go the route of everyone else—admit guilt and cough up—but instead to exercise my citizen's right to make a challenge.

I show up at court. Except that on my appointed date, the judge wasn't there. Why? They wouldn't say. Is he sleeping in? No. Taking a family vacation? Outrageous that I should even ask! Ok, then, how about I see the substitute judge? There is no such thing. But if I hadn't shown up I would go to jail for "failure to appear." How is it that he can fail to show up and everyone acts like this is normal? The clerk rolled her eyes.

Silly me. This is the state. Different rules apply to it as versus me. So I am given a new court day, six weeks later.

I show up again, and tell the clerk that I plan to say that I am not guilty. This moved my papers to the bottom of the stack, which is a very bad omen. I would end up sitting in the court room all morning, listening to some 40 cases of people who are not so foolish as to protest the judgment of the officer of the law.

But then again, it wasn't so bad. I got an education. It turns out that in a courtroom packed with purported criminals, not even one of the people who appeared before the judge was a danger to society. Nearly all were in for victimless crimes. The two who had perpetrated actual crimes—petty theft from Wal-Mart and the local mall—could have easily been dealt with without involving the state. So far as I could tell, the place could have been emptied out completely and our little community would have been no worse off, and massive human suffering could have been avoided.

But that's not the way it works. These people, overwhelmingly black and poor but dressed very nicely in the hope of impressing the master, found themselves entangled in the web, and thereby elicited the glare and killer instinct of the spider. How painful it was to watch and not be able to do anything about it.

The first case turned out to be typical. This was a person picked up for "public intoxication," which amounted to overcelebrating following a football victory and daring to walk on the government's sidewalks under the influence of one too many. Arrested, jailed, bailed out. Now was the time to face the judge.

What is your plea? Guilty, your honor.

What do you have to say for yourself? I'm so sorry that I did this and I won't do it again.

The judge then decides to be lenient. He gives the minimum fine plus court costs. I couldn't find any consistency in this pricing scheme, but generally it amounted to between $400 and $1,500. The judge asks the person to pay it now. When he says that he doesn't have the money, the judge considers a payment plan, contingent on the guilty declaring his income to the courtroom; it averages $400 per month.

How about you pay $100 per month? Fine.

Oh, and there's one more thing. The criminal's driver's license is suspended for six months. How can he get to work? That's his problem. It is a very special problem since the court has decided to loot the person of a quarter of his income during this very period. How can you keep your job?

Hard to say. Life is tough. And that's the price you pay for drinking a few beers and daring to walk on the sidewalk.

So on it went for person after person. Tragedy all around. Pointless suffering. There were other victimless crimes. There were a few people who smoked pot—and one who had carried a joint clip or some other drug paraphernalia in his car. There was a person who made a "false report," which seems to be lying to the policeman. He was dragged off to jail on the spot.

Another victimless crime of which these people tended to run afoul: "resisting arrest." I'd never thought about this charge much, since it is a rather stupid thing to be disobedient to the police. Still, we must ask questions. To protect oneself from danger, threat, and capture is the most basic of all human instincts. We resist criminals. We duck when someone tries to hit us. Maybe we fight back if we think we can win. We lock our doors to deter invasion and to protect our property and person. The right to resist being captured is the very heart of the idea of security.

Why is it that we are expected to utterly gut our instinct for self protection when the cops, for any reason they happen to manufacture on the spot, say we must? It doesn't matter if we are guilty or innocent, whether the cop is wonderful or wholly corrupt, or whether the crime was tiny or big: we must immediately turn into human rag dolls and obey our masters. And if we do not, and instead we walk away or run, we can be tasered and shot unto death. (The highly disturbing video of the Utah cop tasering the fellow who didn't want to sign a ticket provides fundamental insight here.)

Think what it means to criminalize what they call resistance. It means what we believe to be our rights and our freedom are really grants of privilege by the state and they can be instantly revoked on the whim of anyone with a badge. These poor souls in the courtroom were all under the illusion that they were free agents; they therefore ran and resisted when confronted with danger to themselves. Now they are learning otherwise.

But what about the actual crimes in the courtroom that day? A lady had stuffed a package of sliced ham or something into her purse while shopping at Wal-Mart. She was fined $800 and had her license taken away.

What do you have to say for yourself, asked the judge. "I'm very sorry. I need to find other ways to deal with my lack of money," she answered.

Yes, you do, because "we will not tolerate theft in this town," unless, he might have added, it is done by the judge under the cover of the law.

Oh, one more thing. This lady was banned from Wal-Mart for life. Now, this sounds extreme, but it was the only decision taken that day that had the feel of something potentially reasonable. Might Wal-Mart have handed down this penalty itself? Isn't this a good principle, keeping the thieves away from its store? Makes sense, perhaps not for a lifetime but perhaps for a year or two.

But there is one problem. Wal-Mart can't do that. Its shopping space is considered under federal law to be a "public space," even though it is entirely privately owned. You can't decide who you are going to let in or out so long as you charge no membership fee. You have to accept all comers. Only the state can ban people from public property. And so Wal-Mart must use the state's services. It is coerced like everyone else. A compassionate and reasonable private solution is against the law.

But keep in mind that this was a case of theft. The others had done no harm to anyone.

The machine continued to operate. The judge hardly looked up, not even to notice how well these nice but exceedingly poor people had dressed in an attempt to impress him. They and their lives meant nothing. It was all about keeping the machine working.

Finally 11 A.M. rolls around. The court has already raised for itself some $20,000, from my calculation. The judge says that there will be a short recess before he hears the not-guilty cases, mine among them. He will then assign public defenders to those whose income is low enough and then schedule jury hearings.

In other words, I would have to wait and then return at some later date. I realized that there was more involved in beating tickets than I knew. I would need to make it my vocation—and might not prevail.

My kids, who had come with me, persuaded me that this was hopeless and ridiculous and very costly. I should declare my guilt and pay the $200 and be free. They didn't want their dad entangled anymore in this system. This is what I did, and I was free to go and join the multitudes who put up with this system of blackmail and money extraction every hour and know better than to attempt to use the system to challenge it.

Most people in my position would have never gone to court, and they will never see just how cruel this system is for the poor, for minorities, and for everyone who gets tangled up in this web of coercion and legalized plunder.

But now I understand something more fully that I once only understood abstractly. I see how utterly ridiculous it is to think that the state can be the right means to help those who are poor or living at the margins of society. The state is their enemy, as it is for everyone else.

34

Officer Kanapsky, is it?

September 9, 2008

It's a suburban neighborhood, on Sunday morning. There is a three-way stop at which hardly anyone ever goes the other direction than the main one. But you often see a police car in the nearby parking lot, keeping his sharp eye out for evil lawbreakers. These are the dangerous criminals who slow down almost to a full stop that causes the car to shift back the other direction, but don't quite do this. Instead they do what is sometimes called a "rolling stop" which stops short of full immobilization. The policeman in the car regards this as "running a stop sign," as if you paid no attention to it at all, and he'll give you a ticket whenever he catches you doing it.

From the policeman's point of view, it's like shooting fish in a barrel. One recent empirical accounting at this intersection (I dragooned some neighborhood kids into keeping count) observed that more than 9 in 10 people do not come to what the law regards as a "full stop."

I should know about this because, try as I might to be a law-abiding citizen, I have now received my fifth ticket this year at this very intersection one block from my house. That's not a typo. Five! I know it sounds crazy—why the heck can't I obey those who are ordained to keep me safe?—but when you consider that I go through this intersection several times per day, I'm actually doing rather well.

It goes without saying that this is a racket. The city is many hundreds of dollars richer because of my penchant for lawbreaking alone, and probably hundreds of thousands richer if you include everyone else's.

But it wasn't until someone drew my attention to this link, (http://www.motorists.org/blog/traffic-tickets/police-officer-raise-stop-sign-tickets/) that I understood the full extent of what this whole racket is about. Yes, it's about money. But there is more to it than that. You see, it turns out that I'm an archetype, a person who rolls through stop signs in my safe neighborhood and then gets outraged when the ticket is issued and attempts to "fight authority" rather than pay up. So, fool that I am, I actually believe in "challenging the system." I take seriously the claim that I'm innocent until proven guilty. Can you believe the naïveté?

It's typical of suburbanites. We challenge tickets, especially frivolous ones. And this, it turns out, is precisely what the police want us to do, for reasons explained below.

So on the appointed court day, I leave the office to go to the courthouse to fight this ridiculous ticket. I sit for hours and hours until I'm given a chance to declare my innocence. All the while, the cop who stopped me stands at the back of the courtroom with his arms folded over his bulletproof chest. He is heavily armed. I, on the other hand, was searched before I even walked in.

If at this point I declare my innocence, I am given the opportunity for a trial with my own attorney, whom I must pay because I'm not poor enough to have the court appoint a lawyer even if I wanted it to. This trial is scheduled for sometime in the future, which means another trip to the courthouse, and another opportunity for the cop to enjoy the air-conditioned surroundings of the courtroom he rules. What chance is there for me? In the end, I would probably have to declare myself guilty of something or other, and pay a lesser fine; meanwhile I will have missed at least two days of work.

What's going on here turns out to do with the way policemen are paid. According to federal labor law, they are only allowed to be scheduled for patrolling up to 40 hours per week, just as the rest of us can only be scheduled to work up to a certain number of hours. Courtroom time—and by subpoena, they have to be there—often counts as overtime, meaning 50 percent more than they are paid for patrolling during regular hours.

In the case examined by John Stossel on *20/20*, a policeman named Officer Kanapsky made an additional $21,562 over his regular pay just by standing around in court. The more tickets he issued, especially for minor issues that outraged people are likely to challenge in court, the more money he made. This is a result of labor law. As the Department of Labor says, "An employer who requires or permits an employee to work overtime is generally required to pay the employee premium pay for such overtime work."

Now it starts to make sense. You and I—his employers, so to speak—are paying a premium for his court time, which is why he spends his patrolling time trying to goad people into going to court. The policeman is being paid time and a half to waste our time and to cause our insurance rates to rise.

In the private sector, permission to work more than 40 hours per week is a real benefit to the employee and the employer, though the terms ought to be left to the contracting parties. But in police work, this overtime permission results in a scam that causes police to engage in low-risk, high-revenue-earning activities that exploit the population.

It occurs to everyone who is given a frivolous ticket: surely the cop's time would be better spent stopping real crimes, not harassing nonthreatening citizens. Now we can better see why they do this. It may be a product of federal overtime rules, another case in which the ghost of FDR haunts us every day.

But what to do about it? Denounce the cop on the spot? That's not a good idea. It strikes you immediately when you are stopped by a policeman that there is a huge disparity of power at work here. You are effectively captured by them. You must comply no matter what. They have the legal right to use any method to keep you quiet and docile and to punish you to the point of death if you resist.

YouTube is filled with clips showing people being subjected to the latest weapon of choice: the taser gun. The police love the taser gun. It leaves no trace of physical injury. You are shot through with electricity, which causes frightening physical and mental convulsions, but there is nothing you can take a picture of. No bruises. No wounds. No broken bones. This is all the better for them—and all the worse for you.

Never forget what happens to you if you decide to run instead. That's a death sentence. Forget that the instinct to evade your captors is universal and deeply embedded in our mental/biological equipment. The state operates on the assumption that you are its slave when it wants you to be, and otherwise free in name only. This is especially true in the age of Bush, in which all police at all levels have morphed into militarized "security personnel." The friendly, helpful policeman of old civics texts seems to be a thing of the past.

In any case, the phenomenon of Officer Kanapsky raises fundamental questions not only about federal labor law but also about the role of the police in any community. Do they really stop crime? Sure, they arrive after a crime has been committed; they take fingerprints (those only seem to work in the movies) and file reports. In real life, however, crime prevention is due to the private sector: locks, alarm systems, and the like. This is what prevents crimes from taking place.

The police aren't so hot at prosecuting crime either, but for people who commit crimes like slowing down at a three-way stop. Yet we are all somehow under the illusion that the police are the reason we are safe. It is the core mythology of our civic religion.

If you do not believe that they do more good than harm, consider the unseen costs. What kind of private alternatives are being crowded out by the very presence of the police?

It is also deeply troubling that most people believe there aren't too many police but too few. How many are too many? What if one in three people were a cop? One in two? Maybe we should have two cops for every one civilian. How safe we would be! Really, there is an ethos in this country that you can never have too many cops on the street, and the idea of hiring more nearly always garners public support.

And yet, when it comes right down to it on the particulars, we can't stand the police. We keep a constant lookout for them when we drive. We dread being pulled over. We know in our hearts that they are out to get us, and represent more of a threat than a security for our freedoms.

In the end, we need to realize that the police are like all other government employees: self-interested, living off tax dollars, parasitical on our liberties. The case of Officer Kanapsky shows precisely how and why.

35

The Creation of the Bureaucrat

August 29, 2003

During the airport-security reform debate of 2001, Congress had the option of permitting the airlines more discretion in securing themselves from the threat of hijacking. Airline security had been imperfect—Federal Aviation Administration regulations prohibited commercial pilots from carrying guns, for example—but airlines themselves were capable of improving, and had every incentive to do so.

With the experience of September 11, airlines learned that the old wisdom concerning hijacking (calm the hijacker down and get him to land the plane) no longer applied. Instead, pilots needed the ability to protect person and property. Airlines discovered the dangers that might lurk in luggage and passenger carry-on bags. They were ready to screen passenger lists more carefully. Consumers, meanwhile, were more alert to security issues, and the airlines would have had to compete on the basis of the most superior security, in addition to the usual considerations of price, reliability, and comfort. The industry could have responded to real threats without creating unnecessary passenger inconvenience.

But instead, Congress, with the blessing of the White House, short circuited the market process. Paid by government, working for government, and identifying with its interests, the bulk of political decision makers naturally see government as the answer to every major problem. They view the "market" as uncertain and untrustworthy, something to be granted liberality on unessential matters but to be restricted and restrained in all essentials.

Hence, the laws regulating airline security were not liberalized. Instead, Congress created a new bureaucracy, the Transportation Security Administration, to be put in charge of airline security. A National Screening Force was established to examine all bags. Not only that: the government decided to charge consumers a fee (who could object?) for the right to enjoy its newly provided security. This is after taxpayers had already shelled out trillions of dollars to the government to provide defense against terrorism, only to discover that there really was no security against suicidal militants carrying box cutters.

At the time when airport security was nationalized, John McCain said: "This, I think, with the president's signature, will give Americans confidence that their government and their Congress and their president are doing everything possible to improve airport security as rapidly as possible."

But doing everything that the government finds *possible* isn't the same thing as doing what is *necessary* according to the assessment of the owners of the airlines and the customers who use them. The TSA has no connection at all to owners and customers. As a result, it is now common for people who fly to return with amazing stories of humiliating and unwarranted intrusions, harassment, and bureaucratic delays. As to whether security has actually been enhanced, it's anyone's guess.

Most pilots are still unarmed. Those that are had to face a thicket of red tape, including an intimidating psychological evaluation, in the course of a government training program undertaken on their own time. Once they are given the right to protect plane and passengers, pilots must still carry their firearm in a lockbox. Meanwhile, federal flight marshals are still rare.

Average passengers, who have borne the brunt of the costs of security guidelines, must obey a codified list of items that can and cannot be carried on planes. Box cutters are outlawed for politically understandable reasons—given government's propensity to protect us all from past threats. Why are people allowed to carry cigar cutters but not razor blades, knitting needles but not ice picks, and nail files but not tiny scissors is anyone's guess.

What makes the people who drew up the list, as versus the airlines themselves, any greater experts on the likelihood that these objects will or will not be used in terrorism? A person who intends to do harm in the sky isn't likely to be deterred by having his cuticle scissors confiscated. Remember too that any object that can be used for terrorism can also be used to protect *against* terrorism; stripping passengers of anything that could be used as an offensive weapon also takes away items that could be used for defensive purposes.

As for bureaucrats now running airport security, they are obeying orders from above, not responding to market needs. They face no competition, have no access to a feedback mechanism of profit and loss, and they lack every incentive to actually make good managerial judgments that would lead to enhanced security. They are not owners but rather outsiders to the market process, blind to the needs of consumers, inattentive to the interests of the airlines, and disregarding of the various tradeoffs associated with choosing one method over another.

All of these results could be known in advance, and critics of the program warned that this would be the result. But it is still something remarkable to observe in real life, as I did on a recent flight. Upon entering the airport, confusion was everywhere. No effort was made to make the system transparent to regular people. There were huge scanning contraptions with bags sitting on the conveyor belt (who owns the contract for those and how did they get it?) but it wasn't clear whether one's own bags were supposed to be placed on them or what would happen to them after. What was clear, given the employee badges and demeanor, is that passengers would be in lots of trouble if they did the wrong thing.

The bags took an age to go through, and anything suspicious would prompt the federal employees to open up the bag and wipe a tiny cloth on the contents inside, in four different places. I suppose this is to check for explosives. They then examined the cloth to observe any discoloring. The whole process had the appearance of silly ritual, not an actual security check. What was especially striking was the speed of the operation. The entire airport had passengers and airline employees bustling about here and there. But the federal employees seemed to work outside of time itself, completely oblivious to the tempo around them. They lacked any sign of vigor or initiative.

These federal employees seemed to be vaguely in charge of all things between the time the passengers entered the airport and when they did the final pass beyond the last X-ray machine. They seemed disparaging of the needs of passengers, stationing five employees in a spot where it should take one, and assigning one employee to do a job that should take five. They were probably all nice people but they acted like caricatures of government bureaucrats: at once belligerent and ignorant, threatening and uninterested, detached and intrusive. Their main job seemed to be to muck up the system, and revel in the fact that they were in charge. This was Martin van Creveld's "impersonal state" at work.

Security is a service like any another. When the market is in charge, it is something provided when, how, and to what extent it is needed. Risk assessment is crucial. There is no sense in wasting resources on nonexistent threats. Those contracted to provide security must be in a position to respond to the needs of the moment, change their tactics, and outwit the threat. Those who do the job best are rewarded and those who fail are weeded out of the market. Competitive pressures lead to constant improvements in methods and continually falling costs.

The bureau in charge of federal security today bears none of these traits. This isn't because of culpable negligence or incompetence, though surely these factors play a role. It is because they stand outside the market system and are not thus responding to the needs of producers and consumers. Though it is a new bureaucracy, its employees already fit the classic description as given by Ludwig von Mises: "they shun innovations and improvements. They look on every project for reform as a disturbance of their quiet." The absence of market mechanisms "creates insoluble problems. It kills ambition, destroys initiative and the incentive to do more than the minimum required. It makes the bureaucrat look at instructions, not at material and real success." (*Bureaucracy*, 1944, pp. 60–61).

Sullen and incompetent employees are a feature of the private sector too, of course. The crucial difference is that in the market economy, forces are at work to systematically punish the bureaucratic impulse and replace it with something more spectacular: vigor, innovation, and genuine public service to others. In the private sector, failure is punished with losses. After 9-11, we saw what happens when government-provided security fails: government grows.

The success or failure of the Transportation Security Administration will come up for review in a couple of years. We already know what will happen. Plenty of failures will be spotted, as well as many imagined successes.

Regardless of the record, the bureaucracy won't be abolished. It will be "reformed," especially given that a huge new lobbying force now has every reason to push Congress to retain the system. The one reform that the system most needs—namely, to be subjected to the competitive pressures of the market—is not possible in the current framework. The only real solution is the one that Congress rejected back when it had the chance for real reform: total privatization.

36

Stop Signs and Liberty

July 14, 2009

And then one day the stop sign was gone.

It was the very stop sign one block from my house that was oddly stationed at a low-traffic, three-way intersection, tempting every driver to slow down but not come to a complete stop.

How the city cleaned up on that one! I have personally coughed up in excess of $1,000 for tickets there, one time receiving two tickets in as many days. This sign was even the reason that I spent a day in jail for failing to fork over when the judge said I should.

I'm not alone: 93% of the drivers failed to come to a complete stop. Even so, I'm routinely lectured that my job as a citizen is to do precisely as I'm told. I've learned to habitually stop completely, even when the place looks like a ghost town, with no cars anywhere in view.

Then one day the stop sign vanished.

What happened here? Did the cops finally get all the citizens trained to stop and thereby dissipate their opportunity for rents? Was there just no more money to be made from the disobedient?

Do I get a refund? How about compensation for the day I spent in jail? What about everyone else?

The local government must have extracted tens of thousands of dollars before good sense overcame our overlords and they decided to relent to reality. But no, there will not be compensation. The law changed its mind, and we are supposed to just deal with it. Now I must rehabituate myself to breaking—I mean keeping—the law.

One day, I'm jailed for failing to stop. Presumably, I could now get a ticket for stopping, since surely there is a law against suddenly stopping on a public road for no reason other than some vague memory than one had to in the past.

What is evil one day is mandatory the next.

Now, I know what some readers are thinking: here we go with the libertarian wacko complaining about the "coercion" of stop signs. For decades, conservatives have been poking fun, caricaturing libertarians as people who rail against stop signs and thereby reveal their personal problem with authority—even such obviously justified authority as government stop signs.

Don't we understand that these keep us safe, and so surely we should be willing to give up just a bit of license to speed around with abandon in the interest of the common good?

Even now, a quick google of "libertarians" and "stop signs" reveals many people on the Left and the Right who think it is just stupidly hilarious that libertarians talk about these issues.

As a matter of fact, the management of the roads is a hugely important issue, given that tens of thousands of people die on government roads every year. Private ownership would in fact lead to greater liability for the road owner—and also more rational rules of the road. The private road would be devoted to serving the customers, not looting them at the point of a gun. And not only are private roads viable; there is a long history and a present practice to draw on.

Walter Block's new book on road privatization makes the case that this is not an issue to ignore but one to solve through free enterprise.

In some ways, then, it is true that the stop sign—as with every regulation by the state—embodies all that is wrong with the public sector. The rules are made to benefit the state. You are on the hot seat if any policeman says that you have done wrong. The pretense of a fair trial is a complete farce, as you have to tangle with judges who hate you, waste several days of work, and throw yourself on the mercy of the court. Once you are entangled in the web, you can't really get out.

And who makes the rules? The central planners make the rules, and the public be damned. The rules are there to serve the state, not us, and the stop sign that is oddly placed in order to extract revenue makes the point very well.

When you are stopped, you become aware that the imbalance between the citizens and the state couldn't be more obvious. Deliver an insult and you are arrested. Try to run and you are gunned down. Fail to pay and you end up in the slammer. And maybe the cop will find something else about your life to be suspicious of. Whatever they want to know, you must tell them.

Government is not reason; it is force. What was the actual social rationale for that stop sign in the first place? You dare not ask, for then you are questioning the elites who are in charge of your life. And why was it removed? It's not for you to question why; it is for you to do or die. It was there and now it is gone. All "law-abiding citizens" must change with the arbitrary dictate of the traffic masters.

Now, I'm not saying that we don't need rules in society. But the question of who makes the rules and on what basis becomes supremely important. Will the rule-making flow from the matrix of voluntary exchange based on the ethic of serving others through private enterprise? Or will the rules be made and enforced by people wearing guns and bulletproof vests with a license to shock or kill based on minor annoyances?

Something as seemingly innocuous as a stop sign can become the occasion for the use of terrible violence and terrible oppression. And think about it: we are talking about local government which is especially sensitive to public opinion. If we see corruption here, what about at the national level, where the citizens are nothing but an abstraction?

So, no, I have no problem with making the stop sign a symbol of the fight. It shows that even the least objectionable aspects of the state can mask despotism and that we should think hard—very hard—before ever ceding control of even the smallest parts of life to the state.

Ultimately, the state is in control or we are.

There is nothing in between.

37

Dress Like the Great Depression

March 9, 2009

A conspicuous cultural change we can look forward to is a dramatic change in men's dress style. Guys, you might as well get ahead of the curve. The free-fall economy means a boon for better fashion for men who intend to survive the onslaught.

We will be highly fortunate if the second Great Depression turns out to be as stylish as the first, in which even the bums sleeping on the park benches looked better than the average workers and even CEOs today.

I am looking at this guy in a Depression-era photo. I see the 1¾ inch cuffs on his trousers, the snappy crease in his pants, the great hat, and the woolen trousers. And the shoes: leather and laces, resting on a solid foundation. If I found any of his clothes in the vintage shop, I would snap them up and be ready for today's tight job market, which seeks serious men, not goofs in sweats and polos.

The boom times led to great shabbiness. Workers have lived in wrinkles and jeans. The guy with the shirt with buttons is derided by others—"You going to a wedding or something?" We were all encouraged to look up to the slobwear of hotshot traders and stock jobbers and the others, who revel in the fact that they look like heck all of the time. Even the billionaires have looked like hobos (who themselves looked pretty great in the 1930s).

The idea behind shabby vogue was to give the impression that you don't really care what others think. You are the cutting edge, the smasher of idols and conventions, a person who doesn't give a flip about how society judges such artificial external superficialities as pant creases and ties and things. Your value is in your very person, the fact of your existence on this planet. In the boom times, the message of fashion is "It's all about me!"

Now all of this has come into question. How much value did this jeans-clad generation really add? How much of it evaporated? How much was illusion all along? Maybe all this hype about intellectual capital is poppycock, and what matters is what one actually does, and not only for oneself but for others, such as customers and bosses and fellow workers.

As Trevor Kaufman, the guru of "CEO Casual," told the *Wall Street Journal* in an article written at the top of the boom, "A suit has become something you wear when you're asking for money."

Uh, right.

In the bust, your clothes need to send a different message. There are fewer resources to spare. Everyone is conserving. The goal of your life becomes different. You are no longer permitted to pretend that your very existence is a blessing to the world. Instead, you must add more value to the world than you take from it. This is especially true in your work life.

In fact, this should be your professional motto: *I can add more value to this firm than I take from it.*

This is what every employer—who these days is reluctant to hire and reluctant to promote and pay—is actually seeking. No more fluff in the workforce. No more fluff in fashion either.

Right now, with unemployment moving into the double digits, it is becoming a dog-eat-dog world in labor markets. You must stand out. You must find ways to show that you are not expendable, that tossing you out would do more harm to the company than good. You must show that the company will risk losing more revenue by sending you away than by keeping you.

Clothing reflects this. There is no sense in disadvantaging yourself in this struggle.

Just have a look at what all men in the Great Depression wore. They were smashing. The suit. The hat. The shoes. The ties. Everything was well put together, among all races and classes of men. This isn't just because all this stuff was intrinsic to the culture. Men in all times and all places have had the option of looking ridiculously unkempt. The point is that these men were under pressure to perform, to show that they were valuable, to demonstrate on sight that they were desirable commodities as workers.

So let us plunge back in time to examine modern needs in light of historical precedent, with some tutorial along the way.

Let's start with the suit. It should be made of wool. It should be gray or blue. It should not have that strange Euro fit but rather have the loose-but-neat fit of the traditional American suit, which was never designed to show off your body, but rather your character.

Thus must it be sturdy and serious. The jacket can have two buttons, three buttons, or four buttons. When you are standing, all but the bottom button should be buttoned. You need to work on the habit of unbuttoning these buttons when you sit down and rebuttoning them when you stand up. Yes, you have to do this each time. Try it consciously over the course of a day and it becomes habit. The only exception might be at dinner, during which it is permissible to keep the coat buttoned.

Never take your jacket off, no matter how much you want to, no matter how hot it gets, no matter how much people plead with you to do so. The jacket is part of your clothing, and gentlemen don't take their clothes off in public.

Just so that we are clear, the sport coat and pants combination is not a suit. In other words, a blazer and khakis don't work. A suit has a jacket and pants, and sometimes a vest, that match. The fabric and color of the top and the bottom are the same.

You can buy great suits in thrift stores or on eBay, but you have to have a sense of what you are doing. If you don't, you have to go to a nice men's store, where you will have to pay the big bucks. However, you can get by on two or three suits, essentially forever. Wear one on Monday, Wednesday and Friday and the other on Tuesday, Thursday and Saturday.

Shirts, always worn with an undershirt during the bust (because people who really work also really sweat), should be white, blue, or light tan. Everything else is a risk. It can be straight collar or button-down. Lose the fancy "collar bars" and things until you are CEO. They look pompous most of the time.

For fit, the pants length should grace the top of the shoe, and the cuffs should be more than 1¼ inches but less than 2 inches. The shirtsleeves should fall ¼ to ½ an inch below the jacket.

Now consider the shoes. They should lace up. They should have leather soles if possible. Loafers are for loafers, and you don't want anyone to think you are among them.

And hats! This might be the most exciting of the restorations of our time. Men haven't really worn them since the 1960s, and that's not just because JFK didn't wear his. It's really because we don't get out much anymore. We go from the house to the car to the office and hats don't serve that much function anymore.

And I hate that I even have to say this, but hats are not to be worn indoors. The only exceptions are large public spaces: malls, train stations, airports, and hotel lobbies. Otherwise, they are always off: restaurants, homes, offices, elevators, etc.

However, the hat serves more than a pure utility function. It is a thing of beauty. It is as valuable, in this sense, in the hand as it is on the head. A hat changes everything about a man. It elicits notice and respect, and the man with a hat knows this: he is complimented on it constantly. And let's just tell the truth here: it raises you above the rabble quicker than any other article of clothing.

There are two general colors of hats: browns and blacks. You choose your hat the same way you would choose your socks, by picking up on general hues and themes. They are made of wool and sometimes pelts (fancy stuff). They can be stiff or crushable. You know the style that is right for you by trying it on. Different head shapes require different styles, so I'm not sure that online shopping can really work here.

In any case, despite our indoor culture, the new Great Depression stands a good chance of finally smashing the legacy of JFK: the hat might be restored.

Please note one final point: dressing up doesn't mean adopting a stuffy personality with a stiff way about you, or walking around like a tin man. Good clothes provide the freedom to express yourself in other ways. You can be casual-acting and normal-behaving, and it is all the more important to be this way when you are dressed up. You can still move about normally, and do all the things you would otherwise normally do.

Clothes on a man should look and seem comfortable no matter what they are. You must be confident enough to wear them as if you belong in them. The more you can look like your clothes are in fact no big deal, just part of your life, the more compelling the message will be.

The way you dress can make all the difference. If it doesn't work to boost your professional life, you can always count on looking fantastic when you march on the White House and protest against its occupants for robbing you blind in the name of saving you.

38

Protectionism and My Stuffy Nose

December 26, 2007

There I stood at the pharmacy counter, with a head cold, sniffing away, and begging for some product that contains pseudoephedrine, which works like a magic nose unclogger. The stuff you can get off the shelf now contains the similar-sounding drug called phenylephrine, but it might as well be a placebo. It just doesn't work, and most everyone knows this.

You can still get the good old stuff from the pharmacist but you will be suspected for this grave action. The government, you see, says that people have been buying the old stuff and turning it into methamphetamine. This is why Congress and the administration passed the Combat Methamphetamine Epidemic Act of 2005, which rations the amount you can buy and requires that you prove your identity and sign a special form.

And, yes, this act is now part of the monstrosity called the Patriot Act.

"Thanks Bush" I muttered as I signed the form under the glare of the pharmacist who has been trained to treat me like a possible criminal.

It's remarkable, really. Two years ago, buying Mucinex was no different from buying toothpaste or shampoo. Today, it is a big deal and you get on some government list as possible suspects. And yes, they do arrest people for buying too much, as the stuffy-nosed William Fousee of New York found out earlier this year.

The data that demonstrate a national crisis of meth usage seems pretty darn thin to me, with reports of increased workplace positive tests balanced by reports of decreased usage among the young.

In any case, one has to wonder about a national law that would so dramatically affect the health of millions in order to stop some guy from making meth in his basement. In the name of saving us from ourselves, the government has made it far more difficult for us to stay feeling healthy.

Laws are passed for a reason. If not health, what possible motivation could the government have had for imposing this law? Possibly to create a national database of the stuffy nosed? Not likely.

Let's follow the money a bit. It seems that most all pseudoephedrine is manufactured in China and India, and very cheaply, much more cheaply than it can be made in the United States or Europe. What that means is that these companies don't have lobbyists in Washington who can make an effective case for their product.

Contrast this was phenylephrine, the world's largest manufacturer of which is located in Germany. The company is called Boehringer-Ingelheim, according to MSNBC. It developed the drug in 1949 for use in eyedrops. In the last two years, virtually every manufacturer of cold medicine has changed its formula to include the Boehringer drug. Some continue to make the old formula available but only with special access.

Is it possible that the move against wonderful pseudoephedrine and in favor of useless phenylephrine was really a form of protectionism in disguise? That it was really about rewarding a well-connected company at the expense of companies without connections?

If that sounds cynical, take a look at this (http://www.fecwatch.org). It seems that our friends at Boehringer Ingelheim are rather interested in American politics, with 73% of their donations going to Republican candidates for federal office. You can see here that Boehringer even has a PAC, located in Ridgefield, Connecticut. Someone with more time than I have ought to check to see how the people it supported for Congress voted on the act that resulted in a massive shift toward their product, and has nearly kept its competitive product off the market.

Oh, and look here (http://www.opensecrets.org). It turns out that this company spent $1.85 million on lobbying in 2005, and this was a huge upsurge over all previous years.

The following year it spent $922,000, and spending declined further in 2007.

And here is the Boehringer 2006 annual report, (http://www.boehringer-ingelheim.com/corporate/download/ar/summaryreport2006.pdf), which triumphantly announces that "the phenylephrine business continued growing at a high level." (Their 2007 report is not yet online.)

Now, before you call me a crazed conspiracy theorist, consider this amazing coincidence. The main company that stands to benefit from a law—passed in the name of the patriotic war on drugs—that effectively marginalizes in its main competition and gives a boost to its inferior product spent millions in lobbying and campaign donations in the very year that the law was passed. There is no record of any substantial spending before the push for the law began, and spending has been declining since the law passed.

So let me go out on a limb here and say what any reasonable person would strongly suspect. The reason you can't get Mucinex and Sudafed that work without jumping through hoops isn't really about stopping basement meth users. It is really about the racket going on in Washington in which the law is used to benefit influential producers in cahoots with the political class at the expense of less influential producers and the American people, who should have the freedom to choose.

Remember: there is a story like this behind just about everything government does. If you comprehend that, you can understand why people like Albert Jay Nock said that the state is always and everywhere the enemy.

39

Bush's Fowl Play

November 9, 2005

In a classic case of News of the Weird, President Bush gave a press conference the other day to announce yet another central plan to deal with yet another disaster—this time an impending disaster, or so he claimed. It seems that some birds are catching a flu called Avian Influenza or, more commonly, the bird flu. It causes ruffled feathers and a drop in egg production. It can kill a chicken in two days flat. Scary.

The Chicken Littles at the White House got wind of this and decided to hatch a plan for dealing with the eventuality that it will wipe out whole cities inhabited by people. That's people, not birds. Bush wants $7.1 billion from you and me, in emergency funding no less, to protect us from the wrath of this disease, which, he says, could sweep the country and kill 1.9 million people and hospitalize another 9.9 million. Part of the money will go for "pandemic preparedness," and part will go to individual states so they can cobble together their own plans for our health and well-being.

As part of this plan, there is a website, pandemicflu.gov, which is also a helpful link if you haven't so far believed a word you have read. Here you can click around and find the Mother of All Flu Reports: The National Strategy for Pandemic Influenza. Be assured that "the federal government will use all instruments of national power to address the pandemic threat." That includes FEMA, the Department of Homeland Security, and a hundred other concrete palaces in DC.

In this report you will find what you must do: be "prepared to follow public health guidance that may include limitation of attendance at public gatherings and non-essential travel for several days or weeks." The government, meanwhile, will establish "contingency systems to maintain delivery of essential goods and services during times of significant and sustained worker absenteeism."

Yes, we are really supposed to believe that the government will "maintain delivery" of "essential goods and services." Your job is to sit in your house and wait. Let's just say that government has a credibility problem here.

Also, the Bush administration has a role for the military to do for the flu what it did for terrorism in Iraq: "Determine the spectrum of public health, medical and veterinary surge capacity activities that the U.S. military and other government entities may be able to support during a pandemic." Remarkable what the military can do, from spreading democracy to liberating the oppressed to curing the sick—that is, when it is not making people sick or killing them for their own good.

Just to show that this isn't merely a perfunctory line, Bush went out of his way in his press conference to defend the role of the military. "One option is the use of a military that's able to plan and move," he said. "So that's why I put it on the table. I think it's an important debate for Congress to have."

Now, should this mass death come about, our future would be rife with many uncertainties. But one thing we can know for sure: any attempt by government to manage the crisis will add calamity to disaster. It will be 9-11 plus New Orleans plus a few other amazing failures all rolled into one.

And the worst part of government failure will present itself: rather than make a mess of its own responsibilities, the government acts to prevent people from doing what they should be doing to deal with the crisis. "Stop in the name of the law" isn't just a slogan from cop shows; it is the sum total of everything the government does.

The Bush administration, however—which is supposedly staffed by people learned in the wisdom of classical conservative thought and informed by revelation from America's traditional religious heritage—is just darn sure that the government is the best and only means to handle a crisis such as this.

A dazzling display of absurdity and *chutzpah*—that's what the Bush press conference on the flu was. Even if the flu does come, and taxpayers have coughed up, the government will surely have a ball imposing travel restrictions, shutting down schools and businesses, quarantining cities, and banning public gatherings.

It's a bureaucrat's dream! Whether it will make us well again is another matter. And why should individuals on their own have no incentive to deal with disease? Why should the private sector have no reason to make cures available if they exist? Why are we to believe that the government would somehow do a better job at this level of crisis management than the private sector?

None of these questions have been asked, much less answered.

So I'm reading along in *The New York Times*, and it casually says this: "This bird flu has infected about 120 people and killed 60. But the virus has yet to pass easily among humans, as is necessary to create a pandemic. Experts debate whether it ever will, but most believe that a pandemic flu is inevitable someday."

Well, as Roderick Long often says about such contingencies, anything *can* happen. Men from Mars could land in capsules and plant red weed all over the world. The question we need to ask is how likely is it and who or what should address the problem should it arise.

The World Health Organization provides a link to data about human infection. It says the following: "Although avian influenza A viruses usually do not infect humans, several instances of human infections have been reported since 1997."

So we've gone from hundreds of infections to "several." And when you look at the specifics, most were not human-to-human infections but people in closer contact with sick birds than most anyone ever is. And even among them, most patients recovered. For example: "A (H9N2) infection was confirmed in a child in Hong Kong. The child was hospitalized and recovered." In another case in Canada, infections resulted in "eye infections." Among those who did die, it was not a clear case of Avian, though the site offers the following odd phrasing: "the possibility of person-to-person transmission could not be ruled out."

For this, we get a presidential news conference? As far as I can tell, the prospect of millions dying from bird flu is pretty remote. If it does happen—and anything *can* happen—why must government be involved at all? Economists might invoke a public-goods rationale: pandemic disease protection is a service that can be consumed by additional consumers at no additional cost and the beneficiaries cannot be excluded from the good once it has been produced, and thus this service will not be produced in sufficient quantity in the private sector.

The point is so farfetched that it makes a case for Randall Holcombe's theory of the theory of public goods: "it is in the best interest of the those who run the government to promote public goods theory" and so the best way to understand the theory is as a justification for the legitimacy of the programs the government wants for itself. It is a tool the government uses for its own benefit.

What about the private-sector alternative? It will manage it as well as can be expected. The price of vaccines will rise and draw more producers into the market. Businesses will establish their own rules about who can come and go. Private charities will deal with sickness. It isn't a perfect solution but it is an improvement on dispatching the Marines or having the government provide "essential goods and services."

What's more, the problem of the bird flu isn't even news, since the incidents of human infection are several years old. Why does the Bush administration choose right now to make such a big showing of its preparations for mass death by bird?

Could it be that it is running out of other pretexts for expanding power? Terrorism is getting boring, floods come only rarely, communism is long gone, the China "threat" is no longer selling, the Middle East is dull, global warming is just too silly, and people have gone back to ignoring most anything that comes out of Washington. Meanwhile, the regime is desperate to be liked again, and forever relive its salad days after 9-11.

That still leaves the question of why so many public health officials seem so hopped up about the bird flu, even though the data doesn't come anywhere near supporting their frenzy. The answer is buried somewhere in those gargantuan budget numbers. Someone somewhere is going to get that $8 billion, and it is not going to be you or me.

What's remarkable is how little comment the bird flu plan provoked. We seem to have reached the stage in American public opinion where hysterical frenzies by government and totalitarian plans to take away all liberties are treated as just another day. We see the president telling us to fork over billions, and we turn the channel. Was it this way in the old Soviet Union or East Germany when the state newscasts went on every night about the march of socialism? Has crisis management become the great white noise of American life?

It is a serious matter when the government purports to plan to abolish all liberty and nationalize all economic life and put every business under the control of the military, especially in the name of a bug that seems largely restricted to the bird population. Perhaps we should pay more attention. Perhaps such plans for the total state ought to even ruffle our feathers a bit.

40

What Men Want

August 10, 2005

You know why so many men walk around with sloppy hair? We hate haircuts. You have to drive there to get one, which represents decline, because if you know about Figaro from Rossini's "Barber of Seville," the barber came to your home (but then he also pulled out your teeth and passed on furtive notes arranging encounters of various sort, etc.).

In any case, you have to drive there to get a haircut and you would rather be doing a thousand other things. Then you wait. Wait! Oh sure, there was probably a time when men would meet at the barbershop to talk about the crops, the harvest, the rain, fishing, or whatever. No one wants to talk about that stuff anymore.

Now they talk about sports. It can be very intimidating. I used to read the sports page before my haircuts so that I could say something, anything, if only to prevent the men from muttering about the odd bird in the bow tie after I left.

Once time, though, I really messed up. I noticed that no one was in the barbershop and said, hey, what's going on? The barber said there was a game going on in Auburn right then. I said yeah? And then warming up to the idea of sports talk I said: "who we playin'?" His answer was devastating and exposed my affectation immediately: "Alabama." (If you don't understand why this answer would be humiliating, you know even less about sports than I do.)

There was once a charming old-world Texas frontier town with a barber whose trade went back generations. He was the only one in town. But woe for the people who had the misfortune of getting a haircut the day I was there. Arriving mid-morning, it was noon before my time came and then he had to step out to get a bite to eat. He didn't come back for an hour. By this time, I was so demoralized that I had to wait it out. My hair was finally cut—after several naps, major depression, suicidal thoughts—at around 2 P.M. I was too defeated to complain.

If there had been anything to talk about with those other cobweb-covered men, it was done after 10 minutes. In any case, the truth is that there is nothing anymore to talk about in barbershops. You learn nothing, nothing that you can't get from Google in half a second. We have nothing to gain from these strangers, and we have no interest in telling the barber the ins and outs of where we are from, what we did on our vacations, and like that. Why should we?

We don't "get to know" the guy who processes our one-click Amazon order. The modern age allows us to pick and choose our associations very carefully, and this should extend as far as possible. Even our doctors have speeded up, thanks to urgent care clinics that have liberated us from the family doctor who is glad to waste a half a day of our time at his convenience.

In any case, what the world needs very badly, I have just found: the three-minute haircut. Can you imagine? You drive up and park and walk in and sit down. Becky Boss at Fantastic Sams in Westerly, Rhode Island, gets the job done in three minutes for men and five for women, and it is a great cut! Not a lot of fussing and poking and flicking your precious locks around. She understands that your time is costly. And her speed helps her get customers in and out.

You can leave your car running! And what a great sense of life this Becky Boss has. No unanswerable questions about whether you would like her to use scissors or an electric razor: she just does what is best. We are not expected to conjure up a panoply of preferences that we don't really have, e.g. do we want it "blocked" in back or "shorter on top." She sees what needs to be done and does it. The critical thing is that she knows what really matters: your time. There is just enough time for a first impression and you are gone.

So I'm wondering why there isn't a chain that advertises three-minute haircuts. I guarantee that it would do very well. Every guy dreads getting his haircut. For that matter, women report that the longer a "stylist" takes with their hair, the more worried they become—and the worse the cut ends up.

Someone told me about a place where you can get your oil changed and get a hair cut at the same time, which seems like a step in the right direction. But still, you don't need your oil changed as often as you need a haircut. So the three-minute haircut is still the answer.

Let's say the haircut costs $12. That's $4 per minute that the barber earns. That's $240 an hour, or $1,920 a day, and $9,600 a week, and—wait for it—$480,000 per year, plus tips! You can be a millionaire in two years, and that's with two weeks of vacation each year! Yes, yes, there are also taxes and the costs of doing business, but the point stands.

I've seen the future and it works!

41

The Shaving Cream Racket

April 22, 2006

Look, I'm the last guy to trash a consumer product. I'm disinclined to blast the manufacturers of a beloved bathroom gel as deceivers who make money off people's ignorance and perpetuate the problem they are supposedly solving, or charlatans who deliberately hook people on some chemically produced gunk solely for the sake of profiting from repeated uses.

But someone has to say it: shaving cream is a racket.

Why don't people know this? It's just part of the lost knowledge of our time. Wean yourself from it for a week, and you will find that your shaves will be closer, unbloody, and quick. Imagine a full shave in less than a minute, with no cuts, gashes, or discomfort. It is within your grasp.

You won't have the face of a tenderized chicken breast. Your skin will be solid and robust. You will feel the same revulsion I do as you encounter that long row of shaving products at the drug store. You too will feel pity on the seventh eights of the human race that does not understand this simple point.

Why is the world hooked on this stuff? Here's what happens. Early on in a person's life, when whiskers and stubble begin to appear on the skin, the young teen is presented a razor and a can — a can with a squirting top that releases a foam. It is a charming little foam. The child is taught to rub it on and then shave it off.

Oh how funny looking it is when the foam is on us! And how fun to zap it off. We are left with clean and smooth skin. Pure magic. But the magic doesn't last.

It never occurs to this child — so innocent, so naïve, so trusting — that he or she has been hooked into a lifetime of shaving hell. That foam, that sweet looking puff of magic, is in fact the great enemy of a good shave — black magic that relies on perpetuating dependency and ignorance.

The problem is this. Shaving cream does something evil to the skin. It somehow weakens the pores and makes the top layer mushy and unresponsive. The kid comes to believe that somehow the foam is essential to the experience. Without it, surely the razor would leave a trail of blood.

But then strange things start to happen. Red lumps appear. The shaved skin comes to feel sort of strange, oddly sensitive to temperature changes and ever more vulnerable to being sliced and diced.

People think: oh I need a new razor! So they go out and buy ever more fancy brands, with multiple blades, pivoting heads, strange lubricants, and push-out tools to deposit the hair remains in the sink.

They don't consider that it might be the shaving cream that is the source of the trouble.

Why don't people imagine this possibility? Because shaving cream seems so frothy and innocent, the glorious barrier that stands as a guard or shield between your skin and the sharp blade. The cream is our valiant protector, so surely that is not the source of the problem!

In fact, it is not our protector. Shaving cream is destroying your skin, turning it into a whining, pathetic, dependent, beaten, insipid layer of pasty pulp. Your skin has become the fatted calf that has been killed, the lamb slain on the altar, the virgin sacrificed in some ancient cannibalistic ritual of an uncivilized people.

Of course the problems persist — and get worse.

There are many attempts to avoid them along the way. People try aftershave, more and more and more of it. Pretty soon, they are tossing handfuls of the stuff on their skin, putting alcohol all over tenderized and sliced up skin. Then they become attached to that too. But it is not enough. The redness and pain are still there.

There are those who believe in hot lather. They buy fancy machines and rise extra early to warm them up. There are those who make the leap toward electric razors that swirl and buzz around in a creepy sort of way. There are those who believe the key to shaving is time: I've heard the preposterous claim that a good shave should take 12 minutes.

Stop the insanity!

The core problem is shaving cream itself, and the solution is a radical one: throw it out and never buy it again. It is destroying you and making your skin weak and sickly.

But you say: surely if this were true, it would be common knowledge. Not sure. There are many thing that are true — the state is a parasite on society, private property would solve most social problems, rock music is tedious and stupid — but are nonetheless not generally known or applied. The truth that shaving cream is a racket should be added to this.

Many problems in the world cannot be solved by one person. But this one can. You can begin the process of letting your skin become normal again. You can restore your skin's health. It won't take longer than a week or so. Stick with it and you will see what I mean.

The first stage of freedom uses only a razor (double blade is fine) and a bit of baby oil or mineral oil. While in the shower or soon after you get out, put some oil on the skin area you want to shave. Then shave it. The end.

At first, it won't feel right. You might cut yourself. It will be scary. Your skin might hurt a bit. It might swell up. Why? Because you have turned your skin to mush for decades of shaving cream use. It needs time to recover from this. You need to do this for days.

This is your first day of relief from shaving cream hell. Your skin is recovering. Do the same the next day. And the next. And the next. After 5 days, normalcy will be almost returned.

After a week, you can even give up the oil and use only warm water. You will find that you will be able to shave ever more swiftly and with ever more abandon. A man can shave his whole face in 20 seconds without a single abrasion.

My freedom from shaving cream began twenty years ago after a friend uttered to me the great truth that shaving cream is a racket. Ever since I have exulted in my knowledge and felt deep pity on the rest of the world for languishing in unknowingness.

To my knowledge, this is the first and only time that this great truth has been revealed. May this short article serve as a hinge of history.

42

How To Dress Like a Man

July 16, 2003

Guys, here is your one-article guide to dressing, based on many years in the rag business and a lifetime of observing the sheer ubiquity of error.

There are two general types of men's clothing.

First, there are clothes for public consumption: clothing in which to present yourself to others and thereby convey an elevated message about yourself. These are types of clothes you wear to work, to the store, out on the town, at a wedding, at church, at parties, or wherever people are going to see you. The primary objective here is that you look presentable, that you be civilized, a gentleman and not a beast.

The other type of clothing is that which serves a pure functional purpose: that is, that which you wear for yard work, fixing your car, an evening at home, a Saturday washing the house or cleaning, or just knocking around the park with kids. Everyone knows what type of clothes these are. They can all be bought at Wal-Mart or thrift stores, and they are made of cotton.

The great dressing error of our time is to confuse the two. Or more precisely: people think that it is perfectly okay to present yourself to others in clothes which serve a purely functional purpose. They say this is fine because it is comfortable—as if the only thing that matters in life is comfort. Well, it is also comfortable not to shave and not to bathe, and we have a word for people like that: slobs. If you don't want to be a slob, you have to live with a bit of discomfort.

If men could absorb that simple lesson, the world would be a much more beautiful place in which to live. Elevated dressing causes people to behave better. Crime might fall. Manners would begin to come back. People might clean up their language. They might listen to better music and read better books. Something resembling civilization might return.

Now the next step: how do you look presentable? For a man, it is a snap. Your full wardrobe need not take up more than 12 to 18 inches of closet space. You need:

- one or two suits in blue or grey
- a blue or black jacket or sports coat
- a jacket for Summer (khaki or blue cotton or, if you want to be really fancy, seersucker)
- a tweed jacket for Winter
- year-round grey wool trousers (light or dark or both)
- a few pairs of khakis
- Three white and three blue shirts
- a selection of ties

That's all. That will get you through a lifetime, replacing them with something similar when these wear out. Mix as necessary. If you have chosen well, just about any jacket will go with your trousers. Just about any shirt will go with any jacket. Ties should be chosen with an eye to color, making sure that the tie stands out and does not blend in with either jacket or shirt or trousers. Men's clothes should *not* "match"; they should go together, which is something else entirely.

But, you say, I'll look the same all the time! Right. This conveys an impression that you are a wise and stable person, not prone to flights of fancy and fits of fashion. There is a practical aspect here. You don't really want to wear clothes that cause people to comment: hey, that is a really nice forest-green, window-pane, double-breasted, peak-lapel, side-vent hunting jacket with leather patches! The next time you wear it, the comment will be: oh, you wore that last week! No, you don't really want people to zero in on your clothes as if they have an existence apart from you and your character. Clothes should not *make* the man; they should *be* the man.

As for adjustments, there are many things you can do to vary your wardrobe. The main trick here is obvious: you can switch ties around (only two knots are permissible: the four-in-hand or the half Windsor.) You can wear suspenders. You can have button-down shirts or plain collars. You can stick a linen handkerchief in your pocket. You can add a hat. All these things can make a world of difference, and make you look just different enough to make it appear that you have a huge wardrobe, but not so different day to day that you come across as a loon.

Is this an expensive undertaking? Not in any way. Unless you have some size issue at work, most of this can be purchased at a thrift store. The other day I bought a pair of grey wool trousers and a pair of olive wool trousers at $3 a piece. The same items were available at a local men's shop for $90 and up. Down with retail! Sports coats are the same: unless you have some size issue to deal with, most are available at thrift stores. Shirts? Same. A buck a piece. Another option is the wonderful shirts from Lands' End. Why spend $65 for a Gitman when you can spend $25 at Lands' End?

Note that wearing a sports coat is not dressing up. A sports coat and trousers are casual wear. It is mostly what you should be wearing to light parties, to most jobs, to the store. It is perfectly presentable for public consumption. But do not be deceived into thinking that you are "dressing up" when you wear them. A sports coat and trousers are the official uniform of a man who is just going about the business of life. When someone says, come casual!, this is what you wear.

Jackets can have two, three, or four buttons. They can have side vents, center vents, or no vents at all. Avoid double-breasted until you have everything else. Americans do not wear hard shoulders! Nor do Americans wear those crazy drop-lapel sexy-style models that Bill Clinton wore. Do not buy these under any circumstances. They are ridiculous. Finally, always prefer natural fibers over synthetics.

Suits are trickier. You can get them at thrift stores, but they are harder to come by. You can also see eBay, which has an amazing selection of suits that you can buy for $20 and up. If this doesn't work, you have to go retail, and here you have to spend $450 and up for a decent suit. The worst thing to do is go to a department store and buy a $200 suit from the likes of JCPenney. These look horrible and they will fall apart. If you can't go thrift or eBay, prepare to spend. It is worth it. A special note for older men: wear suits most or all of the time, and always ties. Ultimately, it is the *only* thing an older man looks good in.

If you are wearing a suit, you are dressed up but you are not formal. For formal wear, you need a dinner jacket and black tie. That is another subject entirely. These days, most people don't need formal clothing. If you do need it once or twice in a year, it is worth it to buy the whole package. Don't spend a lot of money! On formal occasions, guys all look the same anyway, and you don't wear it enough to wear it out. You can get away with spending $150 in some discount formal shop. But I digress.

On shoes, there are only two brands that qualify as quality shoes: Allen Edmonds and Alden. All others are junk. Good shoes are expensive. Prepare to pay. The best possible shoe is the shell cordovan from Alden, starting at $440 and up. So it is. They last a lifetime. If you don't have the money, go to the military supply store and pay $10 for some used military oxfords. They look great! Ultimately, you need: a black shoe, a burgundy shoe, and a casual shoe (this, again, leaves aside shoes that go with functional wear). That's all. As for loafers, they are aptly named. The normative men's shoe should have laces.

This takes us to the issue of fit. Most people buy their shoes too small. Get a half size bigger than you think. Shoes should not hurt your feet. Don't believe your shoe will stretch. It should be right when you wear it out of the store.

Fitting a shirt is not hard. Measure your neck with a tape measure. A shirt should not be too loose around the neck (you should not be able to stick your whole hand in your collar!) nor should it be too tight (when you turn your head, your shirt should not turn with it). The sleeve length should be such that the cuff hits that bone at the top of your hand some four inches above your thumb.

Do I really need to say it? No short-sleeve "dress shirts" in public, ever! Also, do I really need to say this? Shirts are not supposed to be worn against the skin. Wear a T-shirt, please.

Jackets: most men wear them too tight! Resist the temptation to get them taken in. They should be loose and comfortable. Jacket sleeve length: men tend to wear them too long! One-quarter to one-half inch of your shirt cuff should show below the jacket. You should measure this standing in place.

It doesn't matter what your life activities are: fit is fit! I once had a drummer tell me that he needs his jacket sleeves long in order for them to look right as he plays his cymbals. Well, if so, I should make mine long to change a lightbulb! This is nonsense. There is only one way a jacket fits: properly.

Trousers: they are not supposed to fit like jeans! They are supposed to be loose and even billowy by blue-jean standards. Do not have the seat taken in. Do not have the back leg taken in. Just wear them as they come. The length of leg should hit the top of your shoe. It should not break too much. Cuffs should be 1.5 inches, no less. Older men can get away with larger cuffs but not younger men.

Socks: nothing fancy, please! They should be blue, black, grey, or tan. Anything else, like argyles or other patterns, is too fussy for a gentleman.

They conjure up an image of a guy rifling through a sock drawer try to find just the right sock for the occasion. This is an awful image. Socks should appear to be put on without any effort or thought. But: never wear a sock that is a lighter color than your jacket. No time to explain why. Just trust me on this point.

Finally, never underestimate the power of the iron. The iron is the ultimate tool for dressing well. It puts the crease in your trousers and takes the wrinkles out of your jackets. It flattens the placket on your shirt and puts a point in the cuffs of your pants. Your iron should come out frequently, almost daily in fact. If you are not ironing, you are not dressing well.

Yes, there is much more to say, but this article contains just about all you will ever need to know to look better than most every man in the world. Follow my advice and do your part to save civilization.

43

Do People Secretly Think You're a Pig?

December 1, 2007

You don't want to read this article. But you should and must. It contains some dreadful truths that are universal but no one is willing to talk about them because the subject is so uncomfortable.

I would like to reveal a universal prejudice—it is a cruel and judgmental attitude that is written on the hearts of people in all times and all places—that might very well wreck your life, but which you can deal with rather easily.

The subject is table manners. No biggie, right? Who cares about how one holds a fork or cuts a steak or eats soup? All this is merely Victorian frippery, irrelevant in our days of social liberation.

Here's the truth. You are being judged every time you lift fork to mouth. And not just judged: you are watched with an eagle eye and mercilessly and horribly criticized in the minds of those around you. They are forming extreme opinions about you. Missteps are being chronicled in the personal histories others carry around in their minds.

What's more, the assembly of facts that people hold in their minds concerning your table manners rises to the top. It is more important than what you say, because table manners seem to reveal some inner secret about you, your background, your class, your rearing, your parents, your attentiveness and self-awareness. People are perversely interested in your secrets, particularly those you reveal inadvertently. No, people will not admit it. But they are lying. You are how you eat.

It comes down to this. You can be wearing a $2,000 suit. You can speak with incredible erudition. You can have the whitest teeth, the best jokes, the coolest haircut, and looks of dazzling beauty. But bad table manners wipe it all away.

Worse: the better you look and sound, the higher the standards are for your manners and the more severe people will be toward your slipups. Why? Because people will figure that all the other externals are nothing but a put-on. You will be a living, breathing hoax.

I know that these truths are hard to take. The first thought might be: hey, don't impinge on my eating freedom! I'll eat how I want!

Ok, that's fine. But then you have to live with the consequences. It's the same with dress and language. You can cuss like a congressman, use a vulgar word at the table, stink to high heaven, and wear sweats to a dinner party. For that matter, you can staple your face with 100 metal rings, and stretch your earlobes to your shoulders—but then you have to live with the social fallout. People will shun you. You will be an outcast.

It's not only that. Are you really happy knowing that people who have eaten with you carry around an image of you in their heads that has you eating like a pig? It doesn't take much to cause this: stacking your artichoke leaves upside-down, for example. So even if it doesn't hurt your career (which is does!), are you really happy knowing that people think ill of you?

Fine, you say, but first let's discuss this.

At some point in your life, you will be required to eat in front of someone whom you want to impress. It could be a future employer. It could be a present manager higher up in the pecking order. It could be the dean, your pastor, a potential client or donor. It could be a possible future in-law. Don't think that eating alone in a fast-food place protects you. Someone could be watching. That someone might later find himself or herself in a position to do you a favor.

So let's say you blow it on one of these occasions. There will be no announcement. No explanation. No one will take you aside and say: "Next time, eat your soup by moving the spoon away from your body." No one says: "I like Jane, but she needs to brush up her table etiquette."

You will never know the reason for your failure. But neither will you ascend. You will only rise as high as your manners place you in the social hierarchy. Again, people are horribly and secretly cruel: they will condemn not only your character but your whole family history. It's not just your reputation that stands in the balance but that generation's.

And remember that you only have one chance to get it right, and then you die and your legacy is established for all of history. Your legacy does not need to be less than it could, all because you never put your napkin on your lap.

These are brutal facts, terrifying ones, even. But it's better that you know now rather than blow your one chance to get it right. Remember the quotation attributed to Oscar Wilde: "The world was my oyster, but I used the wrong fork."

There are many guides to table manners out there. But we live in a blogging culture in which all information must be instant and short. So here are the five essential things you *must* do no matter what:

1. Hold your fork and spoon properly. There is only one way: balance them between the first knuckle of the middle finger and the tip of the index finger; the thumb steadies the handle. There are no variations on this, no issues of personal style, and no regional permissions. For some things, such as cutting with the other hand, there are other variations that require turning the fork over. If you are unsure, default to the orthodox way.
2. Put your napkin in your lap after you sit down to dinner. Do not forget.
3. Don't smack. This is easy, right? Apparently not. Smacking is incredibly and disgustingly common. People must suppose that others don't hear it. But they do, and it's awful. There is only one way in the known universe to prevent smacking: keep your lips closed when there is food in your mouth, no matter what.
4. Eat at the margin, not the aggregate. Don't cut all your steak up before you begin eating. Don't butter your whole roll. Prepare each bit separately.
5. If in doubt, wait for others. Don't start eating anything until everyone has been served.

There: that's five hard-core rules. There are a hundred others that you can pick up in time, and it is good to read a book, so that you know for sure that you are doing it right. But you do not want to look like an obsessive rule keeper. Equally important to obeying rules is to look like you are not even thinking about them. You must look comfortable, happy, and relaxed. What's more, this is the only way to be in order that you can be delightful at the table.

Okay, so you are jolted a bit, and offended by this article. You are tempted to forget that you ever read it. You are free to do so. But others are also free to think of you as uncouth, ill-trained, low-born, and poorly raised, and to treat you with all those assumptions in mind.

Yes, there are probably great men and women of the past who ate like pigs. They succeeded despite it. Why take the chance that you will happen to be among them, when minding manners is so little to ask?

44

Ten People I Would Like To Meet

August 1, 2005

Blog memes can be annoying, so this is no attempt to start one. It is merely an interesting exercise that yields interesting information about both the subjects and the person doing the choosing.

The idea is to choose ten people who you would most like to meet in all of history, five men and five women. To make it more challenging, let's exclude family and primary religious figures such as JMJ, etc., and exclude elected politicians and bureaucrats just because their profession is such an obviously shoddy means toward achieving immortality.

The idea isn't to meet them to pester them with some question, like asking Socrates precisely what he was teaching the youth, or Shakespeare whether he really is Shakespeare. Nor is it about some time-travel thing that allows you to ask Kennedy who he thinks shot him.

No, the idea is to meet these people as you might meet anyone today in a casual setting in which you have a few minutes to visit, just to see what impression he or she makes. The goal is to discover what it is like to be in their presence, to hear their voices, to look in their eyes, observe how they manage the space, to engage in polite introductions and small talk and, perhaps, to convey to them what their lives and work have meant to you.

Here are my choices.

Gustav Mahler (1860–1911). In this conductor and composer we have a mind and an imagination that surpasses human understanding, and yet at the same time his art reveals a grinding human struggle. His nine symphonies contain enough depth and meaning to captivate a person for an entire lifetime, since it's my view that it takes ten years to come close to fully grasping even one of them. You sense that if you did succeed in fully grasping all nine, you would know all that it is possible to know about life, death, love, joy, sadness, and the entire range of human emotion and experience. A non-practicing Catholic Jew in Vienna, he drew from all the cultural sources within himself to cultivate the capacity for truly universal expression—it came, but only with intense work and deep pain. He was known more as a conductor in his time than a composer, which is an astounding fact. By the way, I just heard Mahler's reorchestration of Beethoven's ninth symphony. Presumptuous, yes, but somehow with Mahler, it seems right. There are many photographs of him available: dashing, deeply intelligent, far seeing.

Ludwig von Mises (1881–1973). Murray Rothbard puzzled many times how it is that the 20th century gave us this man who seemed destined to resist all the evil of his times, and stand on principle despite every pressure to compromise. He paid a huge price. He was educated in security and spent his early career accumulating a European-wide reputation for pioneering contributions to economic science. He refuted socialism. He integrated money into macroeconomics. He put the whole of the social sciences on a new epistemological basis. Then the tables turned. Positivism advanced, and the liberals began to cave and support the state. The Nazis advanced. He was run out of his native country, run out again of his sanctuary in Geneva, and ignored by academia in the U.S. He had every reason to give in, give up, or regret his fate. But he never did. It's as if his internal constitution would never permit him to relent. This is why he was so hated, feared by some, and also respected. God bless people like this. All accounts report that he had Old-World manners, inner cheer, and surprising warmth. Can you imagine meeting him?

Thomas Jefferson (1743–1826). Yes, I know this seems to violate the rule against including elected officials, but I plead two considerations: his presidency is the least important thing about him, and he only agreed to it because the Hamiltonians were in the process of completely shredding what was left of the founding ideals embodied in the Declaration of Independence, and they had to be stopped. He didn't mention his presidency in his chosen tombstone inscription! All that aside, has American history given a greater gift to humanity than the mind and thought of Jefferson? He was best as a radical libertarian in every sense: secessionist, revolutionary, decentralist. His faith in the capacity of people to organize their own affairs remains the driving force behind political revolutions the world over. His stature seems to grow larger as time goes on. He was a polymath and yet he strikes me as a humble man—not at all the person whom public-school kids study. His letters reveal a very careful writer with no pretensions but an explosively creative intellect who wanted to somehow make a difference in human history on behalf of liberty. He seems so much larger than life itself. To meet him would somehow prove that he really did exist.

Oscar Wilde (1854–1900). The least important thing to know about Oscar is what everyone knows, and how tragic that is. Here is what really captivates me. He wrote plays and books in the late 19th century that were snappy and edgy and funny and triply ironic—and the same plays and books sound just as contemporary and snappy and ironic in 2005. Few writers have ever made humor timeless, but he did. His works are for the ages. And they are all "adult" in the right sort of way: you have to be a certain age to comprehend all the meanings and implications. To read him is to be in the in-crowd, part of a private crowd that knows what's what. He flatters you that way. Also, he had a huge range. *The Picture of Dorian Grey* is as serious a story of the corruption of the soul as has ever been written. His poetry is wonderful. It is said that he had not an ounce of malice in him. I believe that. His teeth were slightly yellowed, and this embarrassed him so he tended to speak with his hands across his mouth. You might think that would be an impediment to communication but no: all reports are that no one in London for generations could so completely captivate a roomful of people. People just adored this amazing man. Star quality doesn't quite describe it. He had god-like ability to enthrall and charm. This was a good man and a great talent. Legend has it that his last words were: "Either these curtains or I have to go." Funny, but not true. His last words were the Act of Faith. May the special interests leave him alone and may he one day be appreciated for the artist he was.

Juan de Mariana (1536–1624). Ah, the Spanish Jesuit priest-theologian-economist who famously advocated the right of an individual to kill the tyrant-king or any despot. His argument was that when a ruler steals, loots, and kills in a way contrary to the natural law, it is in accord with justice to do what is necessary to unseat him. Natural law supersedes state law. Don't feel bad for the despot: power corrupts and with that corruption come risks. As for the worry that good kings would be killed unjustly under this idea, Mariana offered up all history to show that is not the pattern: good rulers are not killed and far too many despots rule. After his book appeared, two French tyrants were slain: Henry III and Henry IV. A mild hysteria against him followed, the Jesuits repudiated his book, and it was burned by order of the Parliament of Paris in 1610. But this book wasn't his most egregious act. The book that really did him in was the one that condemned inflation as theft (he was a great monetary economist). At the age of 75, he was condemned to prison for life. All reports indicate a man of amazing personal fortitude, as unrelenting as he was brilliant.

Mother Cabrini (1850–1917). Shorter than five feet and always dressed in her habit, St. Frances Xavier Cabrini was one of the great entrepreneurs of the 19th century, the Bill Gates of charitable work of her time. From her earliest days she had wild ambitions to be a missionary to the world's poor, starting in China. Instead, the pope sent her to the United States. She founded the Missionary Sisters of the Poor, but this was resisted on grounds that women can't be missionaries. She wrote to Rome: "If the mission of announcing the Lord's resurrection to his apostles had been entrusted to Mary Magdalene, it would seem a very good thing to confide to other women an evangelizing mission." Well, what could Rome do but agree? And so it seemed throughout her life. She overcame resistance everywhere she went and eventually created a vast network of hundreds of orphanages, schools, and hospitals in the Northeast, the South, and even the Far West. She was both worldly and holy, an amazing businesswoman and pious saint. Her business sense was particularly shrewd: she was once donated some gold mines in Colorado, but rather than sell them she sent some sisters there to run them properly.

Clara Schumann (1819–1896). I picture her as a graceful yet powerful personality, with beauty that flows from the inside. Certainly everyone who knew her adored her. Her musical brilliance first struck me when I read a letter to her from Brahms in which he bemoaned the fact that he was doomed to make a living as a piano teacher whereas *she* could grow rich from performing the piano. She had far more invitations than she could accept. Imagine how many virtuosic pianists there were in her time, and yet she dominated the field with masterful performances that drove the likes of Brahms to unemployment! She made innovative contributions to piano pedagogy as well, in her position at two German conservatories of music. She was of course married to Robert, and inspired his grandest compositions, but she is also the reason for the melodies behind many pieces of music from her time. Aside from that, she bore and raised seven children and wrote many creative works for piano. What a mysterious power she must have had, the kind of person who walks into a room and fills the entire space but is not entirely aware of it.

Saint Cecilia (third century). She was a Roman aristocrat who became a Christian and found herself in an arranged marriage to a pagan and refused to consummate it. Her piety converted him, and so an angel appeared and they were crowned with roses and lilies. Later he was killed for his faith, and his brother too. Roman prefect Turcius Almachius had her condemned to death, first by suffocation, from which she escaped, and then by decapitation, which did not work even after three attempts. The executioner freaked out and ran away. Cecilia lived three days and served the poor. The only problem is that none of this is likely to be true. Yet here is what we do know. She lived and was martyred, and her intervention has been credited with supporting the arts and music since her death. There is usually some basis for such stories, either supernatural or biographical. I would not be surprised to find that there was something about her that called her to some massive role in history long past her death. What it is I would like to know.

Rose Wilder Lane (1886–1968). Now here is a wonderful writer, and a true American! The daughter of Laura Ingalls Wilder Lane, some people believe that she had more to do with the *Little House* series than is generally acknowledged. Her writing career began in 1910 and lasted until her last years. She wrote biographies, as well as stories for dozens of papers, and lived a varied and exciting life. Her book *The Discovery of Freedom* is a classic of libertarian apologetics. I've yet to read her novels (the ones she took credit for) but I would like to. I like this passage: "Give me time and I will tell you why individualism, laissez faire and the slightly restrained anarchy of capitalism offer the best opportunities for the development of the human spirit. Also I will tell you why the relative freedom of human spirit is better—and more productive, even in material ways—than the communist, Fascist, or any other rigidity organized for material ends." How dashing she must have been. I've heard reports, though, that she was rather shy.

Bette Davis (1908–1989). If she had never made a movie, one senses that she would have made her mark on history somehow. This was a remarkable woman with the greatest range in her personality. No one so fully dominates the screen as does. One almost feels sorry for her co-actors; they seem to shrivel and dry by comparison. Her voice, her eyes, her walk, her presence and stamina, they all combine into a very powerful on-screen personality. She most famously played ruthless women but this was just a matter of the division of labor because she was just as great in other roles. She is obviously very smart, and must have had an explosive personality. I once met Gary Merrill, to whom she had been married. Actually I was sort of forced to spend several days with him because of circumstances of time and place, and I certainly had the impression that he never really recovered from whatever he went through with her. In any case, how unforgettable it would be just to be in the same room with her.

So that's my list, subject to change, even as soon as tomorrow.

45

The Gay Adoption Conundrum

July 8, 2003

Closely linked to the issue of gay marriage is the issue of gay adoption. The subject raises the stakes in the current national controversy, and, as usual, state intervention complicates the picture enormously.

Below I argue for the political intuition of both the Left (that gay couples shouldn't be prohibited by law from adopting) and the Right (legalization raises the specter of children placed by courts in ethically dysfunctional environments and otherwise used as political footballs). I conclude that the social, cultural, and religious conflicts associated with gay marriage and adoption are best resolved through laissez-faire.

In a painfully circuitous column on gays and marriage, Jonah Goldberg writes: "I remain unconvinced that marriage is a 'fundamental right' and therefore immune to government regulation." Rather than try to sort out the myriad confusions in this sentence, let us just state the obvious: marriage and family, like the ownership of property, precede the state. They are rooted in the freedom of association and the right of contract. They need no state to exist. In a state of anarchy, there would still be property, marriage, and family.

Historically, religious institutions and clan, not the state, had the strongest claim to adjudicating matters involving marriage, though in a free society the decision to marry is the individual's. (The Catholic Church has long recognized the right of the individual in the choice of a spouse, for example, and the sacrament of marriage itself is confected not by the priest but by the couple.) The state took over this power and has made a mess of it. It should be restored to private institutions, and be none of the state's business.

So should gays be permitted to marry? Michael Kinsley is right: government should get out of the marriage business. This answer flows directly from the general embrace of the principle of free association: people should be permitted to do whatever they want provided they aren't violating anyone's rights. They do not have the right to expect the Church, employers, or anyone else to recognize their choices as valid and morally legitimate, of course. If people have a problem with the idea of two men or two women being married—as would practically everyone throughout the whole history of world—there is an easy solution: don't recognize it as a marriage.

We do this all the time in life. I love music but I don't recognize rap, heavy metal, and Christian contemporary music as genuinely musical. I think they're junk and I'm glad to say so. In fact, my opinion is that anyone who listens to this stuff is doing harm to himself, and, in the broadest possible sense, is debasing the culture. But to listen to this music is not harmful to anyone but those who choose to do so, so I am not within my rights to prevent it. As for the culture, I do not enjoy the right to shape it according to my own views of what constitutes beauty and art and truth. (If I did I would force everyone to listen to 16th century liturgical music, properly performed.)

So it is with gay marriage. If you think it's a hoax, nothing prevents a free person in a free society from saying so, just as nothing prevents anyone from calling a union of two persons or more of whatever sort a "marriage." If you don't like that, and believe that society requires an overarching coercive authority to impose the family structure, you do not have much faith in the orderliness of human choice, you are not a liberal in the classical sense, and you won't like the rest of this article. Suffice it to say that the traditional family structure is not a legal artifice; it is an outgrowth of tendencies in human nature, and it is not going to disappear because some men in Texas shack up and call themselves married.

The existence of the state, as well as its benefits and legal rights associated with marriage, add a layer of confusion. The very presence of legal marital protections and benefits cries out for the state to define what constitutes a legitimate marriage. By itself this is a dangerous power. If the state can define a marriage, it can dictate the workings of the marriage and family too. It can police the raising of children, kidnap kids, prevent them from working for wages negotiated by contract, limit or mandate family size, and a host of other interventions.

That marriage should be privatized is clear enough, but it leaves out a crucially important consideration: children. This factor is the main concern of those who would legally prohibit marital unions among gays. The worry is that once the state permits gays to define themselves as married, nothing stands in their way of adopting and raising children—a fact which gives rise to important concerns about the health of children in a setting that in all times and all places has been considered ethically objectionable by the dominant social ethos.

But let's be precise about what in particular seems troubling about this to the point that many believe the force of law should prevent it. It can't be merely the desire for all children to grow up in perfectly stable and moral home environments. Everyone knows children who are raised in less than ideal circumstances, from single-parent households resulting from death or divorce, to poverty, to cases of neglect. As sad as these cases are, hardly anyone thinks that the state should correct every one of them by imposing idealized circumstances, and properly so.

We look at such cases, feel bad about them, but recognize them as part of life—essentially private tragedies (I'm leaving out cases of severe physical abuse, of course). It's true that children need both mothers and fathers, and it is absurd to pretend that anything less is just as good. But when this doesn't happen, we help where and when we can but don't necessarily believe that the state should actively intervene to crush all less-than-ideal family settings.

What's more, it cannot be ruled out that a stable home with two responsible parents of the same sex would be a better setting for raising children than an unstable home with parents of different sexes or a single-parent household. In fact, most people these days know of gay parents with children, and they haven't led to any sort of social calamity. Such families are surprisingly bourgeois in terms of their internal life, and the effects of such parenting on the kids. Perhaps this isn't surprising; the desire to raise an adopted child may reflect a desire for normalization and regularization on the part of gays.

None of which suggests that people should or should not approve of gay adoptions. In all societies everywhere, such cases have always existed under a cloud of some degree of social disapproval and they always will. The only question of any political relevance is whether the state should actively intervene to prevent them or whether this is an issue that should be dealt with through non-violent means. As it is, there is nothing the state can or should do about single people having and raising children outside of a conventional marriage (of course it should not be subsidized by the state either). So it is unclear why adoptions should not be similarly permitted as merely the consequence of voluntary choice.

A main problem that inchoately exists here is the sense that gay adoptions would be somehow foisted on society via the court system, as an imposition, just as the courts are working to grant gays many special preferences in the law (e.g. the alleged right not to be discriminated against). We can easily imagine state adoption agencies, and those licensed by the state, adopting a rule of "non-discrimination" between gay and non-gay households, a completely preposterous rule but one that would be lobbied for by organized gay activists. Political pressure to relent in any such discrimination for or against gays would be intense.

Foreseeing an adoption system as politically poisoned as the current foster-care system, many people suspect that the demand for the right to marry and adopt is merely a ploy to have the state intervene yet again against bourgeois values. This is not an unreasonable assumption. The state adoption agencies in question, if they are permitted to choose gay parents, will not be wholly concerned about the well being of children or the desire of the donor mother. The children will be placed with a variety of other bureaucratic and political considerations in mind.

Even now, the entire adoption process is fraught with interventions that impede its development. Adoptive parents cannot purchase parenting rights, so there is no market as such. Agencies are hindered in their ability to make contracts in all directions. Private services, including those that would pay mothers to carry children to term, are either forbidden or crowded out by public services. The first step to clarity, then, is to abolish all these interventions and not impose new ones, legislating neither for nor against additional rights for gays. The entire problem could be left to (unregulated) private organizations.

How would adoption work in a free society in which gays were permitted to call themselves married? The donating parent is a contracting party and would only give up a child provided certain conditions were met. That the child grow up in a regularized family environment is a minimum expectation that most all donating mothers (and fathers) would ask. If her child were to be raised by a two-person, single-sex household, she would surely have to approve it. In general, who is in a better position to want the best possible environment for a child than the mother?

In a free society, there are no grounds to prevent women who bear children from arranging peaceful exchanges and cooperative arrangements concerning the parenting rights they own from the outset. If a woman conceives a child, she owns the parenting rights and can choose to give them away or sell them as she wishes. In this case, it is highly likely that the mother would seek conventional families to adopt her child. It might be that single-sex, two parent households would face a dearth of available children for adoption. Certainly they would have to pay a high price for the rights, given that we could expect far fewer mothers to approve these conditions than more conventional families.

It's true that gays have a higher income than non-gays and could well afford the price. But there is another price tag to consider in a free market: the mother herself would be in a position to earn money from contracting with parents over parenting rights. Donor agencies concentrating on non-gay parenting might find themselves in a position to outbid the donor agencies concentrating on gay parenting.

In fact, we might expect that agencies and donors would have every incentive based on deep moral conviction to outbid the offers of pro-gay adoption agencies, and convince risk-averse mothers-to-be that their child should be adopted by non-gays. Each side would have every incentive to make the strongest possible case for or against gay adoption, thus providing an environment in which the research and findings on prospects for gay parenting would receive maximum encouragement and exposure.

We can see, then, that the free market might end up seriously discouraging gay adoptions, simply because mothers who relinquish parenting rights would likely prefer non-gay to gay parents. Would households in which gay couples raise adopted children continue to exist? Most certainly, but the crucial thing here is that all parties would have to agree to the arrangement. Would there be abusive settings and morally objectionable environments for kids? Certainly, but those exist now, whether the families are gay or non-gay.

Under the principle of laissez-faire, all parties would have every reason to want to continue to monitor the arrangements once they are agreed upon. Moreover, the experience of present and future gay adoptions would have a big influence on their prevalence in the far future. The feedback works here too: gay parents would have every reason to do the best possible job so as to improve the reputation of gay parenting.

Of course those who object on moral grounds would continue to be free to decry such arrangements, just as gay parents would have every reason to dispute their claims. This solution doesn't solve every problem but neither does freedom itself. Freedom at least takes politics out of the question, which is the first step toward finding the truth in an atmosphere of peace.

Thanks to Stephan Kinsella, Walter Block, and Joseph Stromberg for their comments.

46

Madmen and Government Regulations

August 18, 2009

The AMC's *Madmen*, themed around New York advertising executives in the 1960s, captivates viewers for its plots, fashions, shocking levels of political incorrectness, and, most of all, and with the way it draws viewers so closely into a world of the early 1960s that they never knew.

It seems like time travel, like all of this is really happening. It's so realistic that 20-something bloggers constantly talk about how "dead on" the show is, as if they would even know. The whole show has become such a culture phenom that it defines for the whole generation the way it views the postwar/pre-Woodstock era of America.

Having some affection for those fashions and times, I was prepared to like the show, and there is no question that the production values are the tops. But hidden inside the show turns out to be another agenda, which seems designed to glorify the regulatory state that came after the times featured in the show.

A few specific instances. Everyone is smoking, mostly chain smoking, and mostly indoors. It gives today's viewers a sense of creeps to observe the extent of it, as if everyone is working on making an early grave for themselves. And you get a sense of what must have been an overwhelming stench of stale smoke. Hardly anyone can watch scene after scene of this without a sense of discomfort, even to the point of feeling grossed out.

A hidden aspect of watching this is to think: thank goodness for the bans on smoking today and thank goodness for the warnings on cigarettes that tell consumers what these people didn't know.

The ubiquity of cigarettes is only the most conspicuous aspect of the overall feeling of danger and creepiness that appears in scene after scene. There is daytime office drinking to an extent that would surely raise questions in the context of modern workplace regulations.

The treatment of women in the movie is egregious and shocking, with every office girl getting ahead by slutting around and dressing mainly to please the men. They are overtly treated like toys, not humans or professionals. Harassment doesn't quite describe it. It is nothing short of ghastly.

Was this really the plight of professional women in those days? Well, the message goes, thank goodness for laws against discrimination and also laws against sexual harassment. If we took even one step away from the regulatory seizure of American business life, we would surely be back in this Hobbesian jungle of booze, abuse, and early death.

But a woman in the show can avoid this hell by choosing instead to be a "housewife," which means making the perfect home for her hubby, and otherwise standing around gossiping with the neighbors and going to tea and growing increasingly lonely and desperate. Meanwhile, her working husband at the office is carousing around and sleeping with the office girls while she pretends not to notice, since—what other options does she have?

Here again we get a picture of a wild world of patriarchal domination and savagery before the federal government tamed it.

This theme appears in scene after scene. The kids in the house are constantly doing dangerous things like wearing plastic bags on their heads, since this was of course before federally mandated warning labels appeared telling us not to do this. Mothers, you see, are way too stupid to know to tell their kids not to suffocate themselves with plastic bags, which is why we need a Consumer Products Safety Commission.

The same is true with cars. And with drinking. And seatbelts. And every other thing big and small you can think of. Every high-profile federal intervention is given a subtle endorsement because we are shown in high relief the sheer awfulness of the world before Leviathan took over our homes, businesses, and public and private lives in every respect. Without them, we would surely be blow-drying our hair in the tub.

This was the constant theme I observed in the several episodes I watched. I'm sure others can think of examples that appear in every episode. It is a Hobbesian tale that posits the inability of society to improve itself without the helping hand of the master.

The truth behind most of the regulations we have today—laws against discrimination, harassment, safety rules, and even smoking—is that there was already a social and cultural movement against the dangers featured in *Madmen*. This support for change was effectively nationalized by the federal government in the form of coercive rules, rather than permitting social, economic, and cultural pressure to bring about its own noncoercive solutions to social problems.

It is easy to forget while watching the show that this is, after all, fiction: a story made up by writers and producers with themes chosen by them for a purpose. Call it a libertarian-induced paranoia if you want, but I strongly suspect that a part of the agenda of this show is to propagandize for the regulatory world that came after, as if it, and only it, saved us from an eternity of grave social injustice and mortal danger to our lives and dignity.

I'm still waiting for a show about the real madmen of the era, those who imagined that fastening a noose around the whole of business culture was the only way to get us to behave in a civilized way.

47

Avoiding Austro-Flamewars

December 18, 2009

Digital media—particularly "social" media like forums, wikis, blogs, and tweets—have forced all people, including intellectuals, to engage each other as never before in human history.

And yet, people have discovered that to know others is not necessarily to love them. Conflicts and confrontations are a regular feature of daily discussion, which is all fine; but sometimes these can become personal and hysterical, and lead to lifelong hatreds.

People who frequent forums and other such venues know all about this. It is often the "noobs" who are at the forefront of the flamewars, getting their feelings hurt and lashing out, creating a spiral to the bottom. More experienced users learn to distinguish substantive discussion and argument from personality clashes.

At the Mises.org forums, for example, the periodic flamewars involve claims that a post or comment is too brassy, or too studied, or too far afield. This may or may not be true, but from where do we draw these impressions? And what standard is available to decide what is and what isn't tolerated?

I've noticed three personality types based on three archetypes or muses in Austrian history and tradition: Ludwig von Mises, Friedrich A. Hayek, and Murray N. Rothbard. This thought occurs to me as I reflect on a type of complaint that comes to us often about Mises Dailies, as well as controversies that come up in blog comments and discussions, many of which concern the proper style and tone (and content) of a site such as Mises.org.

The complaints run something like the following:

"Mises would never endorse such inflammatory rhetoric, and he was no anarchist. He must be turning in his grave after the article you ran yesterday."

"How can you run an article on the Fed that sticks to only economic analysis without pointing out the insider scam artists who are getting away with robbery on a gargantuan scale?"

"The site's recent obsession with [fill in the blank] is a huge departure from anything the Austrian economists of the past talked about."

The points here are not completely invalid, though surely not every article has to say everything or be everything. There are times for power-elite analysis and times for advancing pure economic understanding. There are times to denounce war and times to reflect on methodology in the social sciences. The Austro-libertarian perspective is vast and varied, with implications for the whole world of ideas.

And it is true that articles here can be rather speculative (Block on private roads, Kinsella on intellectual property, French on the downside of bank deregulation), but there is nothing wrong with pushing a paradigm further down the road. Nor is there anything wrong with passion in defense of freedom.

Is there really a need to choose one approach to prevail? Why can't they all work together, provided people can be tolerant toward different temperaments?

These three types generally follow the styles and approaches of these great thinkers — however different they might be. Let's examine the prevailing models and see which one you might fall into.

Ludwig von Mises (1881–1973)

He was a gentleman of the old school, born into prewar Europe, a brilliant student in every area, with courtly manners that he retained until his death. He faced immense trials in life (two wars, economic depression, two migrations, and relentless professional upheaval) and yet never lost his foundational commitment to reasoned, calm, and relentless argument as the right approach to changing society. Even when he was witness to amazing banking scams, he resisted naming names to focus only on the facts and logic.

His dedication to truth as he saw it was intransigent from the moment he read Menger's *Principles* until his death. His style was firm, dedicated, and forceful—but always of the Old World. He also retained his commitment to 19th-century-style liberalism—despite the totalitarian trends of the

20th century and despite the growing radicalism of his own later students. His method was systematic argument in the form of large treatises in which logic was the engine, and his system of thought was revealed book by book over the course of his lifetime.

He believed that the ideas that people hold were ultimately more powerful than their personal interests. I think of him as the pure intellectual, full of discipline and rigor, but perhaps a bit impersonal. The old-world ways of burying the personality for the sake of science prevailed in his practice. And this was true to the point that when Jörg Guido Hülsmann was writing his biography, he became amazed at how little documentation he found on any personal issues. Mises lived the purest life of the mind, Guido suggests.

Friedrich von Hayek (1899–1992)

Hayek was a colleague of Mises's who adopted a different style and approach, first in Austria as a teacher faithful to the master and then later in London as the popularizer and systemizer of Mises's business-cycle theory. His battles with the Keynesians and the Fabians, however, imparted to him a strong sense of the importance of presentation in the war of ideas. He was temperamentally disposed to seeing his opponent's point of view; he crafted his message in a way that was not merely true but also, in his view, convincing.

He was not a system builder so much as a curious and brilliant scholar who took on topics one at a time throughout a long life, a man whose positions on issues evolved in unpredictable ways. He was a dedicated proponent of the gold standard who later (regrettably) suggested that some reinflation after a crisis might be necessary and (wisely) later came to the radical defense of an immediate end to all central banking.

He penned compromises with the welfare state in one book and later argued the "extreme" view that no forms of intervention can improve on the natural evolution of the social order. He spoke about the common law and the merit of evolved tradition, on the one hand, and in other writings took a strictly libertarian view about property and the state. Then just when you think that Hayek was a bit of a softy, you find an old interview with him on national television holding a hard line on the topics of inflation and unemployment.

Part of what makes Hayek interesting is precisely this sense of struggle that you get in his writings, the sense that he is not presenting a finished package but working through topics in light of his scholarly understanding—as led by evidence and reflection. In this way, he leaves some very interesting surprises. Of all the Austrians, he was strongest against "intellectual property" and, before Rothbard, he might have been the most sympathetic to the idea of a stateless society as a viable option. He never stopped learning and never stopped his intellectual struggle.

Murray Rothbard (1926–1995)

Rothbard was a system builder of a different sort, but more open, more enthusiastic and spirited, a researcher whose theoretical apparatus seems to have been largely in place from the time he put pen to paper, and certainly by the time he finished his large treatise on economic theory. He took his economics from Mises and his libertarianism from Chodorov and the old American liberals, and knitted it all into a dazzling system of thought.

He had this remarkable capacity for teasing out the best from the thoughts of all ages, devouring books like snacks, and putting what he found into a model that applies in our times and all times.

The resulting outlook provided the perfect tableau for historical studies, and here, in my view, is where Rothbard's work really takes flight. There were no taboos, no unthinkable thoughts, no unspeakable phrases, no preconceptions, no sacred cows. He was a discoverer whose books take the reader through wild rides of villains and heroes, frauds and truth speakers, tragic victims and triumphant struggles. Even the longest-dead characters in history were still alive in Rothbard's mind.

As for his rhetorical style, it was pure fire. Progress meant breaking the model. He was committed to science but he was also ebullient in a way that is uncharacteristic of great scholars. Fun doesn't quite describe it. Just his presence in a room made the entire event entertaining for everyone. He was quick to laugh and he did so often and uproariously, and the juxtaposition between radical theory and outrageous fun was irresistible.

Fighting the enemies of liberty was, for him, a gallant and thrilling adventure, and fighting for liberty was pure joy. He had a way of regarding every moment of life as something of historic importance. He could turn a drab academic meeting into a memorable occasion, writing about it later the same way that others might write about wars and revolutions. This is far from Hayek, far from Mises, but completely captivating and thereby essential to the Rothbardian way.

Three in One

So there we have it: the three tendencies of the Austro-libertarians I've seen online. We might sum up the dominant traits as reasoned, reflective, and radical. That's not to say that each of these three thinkers did not embody all of these traits. We are speaking here of large tendencies stretching over three long lives, about dominant characteristics that one might take from each thinker.

Nor is it the case that people working within this tradition must always fall into a single category. Some days, we feel as radical as Rothbard, others as reasoned and cool as Mises, and others as speculative and searching as Hayek. Sometimes it depends on whom we have most recently read. Great thinkers tend to have this effect on the world, transferring not only their ideas but also their temperaments to those who are influenced by them.

Yes, there are tensions from time to time, but Mises.org communities are proof that all three types can get along just fine, so long as no one is prepared to purge the others, or otherwise push one style, one approach, one method at the expense of the others. We can look at other figures in the history of the school, people like Hazlitt or Hutt, or at modern thinkers like Salerno or Hoppe, and see that they too embody a variety of these approaches.

It is a hopeless task to attempt to impersonate anyone, and Mises.org mavens cannot and should not do this for Mises or for Hayek or for Rothbard. We can only learn from them and be inspired by them. To draw insights from all sources is to create the kind of diversity that makes for a vibrant and productive intellectual paradigm and an endlessly fascinating website erected in the defense of liberty.

48

How to Improve the Culture

December 28, 2009

The culture is going to hell in a handbag, we've been told for hundreds of years, and the free market gets a large share of the blame. The observation stretches from Left to Right and everywhere in between. It is universally agreed that letting markets run loose runs roughshod over all the finer things in life, from books to arts to clothing to manners.

Mises himself traces this ideological tendency to 19th-century critic John Ruskin, who "popularized the prejudice that capitalism, apart from being a bad economic system, has substituted ugliness for beauty, pettiness for grandeur, trash for art." The same argument appears today in conservative periodicals, every week, as a built-in bias; everyone knows that markets have unleashed a race to the bottom.

One response might be to say, This is not decline at all but just difference. Whether it's opera or rap, frescos or graffiti, black tie or grunge, it doesn't really matter. Culture takes different forms in different times, so get used to it.

I'm not really satisfied with that answer, mainly because of my own cultural biases. My tastes in music predate Bach. Dancing to me means ballet. Popular fiction I find insulting in every way. Kids, in my view, should spend their time mastering piano rather than gaming on computers.

I admit that it would not be impossible for me to be mistaken for a snob.

And yet, I would like to offer a contrary view—but not in the form of a big theory. Rather, consider some cases of cultural entrepreneurship that made a real difference by the same means through which every innovation comes about: risk taking, hard work, and marketing.

Let's begin with dance. Some ten years ago, I found myself at a ballet recital for young people. I had expected something like we used to see on GE commercials: little girls in tutus dancing to Tchaikovsky. Instead, the girls danced to ridiculous rock music and danced without discipline at all, flailing around this way and that. It was clear that they were learning no technique at all. And yet the parents were wild for it.

I'm not against jazz and rock dance but to do it right requires a foundation in ballet, which is the fundamental language of all dance in the West. Those amazing dancers you see on Fosse—they knew ballet first. But in these self-indulgent times, no one cares about discipline and hard work. Everyone wants to jump right into the fun thing even if it looks stupid.

I left that recital despairing that another epoch of goodness had passed into the night, replaced by a state of permanent slop. And then suddenly, out of nowhere, a 20-something dance entrepreneur showed up in town and opened a new studio, pricing her teaching below the competition. Through good will, efficiency, low prices, and smiles all around, she attracted a slew of new customers.

But this wasn't just any ballet entrepreneur. She had an attachment to the old ideals, old music, and old pedagogy. This is what she emphasized and pushed. At the first recital after one year of operation, the parents of the students all enjoyed the recital with new standards: the classical training, the old-world music, great attention to costumes, and all the trappings everyone once expected in real ballet. The parents cheered to the high heavens the glories of these kids and the program.

And so, voilà! In one year, thanks to one entrepreneur with a vision and the dedication to carry it out, the local culture is massively and dramatically improved—the Old World and its high standards carried on toward the future. I looked back at my previous despair with embarrassment. It turns out that there was nothing inevitable about cultural decline. All it takes is one person to make the change.

Let's move on to the subject of children's choirs. Since the ancient world, children's choirs have been the incubator of great musicians for the future. But today? It's a disaster. If there are choirs at all, they are taught pop tunes, bad technique, American Idol approaches, all of which end in creating would-be stars who never really do the hard work necessary for serious music-making in any field. The result is inevitable: a musically ignorant culture, and no real choirs at all.

But right here in my own town a woman decided to change that with a civic chorus of children. In the first year there were 25, and in the second that doubled, and then a chorus of older children was split off. They wear concert clothing and sing all the classic repertoire, even music in Latin. They have a rigorous schedule of rehearsals, very much like sports team practices. They learn technique and discipline. The parents love it! And the choir is singing all over town in a wonderful way.

To be sure, the director does not make the big bucks. She works extremely hard, giving private lessons and working with parents and spending far more time on this project than the payoff would seem to dictate. But she does it anyway because she has a passion for it and she is living out a dream.

Because of this one cultural entrepreneur, the community is changed.

Now, in both cases, we see that it could have gone the other way. If these two people had not come along with the desire to raise the standards and provide a valuable service, another generation's cultural education would have been missed. Instead, they both acted and took a risk. As a result, their legacy on this earth will outlive them.

Another case in point concerns a new immigrant family from India who opened a wonderful new Indian restaurant in a town overrun with fast-food chains and chicken-finger shacks. Everyone I know has long bemoaned the lack of great foreign cuisine here. It's the first point cited as evidence that this backwoods place has been given over to the capitalist pigs.

Then one day it was there: an Indian restaurant as good as any that one would find in any major city in the world, with a vast and varied menu and all the ambience one would want. And what made it possible? Not the overthrow of the capitalist order but rather the risk, hard work, and dedication of a single entrepreneur. Again, there was no guarantee that this would happen. It was a choice that was made by one individual. He and his family decided to open the restaurant.

Mises's fundamental point about the cultural critique of capitalism was that capitalism makes more of everything available to the consumer. That means more trashy novels and rotten music, but it also means more great literature and high-level music, all of which is accessible as never before.

But today, cultural entrepreneurs are seriously inhibited in their innovations by high taxes, regulations, and mandated benefits. This produces fewer attempts to improve our world than there would otherwise be. Some markets are hobbled to the point of near inaction, such as the education market, and others are less vibrant than they would otherwise be.

So what we need is not the overthrow of private property but more freedom for cultural entrepreneurship, and more individual initiative to do more than complain that the world is not conforming to your own values. The next time someone complains about what the market is doing to the culture, ask that person what he or she has done to enter the market and make a difference. And ask what that person has done to make the world freer for those who seek to make the world a more beautiful place.

49

Dealing with Failure

November 1, 2007

Dealing with personal failure is one of the great struggles of growing up. When we are young, the possibilities seem without limit, but as the years pass, we face every manner of barrier that causes us to be all too aware that we face a world with many constraints, many of them due to the limits of the temporal world but also, we must admit, many of them due to our own inadequacies.

I'm thinking in particular of my great failure to become a heavy drinker—I mean a serious, quaff-it-down-every-night, devil-may-care kind of drinker. I think back to when I was a young man, and how I split the world between two types of people: those who seriously drink, managing their lives well and enjoying every minute; and the other type who have a "glass of wine at dinner" but nothing else.

How I heaped disdain on the latter type—those puritans who poured up a tiny glass for purely functional purposes only, such as to "relax after a hard day's work," or to "cleanse the palate during dinner." How they collected bottles and talked so sweetly about vintages and labels and smelled their wine long and hard. How pathetic!

At dinner parties, some well-dressed man would refuse a cocktail—you might as well not come at all—and then lovingly take little sips of grape extract with the meal. When the host or hostess offers to pour another glass, the gesture arrives: the hand over the glass! It's as if to say: I refuse to live robustly as part of this gang. I'm too weak, too precious, to handle more.

So many of our influences in life are of a negative kind, people we observe and swear: I will never be like that. But I'm here to confess that I am indeed like that. It is not something I ever wanted. I wanted to be that other man who drank two double scotches before dinner, two or three glasses of wine during dinner, a brandy after dinner, and finally some peculiar liqueur with dessert.

If I drank like that now, I would be in intensive care and miss work for weeks.

I'm not entirely sure when the softening and compromises set in. Instead of two highballs before dinner, I would secretly and inauspiciously have one. Then during dinner, I started to drink more slowly and then use water to quench dinner thirst—a very bad sign. Then the whole brandy thing was cut, as was the fancy liqueur bit. Once I gave up the before-dinner liquor, it was straight into the abyss.

In the course of all of this, there were people who said that the problem was that I was relenting and thereby becoming less tolerant of alcohol. I was digging my own grave, so to speak. So I tried to prevent this by deliberately drinking more than I wanted in hopes of increasing my tolerance. Maybe I had to go through several weeks of not feeling well in the morning before I could restore my old level. Sadly, this didn't work at all.

Eventually I gave in to reality and my own defeat. I became what I had once rightly loathed.

My second major failure in life deals with my lifetime ambition to be a heavy smoker until I died. Here I had many positive influences. These influences were from all classes of people. I've seen men in their eighties who were still pack-a-day smokers. Because they smoked so late in life, they still looked cool. They were good conversationalists because smoking gave them time to think before they spoke. I recall a banker who smoked and looked like a 1930s movie star well into his dotage. Then there was a coal miner who rolled his own cigarettes until his nineties. Every puff seemed to reveal a personal biography of courage and strength in hard times, and a marvelous and manly fighting spirit. He just had a way about him that was fabulous, and that cigarette seemed to sum it all up. Such style!

Like most smokers, I had a promising start when I was young, though of course it was a struggle at first. When you first start, you can't smoke more than five a day without gagging. But gradually, you can increase that to 10 and finally, to the real goal, a pack a day. This I achieved in less than six months. I vowed to keep this up until the last day.

You can only imagine my thrill when I bumped it up further to two packs a day, and finally three. Now, I admit that my bragging rights are limited since I tended to light up incessantly and most of these cigarettes burned up in the ash tray. Even so, I was well on my way toward achieving my dream.

At some point, however, problems began to set in. There were rules, of course, about smoking in the office, and these rules tightened over time. Then the airline restrictions came along. Then restrictions in restaurants. But as much as I hated the state for curbing my ambitions, there was a more fundamental problem developing: my lungs just couldn't take it anymore.

Of course I was in denial, but as the bouts of coughing and sickness increased, I finally had to face the fact that there was a problem. No, I didn't stop altogether. First I smoked a pipe. Now here was a new image that worked just fine! But all that apparatus—the cleaners, the bag of tobacco, the special lighter, the dirty fingers, and bulky pipe itself—became an annoyance. So next came: the cigar! But this introduced other problems. The expense was prohibitive and, frankly, people hated the smell.

Eventually, and much to my dread, I had to face the fact that I would have to quit it altogether. It was a humbling moment but an unavoidable one.

I share all of this in the hope of helping others who have faced similar defeats, and letting them know that they are not alone. We all stumble.

Perhaps too there are lessons here in avoiding defeat itself. Perhaps there is a way to work up to becoming a lifetime heavy drinker and smoker by taking it all at a slower pace.

Perhaps one should set a schedule, and only hope to achieve the height at the age of 60, or something like that.

And a key question will always haunt me: perhaps I should have started smoking and drinking earlier, before I was fully grown. Perhaps then my bodily system might have become more accustomed to the habit and not reacted so negatively by the time I turned 30. Then I might have kept it up until a blessed old age.

Always remember that there is no better time for smoking and drinking than when you are young, when your system can handle it. As you grow older, you never know the ways in which the body will fight back against your dreams to smoke and drink heavily forever.

In any case, there is no sense in giving up hope. There is still the great lift that comes from observing others who have not similarly failed but rather stayed attached to their ideals. Nor will I give up hope in myself. To paraphrase someone, I'm no failure because I'm not yet dead.

50

Fortune Cookie Economics

August 28, 2006

Have you noticed how the texts of the "fortunes" in fortune cookies seem to be improving? In contrast to the old days when the fortune was a mere throw-away, these days, the language is clearer. The thoughts are more profound. Some of them are real keepers.

Is this a consequence of China's having become more capitalistic?

While I can't comment on the "lucky numbers" printed on them—who knows?—the last four fortunes I received in my cookies just astounded me with their erudition (even without adding any words at the end of them). Indeed they seemed to sum up the essence of core postulates of Austrian Economics!

Let's see, and keep in mind that these are real.

The value lies not within any particular thing, but in the desire placed on that thing.
Lucky Numbers 11, 2, 38, 44, 21, 8

Now, here we have a popular summary of the subjective theory of value. Value is not embedded in the material properties of any good or service. Neither does a thing acquire value merely because labor was employed to create it. Value is not dictated by the production process or social conditioning. An economic good is valued because an individual mind values it. It is a product of the human mind.

As Menger says:

> Value is therefore nothing inherent in goods, no property of them, but merely the importance that we first attribute to the satisfaction of our needs, that is, to our lives and well-being,

> and in consequence carry over to economic goods as the exclusive causes of the satisfaction of our needs.

Next we come to a further condition that affects economic valuation:

A bargain is not a bargain unless you can use the product.
Lucky Numbers 17, 31, 7, 48, 41, 5

Admittedly, this fortune is not quite as scientific but it makes a good point. Prices are the result of the interaction of subjective valuation and objective conditions of the relative availability of a good. They represent a historical record of trades that have already taken place. They do not and cannot dictate the future.

And yet even given a good with a certain price on the market, the desirability of a good cannot be imposed on others. It must be adopted and accepted by buyers, who assess prices based on individual usefulness.

Or as Mises says,

> It is ultimately always the subjective value judgments of individuals that determine the formation of prices.... The concept of a "just" or "fair" price is devoid of any scientific meaning; it is a disguise for wishes, a striving for a state of affairs different from reality. Market prices are entirely determined by the value judgments of men as they really act.

Dreams are extremely important. You can't do it unless you imagine it.
Lucky Numbers 37, 2, 17, 8, 49, 4

So let us accept the fortune cookie's implied claim that past data cannot somehow dictate our actions and therefore the future. The market is always looking forward. Our actions to buy or sell or invest or save are always a speculation, a judgment call. Nowhere is this more clear than in the institution of entrepreneurship, about which the next fortune speaks:

Given the forward-looking nature of the market process, and the human desire for economic development, there must be individuals who can imagine a future that is yet to be experienced, invest real resources in seeing their judgment come to pass in the production process, and thereby enjoy the rewards to come from profitability. This person is the entrepreneur-capitalist: the dreamer who imagines a possible future and then commits real resources to making that future happen.

The market process does not stop with one entrepreneurial success. Profits call forth emulators, people attracted to a certain idea or sector because a good or service is yielding high profits. For example, if a software entrepreneur comes up with an excellent anti-spyware program and becomes rich, others will take notice and enter the market and provide competition.

The method of success becomes part of the social store of knowledge that others are free to acquire and employ for their own use. As more producers enter the market, the result will be lower prices (if nothing else changes) and reduced profits for each producer.

In short, the successful entrepreneur will attract many people who strive to be just like him. His sucess in making his dreams become reality provides a model for others who do the same. Following the text of the fortune, we can call these people "friends."

> **In prosperity, our friends know us; in adversity, we know our friends.**
> **Lucky Numbers 28, 33, 48, 9, 40, 37**

The fortune is already ahead of us here, because it also speaks the reality of losses. Let us never forget that capitalism is not only about profits, which win friends. As Rothbard says, entrepreneurs also face the prospect of losses, sometimes big losses. When this happens, people flee our adversity. We lose our friends. We are humbled, and learn from our errors. We then look to others who are making profits and follow their ways, and the process continues without end, to the continual improvement of our standard of living.

If China's path to economic development continues on an upward path, can we expect ever-increasing economic sophistication from fortune cookies? I heartily await other fortunes that discuss capital theory, interest rates, the business cycle, and perhaps even price controls. If some entrepreneur wants to take the risk and create them, and I find them in my next set of cookies, I promise to scan them and make them famous. In your prosperity, your friends will know you.

51

Pound for Pound

September 28, 2005

There's a sense these days that anyone would favor a pie over a cake, and I think I know why. Pies don't tempt household cooks to scrimp on ingredients. That's why pies generally taste better.

If it's apples, it's apples, and most people don't think a half a cup of sugar in something is "too much." So it is for lemon and blueberry and a host of other pies made from fruit. As for the seasonal pumpkin pie, it's just vegetables in a crust, so who is to complain? Even pecan lives in the age of the decline of dessert, since most people think corn syrup is not objectionable, even if the pecan pie requires two cups.

But cake? People don't have the stomach to make a good one anymore. So we buy ice-cream "cakes" for birthdays for kids and otherwise don't bother. When people do bother to bake a cake, they succumb to the temptation to substitute ingredients. Instead of butter, they use margarine or mezoline spreads of whipped smear stuff of some sort or another. And then they cut back the sugar, and use strange sugar-like chemicals. And perhaps instead of eggs, its "egg beaters" or who-knows-what. Pretty soon, there's nothing left but a vague cake-shaped object.

The cake seems to have fallen on hard times indeed! We eat them when we are at buffets and civic events when they are available on paper plates, but that's because we weren't there to see them being made. Cakes have become like sausage: we love it but don't want to know about the process, much less undertake it ourselves.

This is why the world's greatest cake—I speak of the pound cake of course—is so hard to come by in American homes these days. It is contrary to the prevailing ethos, which is all about "substitutes" rather than the real thing. We spritz our pans with veggie oil rather than lard them as we should. We use fractioned rather than whole milk. We fear flour as if it is poison.

Modern civilization has given us glorious ingredients at our fingertips, all of us wherever we are, and what do we do but ungratefully spurn them all as if real food is nothing but a conspiracy to cut our lives short. Then when nature calls us to eat as we should, we give in to temptation and eat ice cream and candy bars in private as if we are partaking in secret sins.

What a dreadful life this puritanical attitude of mind leads to!

The pound cake is the key to breaking this cycle of false piety followed by guilt. It is the cake that embraces our age and says yes to life and love.

To begin with, you have to appreciate a food with a history to its name. In the middle ages, the term cake itself referred to a bread that was sweetened. According to this history, the pound cake dates to the early 18th century, and was favored because its ingredients were easy to remember: one pound each of four things. It was improved immeasurably (in my view) by the invention of rising agents in the 19th century.

Then it became an international food.

In France: Gâteau Quatre-Quarts.

In Spain: Queque Seco.

In Germany: Sandkuchen

Traditions, even international ones stretching back centuries, are great but never decisive. What convinces you of the pound cake's magnificence is the tasting. Here we have the perfect dessert treat. It is subtle, balanced, and robust. The texture is spongy but not flaky. It is moist without having the uncooked pudding-like quality you get from those "extra-moist" box jobs you buy at the store. Nor it is puffy and dry as so many homemade cakes can be (a result of pulling back on essential ingredients).

The other stopping point for many people today is the name pound cake, which sounds like something that will put on *pounds*. It might as well be called calorie cake or scale-busting cake or make-you-fat cake.

So let us be clear: the pound part refers not to its effects but to its ingredients. Now, to be sure, making it is not for the faint of heart.

Pound one: You know those boxes of butter that have four sticks of butter in them? You will use the whole box.

Pound number two: Do you know how much sugar is required to weigh in at a pound? Two cups.

Pound number three: Are you worried about your cholesterol intake from too many eggs? This cake requires half a dozen. That's half a carton.

Pound number four: Flour, Dr. Atkins, and three full cups!

If that sounds alarming to you, and you aren't prepared to face the reality that making something astonishingly delicious requires these ingredients, do not read further. If you would rule out making this just on grounds of its decadent ingredients alone, drop out of this article right now. You can continue to be part of the problem rather than part of the solution, as is your right.

But for those who want to take history in their hands and help bend it back toward sanity in cooking and taste in eating, the pound cake can recapture our history and lead us to the future.

The pound cake can be eaten by itself, or with coffee or hot chocolate. It can have a side of sweetened fruit or ice cream. It can be glazed with sugar or merely dusted with powered sugar. It can be eaten for breakfast, lunch, or after dinner. Can you imagine this as a midnight snack? Even the thinnest slice is satisfying.

After trying other variations, here is the one I settled on (pounds rendered here as normal measurements):

Mixed dry ingredients: 3 cups flour, ½ tsp. salt, ½ tsp. baking soda, 1 tsp. baking powder, 2 cups of sugar. Pour in 4 sticks of melted butter, 2 tsps. vanilla, and stir lightly. Add ½ cup of sour cream, ¼ cup milk, and six eggs. Blend on slow. Bake in tube pan, buttered and floured, at 325 degrees Fahrenheit for 1 hour and 20 minutes, or until toothpick comes out clean. Cool for half an hour.

Now I ask you: wouldn't you choose *this* cake over a pie?

52

The Work of Human Hands

October 9, 2002

War is coming, we're still in recession, the public is still angry about 9-11 (hey, is all this connected?), so we must do something to rekindle a sense of joy in our own private lives. But what? What people on the home front have always done: throw themselves into the domestic arts, preferably something that is beyond the time and connects us with ancient truth. For my part, it is all about bread.

I know that bread is out and meat is in. In the Age of Atkins, bread is the great taboo, the thing that puts inches on your frame. Anti-breadism runs rampant.

And yet, we must keep some perspective here. Some things in life are not dispensable, no matter what the dietary trends. Bread is among them. Man cannot live on it alone, but it isn't called the staff of life for nothing. It is the substance Christ chose to become, through the sacrament of communion, His own Body. Surely that means something.

We should not contemplate life without bread any more than we should imagine living without wine, the choice of which to become Precious Blood makes Prohibition and teetotalism radically objectionable.

Once you accept the inevitability of bread, that it must be fresh from your own kitchen is proven by a taste test of the greatest store bread against bread from even a moderately good home baker. The results speak for themselves.

Now, quick breads have much to recommend them. I favor the mix from the old (and out of print) *Better Homes and Gardens Cookbook* (10 cups flour, 2 cups lard (yes, *lard*), ⅓ cup baking powder, one-quarter cup sugar, some salt) , which turns into biscuits, pancakes, or muffins in no time.

This repertoire is a regional favorite, and the kids love it. It is quick, easy, and versatile.

I don't know if other quick-bread people are the same way, but I've found the prospect of cooking with yeast intimidating. In college, I thought I had it all figured out. On Sundays, I would make six loaves of bread, eat one, and give the rest away. But it only took one bad experience in a mucky coastal town (the bread wouldn't rise!) and I gave it up.

But social and political calamity calls for taking new risks. So, yeast bread it is. And yeast is all about giving life and avoiding death that comes from the wrong temperature. We are fortunate nowadays to have access to electronic temperature checkers. For those of us without infallible wrist-based temperature gauges, these are a godsend for getting the yeast to 100 degrees and the milk-sugar-butter mixture to 110 degrees before the addition of eggs cools it down a bit more. One mistake can kill the yeast, so the gadgetry is a help.

What kind of bread? This is the real glory: the ritual of the dough itself. Once you understand it, and can make this part, anything is possible. Baguettes? Sure. Cinnamon rolls? Homemade are the best. Or make just plain white bread, eat a slice for breakfast, lunch, and dinner, and French toast tomorrow morning. Somehow, just the smell of it provides comfort and security, a sense that all is right in the home even if not in the world.

And as much as we love technology, as much as we favor time-saving devices, ideally bread should be the work of human hands. The mixing and kneading is the very essence of what bread making is all about. Turn the job over to a machine, and you drain the entire exercise of life and joy. Why not just buy bread at the store?

When you give some of your bread away (as you should), you don't really want to say that you used a bread machine, do you? You want to say that you mixed and kneaded it yourself. And why does this please people? Because it suggests integrity and truth, that you care enough to mix your labor with basic ingredients to generate a new creation, and do this for another as a pious act of generosity.

We have all seen those flour commercials that claim that this or that product gives you confidence in what you cook. Perhaps. But it's not really the product that matters. It is the doing itself. When you make bread, you are given a sense of extraordinary accomplishment, as if you have conjured up something spectacular out of nothing. This sense spills over to life itself, granting you an overall confidence, the belief that whatever else is going on around you, you have within you the capacity to create glorious things,

things that rise and grow and become something completely new and life-sustaining.

I'm sorry, but quick-bread just doesn't have these mystical properties. Neither, for that matter, do meats and vegetables. Bread alone among all foods seems to touch the very soul of man and contains within it the power to remake our spirits and bring us life.

Make one loaf, one pan of cinnamon rolls, one baguette, and you have a vision of yourself doing it every week, or every day. It seems possible.

Anything seems possible. Making bread all the time could become a part of the liturgy of life, and then—and then—you are complete. Though the politicians call for war, the stock market sinks, the terrorists plot, as a baker of bread you are the bringer of life and health and happiness to yourself and the world of your own choosing.

53

Bring Back the Breakfast Drink

July 16, 2005

Everyone knows the rule: drink no liquor before noon. How insufferable such advice is! It has caused morning drinkers to hide their habits, deny them when confronted, and otherwise feel like they are doing something wrong or immoral or socially intolerable, a combination which leads to other forms of pathology.

It is time for them to stand up and proclaim themselves and their habit as the noble act that it is. All over the world, there exists a grand tradition of including a bit of spirits with one's breakfast, or at least a bit of beer or wine. How tragic that those who struggle mightily to uphold this practice are reduced to doing so alone, enjoying their pleasure only in the privacy of their own kitchen for fear of inviting public humiliation.

I was reminded of this tradition recently when a friend—a brilliant and productive young composer and musicologist who has to remain nameless—partook in his favorite breakfast, which he does every day insofar as it is possible. The food part is simple: a chocolate cake donut, with or without icing. The drink part: a pint of Guinness Stout. The method: dip the donut in the stout and chomp it down. It is the adult version of the child's milk and cookies trick.

Splendid!

It turns out that in the sweep of history, when water was not always safe and orange juice rarely accessible, this practice of morning drinking was the norm for all classes in society, and remained so for the upper classes far into the modern age. We forget that coffee and tea are relatively modern by comparison. In the middle ages, the typical British breakfast always included a mug of ale or wine.

In the South today, the tradition seems to bypass the middle class completely and last only among the truly well-formed working class blacks and upper class white aristocrats. A maintenance man I knew would never touch the "government's liquor" but he would never start a day without a nice swig of his favorite moonshine.

I tried it once and it took two days for my lips to feel normal again! But he managed it quite well, worked hard, and had a great life.

Also, I know a delightfully old-world Southern gentleman who lives in an antebellum house and studies Holy Scripture every morning, the original Greek and Hebrew, and does this before he ever picks up the newspaper. His theory is that mornings are not for rushing around but rather contemplation of higher things.

One day I came during these early hours just for quick visit, and he invited me in.

"Would you like a cup of coffee, Jeffrey?" he asked.

"Yes sir, I would, thank you," I said.

Then he paused and said, with an impossibly charming flash in his eyes:

"Would you like some bourbon in that coffee?"

Well, of course I would! And so it was done.

Today most breakfast drinking takes place on airplanes. Why? Because we are surrounded by people we are not likely to see again, and so we feel a sense of freedom from artificial social impositions. If you think about it, once the silly taboo against breakfast drinking is crushed, many possibilities present themselves.

If you ask people their favorite breakfast drinks, and press the issue, you eventually find that in addition to the ones above, these are the best beloved:

The Bloody Mary: It is made from a jigger and a half of vodka, a few drops of Tabasco sauce, 3 jiggers of tomato juice, pepper, some lemon juice, salt, and a bit of Worcestershire sauce.

The mimosa: champagne and orange juice to taste. But actually you can add champagne to any fruit juice and create an amazingly festive break of day. It's unclear precisely what makes the difference, but I have a theory that it is just the popping of the champagne cork first thing in the morning. You can try this at home. Wake up late, shower, and then pull out and open a chilled bottle. The action alone creates a bigger rush than you can get from any evening martini.

Both of these drinks today are called "doghair drinks" as in the old saying that one should eat a bit of the hair of the dog that bit you. Strange saying, but it refers to the idea that one should have a bit more of the same drink of which you drank too much the night before, all toward the goal of curing the hangover.

Do you see what is happening here? The breakfast drink is being snuck in under the label of medicine as a way of evading the social taboo against liquor before noon. That's just silly. You don't need an excuse, particularly not a medicinal one. You can have a Bloody Mary or a mimosa anytime!

Along the same lines there is rum and 7-Up, rum and apple cider, and this interesting one just called "the breakfast drink": jigger vodka, jigger peach schnapps, cup of orange juice, 2 jiggers raspberry liqueur, ½ cup of collins mix. Fascinating!

For all the wonders and complications of that latter suggestion, I still can't get past the simplicity and clarity of my favorite of all time: a small glass of port wine.

Maybe it is an age thing. I like the idea of the Guinness, the courage it takes to drink moonshine, the fussiness that comes with a mimosa, the bold stroke of the Bloody Mary, and the sheer decadence associated with "the breakfast drink" but somehow the clarity and stability of the glass of port—which recalls the glory of colonial America—seems just right and just what is needed to join the movement to smash this ridiculous taboo against morning drinking.

A final note on a frequent objection: morning drinking diminishes one's productivity during the day. This is true, of course, but particularly for adults who process liquor more slowly. This underscores a point that cannot be emphasized enough: like smoking, morning drinking is particularly suited for the young, meaning under the age of 25. Their systems are robust and can handle it better. Don't waste your youth: it is up to you to bring back the breakfast drink!

54

Dr. Jekyll and Mr. Government

February 9, 2006

Ever since there has been government, there have been those who want to purify it from its excesses and corruptions, rid it of its grafters and operators, and cleanse it from any taint of the sin of private interest.

Government should serve the people with an eye to the common good, they declare, and it should be part of the solution to the problem of evil in the world, and not contribute to the problem itself. Government, in short, should be good!

The naïveté of good-government ideology is more widespread than is usually supposed. Those who want government to do some things always, but do other things never, embrace the same ideal.

The Left is scandalized by a government that plunders foreign nations and spies on its citizens' private lives, but urges that same government to plunder property owners and spy on their commercial lives. The Right is disgusted by a government that slathers billions on deadbeats and ne'er-do-wells, but wants the same government to squander billions on military contractors and goons that enforce bad law.

If only we could separate the good from the evil!

Of course there is no agreement on what constitutes the good and evil, but both Left and Right will forever agonize about why they must put up with what they don't like in order to get what they do like out of government. But it is an unstable compromise, and thus do both sides work constantly to somehow make government do the good things (however defined) but not the bad things (however defined).

Now to the literary metaphor.

Robert L. Stevenson's classic novel *Dr. Jekyll and Mr. Hyde* was not just about a person whose personality changed because of a potion he drank. Dr. Jekyll was an idealist who was annoyed at the constant presence of the tension between good and evil that lived within him. He sought to separate them from each other, so that Dr. Jekyll could have pure motives in all he did and never be tempted toward evil, while his alter ego could pursue bad works without tainting the good Doctor.

As he puts it:

> It was on the moral side, and in my own person, that I learned to recognise the thorough and primitive duality of man; I saw that, of the two natures that contended in the field of my consciousness, even if I could rightly be said to be either, it was only because I was radically both; and from an early date, even before the course of my scientific discoveries had begun to suggest the most naked possibility of such a miracle, I had learned to dwell with pleasure, as a beloved daydream, on the thought of the separation of these elements. If each, I told myself, could be housed in separate identities, life would be relieved of all that was unbearable; the unjust might go his way, delivered from the aspirations and remorse of his more upright twin; and the just could walk steadfastly and securely on his upward path, doing the good things in which he found his pleasure, and no longer exposed to disgrace and penitence by the hands of this extraneous evil. It was the curse of mankind that these incongruous faggots were thus bound together—that in the agonised womb of consciousness, these polar twins should be continuously struggling. How, then were they dissociated?

Dr. Jekyll finds a way, thanks to a scientific process he fails to reveal that involves some scarce salts. He drinks the potion. Incredibly, he is transformed into another person who is shorter, hairier, more primitive in emotions and desires, and completely callous toward the fate of everyone but himself. Mr. Hyde is a loathsome character who feels no remorse, and whose very presence discombobulates everyone around him. He is the very embodiment of evil. Eventually he is guilty of murder.

He drinks the potion again, and turns back into Dr. Jekyll. But there is a hitch. Whereas Dr. Hyde was pure evil, Dr. Jekyll is *not* pure good. He is the same mix of tensions that he was before. Reverting to his old self, he found few takers in the Cold War era. Meanwhile, his earlier career as a business journalist and wonderful novelist in the 1920s had been entirely forgotten by the 1950s.

This is a tragedy because both his nonfiction and his novels display a most rare talent and offer more than a mere condemnation of the New Deal government. He not only wrote in opposition to war; his entire oeuvre offers a sparkling vision of peace under free markets as well. Whereas many intellectuals on the Right and Left regard the peaceful, bourgeois society as something of a bore—with the middle class amassing wealth and spending it on fripperies—Garrett saw peace and freedom as the essential precondition for the real drama of human life that revolves around creation, association, love, courage, and the full range of human vices and virtues that transform society in spectacular ways.

He began to write fiction after Warren G. Harding had called for a "return to normalcy" after World War I. But for Garrett, "normalcy" was civilization itself. For example, *The Driver* (1922), *The Cinder Buggy* (1923), and *Satan's Bushel* (1924) are novels that tell great stories about American history, with complex plot and character development, in which the glorious drama of commercial life plays the central role. These novels show that you don't need war as a backdrop in order to make a story of national life. These novels chronicle dramatic social and economic transformations in the context of fierce struggle and great risk—all within the framework of peace.

Garrett was not a trained economist but his knowledge of economic forces was so profound that he wrote the first full and widely circulated explanation, in line with the Austrian School tradition, of the 1929 stock market crash. *The Bubble that Broke the World* (1932) placed the blame on an overextension of credit made possible by the Federal Reserve; this created, said Garrett, a false prosperity that led to a correction. This book alone is proof that his journalism continued through the Depression and war, always with a decidedly and even radically libertarian cast.

As an example of his forgotten legacy, one of his last works was a wonderful history of the Ford Motor Company called *The Wild Wheel* (1952). John Chamberlain said that this book "should have been the bible for college students of productivity, but in the 1950s it had been forgotten."[1]

[1] *A Life with the Printed Word*, John Chamberlain (Regnery Gateway 1982), p. 139.

was nothing more than "that incongruous compound of whose reformation and improvement I had already learned to despair. The movement was thus wholly toward the worse."

Well, that's a pretty good description of the results of most good-government legislation. It creates new obstacles for the old evil forms to get through but strengthens the evil by making the public less wary of it. A government perceived as righteous is more dangerous than one that is looked upon with suspicion. Sometimes corrupt government can actually be better than good government, if it means that unjust and unworkable laws can be bypassed through bribes and graft.

Every few years, for example, Washington, D.C., elects a mayor who promises a clean sweep of the bad and a restoration of the good. A bar owner there once told a reporter that he always dreads these changes, because it means that absurd fire codes and license requirements are enforced to the hilt. Under a corrupt regime, he needs only to bribe a few policemen and bureaucrats. Under good government, he has to cough up tens of thousands for lobbying groups, lawyers, and legislative specialists in order to keep his business running.

"Good government" seeks to give us all the government we pay for, and who can but rue the day that this happens?

In the Stevenson book, Mr. Hyde grows stronger as he spends time separate from Dr. Jekyll. He is unleashed, unchecked by conscience. Whereas he was once a temporary indulgence, he eventually becomes a full-time obsession even as the good side of Dr. Jekyll seems to become less robust and shrink.

So it is with good-government movements. Once the state is reformed, the next step is obvious: a clean state that does wonderful things, untainted by nefarious practices, should be permitted to expand to do those good things with more liberality and efficacy. Thus has every government reform movement in the last century and a half ended up expanding rather than shrinking the state. And the expanded state does not end up doing good; it draws ever more evil to its side and results in an expansion rather than a shrinking of corruption.

The same is true of the pressure groups that have a selective interest in the activities of the state. The Right believes the government should provide for the common defense but in so believing turns a blind eye to ghastly abuses that occur in wartime. The Left believes that the government should redistribute wealth, and thereby pretends not to notice that this requires increasing violence against property and subsidizes the worst propensities of human nature.

As government grows ever bigger in the guise of doing good, its capacity for doing evil expands at a far more rapid rate. Whatever true good that government might be capable of doing is swamped by growing levels of corruption, graft, payoffs, violence, arbitrary rule, and all the rest of the institutions that the movement was trying to make go away.

Here we have the real lesson of the misbegotten idea that government can be purified. As Dr. Jekyll admits later: "I have been made to learn that the doom and burthen of our life is bound for ever on man's shoulders, and when the attempt is made to cast it off, it but returns upon us with more unfamiliar and more awful pressure."

Don't administer a potion. Just shrink it until it goes away.

55

Who Is Garet Garrett?

October 25, 2007

If Garet Garrett (1878–1954) is known at all today, it is by those who are captivated by the handful of intellectuals who wrote in opposition to the New Deal planning state and the regimentation of national life it brought about. They were a rare breed, but there is much more to Garrett than people know.

Having spent several months steeped in his work, reading everything by him I could find, I remain completely flabbergasted that he is not better known. We go about our lives assuming that there is some magic force of history that causes quality work to last and inferior works to fall by the wayside. What a myth. Garrett is a case study in a forgotten genius. How did it happen? War? Depression? Politics? I don't know. I can only say that he should rank among the master novelists and politico-economist journalists of the last century.

Ludwig von Mises recognized this: "His keen penetration and his forceful direct language are … unsurpassed by any author." He was speaking in particular about Garrett's book *The People's Pottage* (1953), which is a collection of three powerful essays that had appeared earlier, and was on the reading list of the "Old Right" that died out by the early 1960s. Why did this movement die out? The Cold War against communism became th priority for the Right, while the Left had long ago embraced the New Dea as it its own. Garrett, whose featured writings in the *Saturday Evening Pos* were once read and celebrated by millions, had been relegated to obscurit by a generation that believed they had nothing to learn from prewar popul intellectuals.

Despite astonishing eloquence and prescience, Garrett's stirring attack on the New Deal and condemnations of the American imperial minds

The Life of Garrett

Garet Garrett was born Peter Garrett (he later changed his name to match his pen name) in Pana, Illinois, to Charles and Mary Garrett on February 19, 1878.[2] His formal education was very slight—only through the third grade—but his independent study took him through all the classics, as shown by the remarkable erudition of his writings. His influence in economics came primarily through a book by the American mathematician/astronomer Simon Newcomb: *Principles of Political Economy* (1886). Newcomb was an advocate of the gold standard and laissez-faire, an early convert to the marginalist revolution through William Stanley Jevons, and a fighting opponent of socialism, institutionalism, and historicism. So Garrett's Austrianism is present, but in a back-door way, via William Stanley Jevons and the American hard-money school of the late 19th century.

He left for Chicago at the age of 20 and worked as a reporter for the *Cleveland Recorder* and then later covered politics in Washington, D.C., writing reports on the administration of William McKinley for the *Washington Times*. In 1900, he left for New York. He vanished for three years, or, at least, no one seems to know what happened to him. But in 1903, he joined the staff of the *New York Sun* as a financial writer. He moved on to the *New York Times* and the *Wall Street Journal* until he joined the *New York Evening Post* in 1909.

It was in this period that he met his lifelong friend, Bernard Baruch, who wrote of him,

> Garrett was a frequent visitor.... This small, round, intense dynamo of a man was then with the *New York Evening Post*.... Garrett was one of the few men to whom I could unburden myself. Once, after hearing me express my restlessness with Wall Street, he remarked "I keep telling you, B.M., you don't belong in Wall Street; you should be in Washington." I don't remember my reply; I probably laughed at him. But I thought about his words from time to time.... [They] nourished my discontent.

Biographer Carl Ryant notes that during this period, Garrett probably made an important contribution to the education of Wall Street. In that time, business reporting consisted mostly of reporting prices and dry facts.

---

2 Biographical details from Carl Ryant, *Profit's Prophet* (Selinsgrove: Susquehanna University Press, 1989). Another excellent analysis of Garrett's work is in Justin Raimondo's *Reclaiming the American Right* (Burlingame, Calif.: Center for Libertarian Studies, 1993)

Garrett wrote with drama on personalities and events, infusing the activity of commerce with a fire and passion that later made his fiction so enormously popular.

He moved to accept administrative duties with the *New York Annalist* and then later back to the *New York Times*. During World War I, he was sent to Germany to cover the war's impact on the German people. Following this, he resigned over dissatisfaction with the way the paper was covering the war. This was a period of grim press censorship, and Garrett was probably having trouble getting his stories printed. This experience very likely had the most powerful impact on his views toward war. He later moved to the *New York Tribune* where he was involved in a regrettable tactic to increase circulation of the paper by attacking rival publisher William Randolph Hearst. In any case, he left the *Tribune* in 1919 and here began the work for which he justly became famous.

Garrett began as a featured contributor to American's most successful periodical, *The Saturday Evening Post*, but his contributions were not limited to this publication. He also wrote for *Collier's*, *Everybody's Magazine*, and *The New Republic*. His topics usually centered on financial matters. Garrett was at the top of his game and became one of the most widely read writers on economics in the country.

He developed a close friendship with *Post* editor George Horace Lorimer, who in turn introduced him to Herbert Hoover, with whom he also maintained a lifelong friendship. He traveled the world for the *Post*. Once, on a boat, he bumped into Will Rogers, who later wrote that he was "an awful nice fellow." His works were reviewed with glowing praise in *The New Republic*, *The New York Times*, and elsewhere.

On the night of January 18, 1930, Garrett was shot during an attempted robbery at a New York speakeasy, the Chez Madeleine, while having dinner. He was shot three times: in the shoulder, hip, and lung. He recovered, but his health suffered and he was left with a raspy voice (which wasn't helped by his lifelong chain smoking). Still, his association with the *Post* continued through the Great Depression, and it was he who gave the magazine its pro-freedom, anti–New Deal flavor through the entire period. He became a vocal and aggressive proponent of staying out of World War II.

With a change in editorial direction at the *Post* in 1942, Garrett left, and two years later founded a journal called *American Affairs*. It was funded by the National Industrial Conference Board as a venue for Garrett. He later wrote that it was a "one-man job. The staff consists of myself, one secretary, and one man attending to subscriptions and circulation." This journal by itself is a remarkable accomplishment. In a time of all-around planning and war, Garrett managed to produce a free-market publication that took on labor unions, price controls, inflation, war planning, international agencies, centralization of power, and war propaganda, and to fight for liberty of the individual in issue after issue. A typical issue would open with five to six pages of editorials and then move to correspondence and articles. The publication would print fascinating correspondence between citizens and the government over issues of taxation and monetary affairs. Even in the existing works on the Old Right, this journal hasn't received the attention it deserves. In fact, the entire run of this publication deserves far wider exposure.

The publication folded in 1950, but Garrett did not quit. In 1952, he wrote *The Wild Wheel*. In these years, he paid some visits to offices in New York and Washington but his reputation faded in the postwar world, which no longer appreciated his pro-commerce, antiwar attitudes. He retired to a New Jersey farm, wore baggy pants and coats with patches on the elbow, and was known to love good bourbon. He suffered a stroke in 1954 and died on November 6. He was buried at the River Cemetery in Tuckahoe, New Jersey.

The Novels

Let's take a step back and have a look at Garrett's least-known work, his once-popular works of fiction that heralded commerce as the very pith of life. His first book was called *The Blue Wound* (1921), an impressive effort at writing a history-of-the-world fantasy through the eyes of a dreamy journalist who sought to discover who caused the world war. The book was a literary success but it was less than clear on an issue that would be Garrett's only real ideological failing. The subject in question concerned trade. He rightly saw the dangers of American and British efforts to force open markets abroad, imposing foreign systems of government on an unwilling population; but he failed to clearly delineate in his mind the difference between purely voluntary foreign trade and imperial expansion. This was mixed with a slight protectionist bias that was typical of his generation—a bias that emerges sometimes in his writing, but, fortunately, never overtook his broader analytics.

From a free-market perspective, his next book was a far more impressive effort. *The Driver* (1922), an exciting book that heralds capitalist accomplishment, tells the story of a Wall Street financier, Henry Galt, a shadowy figure who stays out of the limelight as much as possible until he unleashes a plan that had been years in the making: he uses his extraordinary entrepreneurial talent to acquire control of a failing railroad.

Through outstanding management sense, good pricing, excellent service, and overall business savvy, he outcompetes all the big names in the business, while making a fortune in the process. Garrett has a way of illustrating just what it takes to be a businessman of this sort, and how his mind alone becomes the source of a fantastic revenue stream.

But his success breeds trouble. The government conspires with envious competitors to regulate him using the Sherman Antitrust Act, calling him a monopolist and accusing him of exploiting the public. There is a courtroom scene that allows Galt to explain to the assembled legislators how investors and capitalists are helping society in ways that politicians can't possibly imagine. What the politicians see as shady is really a form of public service that enriches the whole country.

A recurring literary motif through the book has people asking, "Who is Henry Galt?" The shades of Ayn Rand here are obvious and some writers have speculated that she borrowed Garrett's literary motif, which may or may not be true.

In one of many asides, this book contains one of the best explanations of the absurdities of "bi-metallism" that fixed the relationship between silver and gold. Indeed, the book is overall quite sound on the money question, showing the inflationist populist movement of the late 19th century to be a pack of fools. Galt himself delivers some fantastic defenses of hard money and free markets.

In any case, the novel is brilliant and thrilling, one that provides an excellent lesson in how entrepreneurship works. Writes Edward Younkins, "Not only is *The Driver* a novel of high finance and Wall Street methods, it also paints a portrait of an efficacious and visionary man who uses reason to focus his enthusiasm on reality in his efforts to attain his goals."

His next novel is his epic story of steel. It is *The Cinder Buggy* (1923), the longest of the three books in this trilogy and his unforgettable masterpiece. With a great story, and tremendous literary passion, it chronicles the transformation of America from the age of iron to the age of steel.

It covers the period between 1820 and 1870 and its march of technological progress. The plot concerns an ongoing war between two industrialists, one the hero who is beaten in the first generation, and the other who is malevolent but wins the first round in the competitive drive. The struggle continues through the second generation, which leads to a titanic battle over whether steel or iron would triumph and why.

The story is set in the iron town of New Damascus. The two men who make it happen are Aaron Breakspeare and Enoch Gib. Aaron is beloved but not a great businessman. He dreams of the steel age but fails to make it economically viable. Enoch is a good businessman but dour and widely loathed for his miserliness and mistreatment of others. A feud over a banker's daughter leads to the initial dissolution of the partnership, and the son of the resulting union, John Breakspeare, returns to New Damascus to enter the iron business.

This leads to a fascinating repeat of events that causes another dissolution, more bitter and shocking than the last. The feud continues over iron and then over steel until steel wins the victory after many fits and starts. In the course of the story, the reader discovers how it is that technology has such a dramatic effect on society, and how risk and entrepreneurship are at the very heart of it all.

Garrett employs every literary device to make commerce itself the setting for great acts of courage, heroism, sacrifice, and tragedy. And as with his other books, the central mover of events is the price system. It is the signal for and cause of the most notable changes in the plot. The reader discovers economics in a way that might not otherwise be possible, and it is hard to imagine that anyone can come away with anything but love for the whole subject of enterprise.

Garrett does not portray the market as some idealized utopia. We have here the full range of human emotion and motivation at work: arrogance, pride, malice, love, compassion, jealousy, rage, and everything else. What is striking is that all these emotions play themselves out in a setting that, despite all the metaphors involving battles and wars, is ultimately peaceful. No one can fully control price movements, and it is these that act to reward victors and punish losers. Here we have the "manly" virtues playing themselves out not on bloody battlefields but in the peaceful marketplace.

We also have here a realistic portrayal of the truth about innovation. It is not enough to come up with a good idea. That idea must be embodied in real production that takes place in a cost-reducing way, and then marketed in the service of society. Technology, accounting, and marketing must all come together to make possible such things as technological revolutions.

The Cinder Buggy could easily be considered the best of Garrett's novels. It is a wonderful novel for anyone who loves, or wants to more deeply understand, American history, economic theory, and the place of technology in the molding of society.

Finally, as the third in this series, there is *Satan's Bushel* (1924), a splendid book, not just from the point of view of economics but also as a piece of literature. What is Satan's bushel? It is the last bushel that the farmers put on the market, the one that "breaks the price"—that is, reduces it to the point where wheat farming is no longer profitable. The problem that afflicts the wheat farmers is that they sell their goods when the price is low and have no goods to sell when the price is high. Withholding goods from the market is one answer, but the farmer lacks the incentive to do that.

As implausible as it may sound, the central figure in this book is the price of wheat. It is the main source of drama. The settings are the wheat pit at the Chicago exchange (circa 1915) and the Kansas wheat fields. Linking those two radically different universes, through speculative buying and selling, is the mission of this book.

The action further explores the meaning, morality, and utility of wheat speculation, which was increasing in sophistication during this period of history. The plot is centered at the turn of the 20th century, a critical period when the agricultural economy was completely giving way to the fully industrialized one, and farmers were panicked about the alleged problem of falling prices. There is nothing lost in the passage of time: the allegory could equally apply to the computer industry today.

The book tells the story of one man's discovery of a brilliant speculator and his relationship with an old and legendary farmer/mystic and his daughter. The mystic embodies both the highest wisdom and the greatest economic fallacies of the day. The question that must be confronted is how to make farms profitable in times of falling prices, and the novel shows that speculation, even with all its human foibles, makes a contribution to stabilizing the market.

Here is one of hundreds of brilliant passages describing the speculator:

> No rule of probability contains him. To say that he acts upon impulse, without reflection, in a headlong manner, is true only so far as it goes. Many people have that weakness. With him it is not a weakness. It is a principle of conduct. The impulse in his case is not ungovernable. It does not possess him and overthrow his judgment. It is the other way around. He takes possession of the impulse, mounting it as it were the enchanted steed of the Arabian Nights, and rides it to its kingdom of consequences. What lies at

> the end is always a surprise; if it is something he doesn't care for, no matter. Another steed is waiting. Meaning to do this, living for it, he has no baggage. There is nothing behind him. If he has wealth it is portable. He is at any moment ready.

In a plot twist that foreshadows the New Deal, one person attempts to destroy the wheat crops with a poisonous fungus, thinking that he is doing the farmers a favor by reducing supply—based on logic he learned from unworkable government schemes. The reader is confronted with the challenge of coming to understand whether this is really beneficial to farmers, and if not, why not? (Keep in mind that *Satan's Bushel* was written a full decade before FDR attempted the same tactics by force from the federal level.)

Another dramatic scene involves the arrest of an opponent of World War I. There are also plot twists that turn on romance, sorcery, criminality, mob behavior, psychological possession, the war, price controls, government interventions, and other surprises, including wholly unimaginable things like water witchery and a teak tree in Burma. The central action, however, deals with the core of economics and the place of production and speculation.

And for financial historians, there is the very special treat of observing the great drama of the early years of the Chicago commodities market—written from the vantage point of one generation later. There are scenes in the wheat trading pit that just take your breath away. This novel demonstrates yet again that no one can make the stuff of enterprise dramatic, tragic, and heroic like Garrett.

The effect is to so closely link the most outlandish and far-flung economic activities to human frailties and uncertainties that one gains not only an understanding of how commodity markets worked earlier this century—and how price movements work in all times and all places—but also a love for the craft of commodities specuclation.

Several passages provide beautiful insight into how the speculator thinks and how the speculator's actions work to reduce destabilizing price fluctuations. But speculation is also a very human institution, subject to whim and learning. Also, the government comes across as nothing short of egregious and destructive.

Garrett's last novel is *Harangue (The Trees Said to the Bramble Come Reign Over Us)* (1927). It tells the true story, in fictional form, of the rise and fall of a fanatic and despotic socialist takeover of a single town, and how it led to loss of liberty and economic collapse. It is, said *The New York Times* in a review, "an analysis of the workings of the self-consciously radical mind and the play of direct action demagogy on the masses ... a first-class study in sociology." The socialist takeover was financed by the heir of a Wall Street fortune, and this provides Garrett an opportunity to explain why the rich are attracted to destructive ideology: it is one thing they can consume that sets them apart from the bourgeoisie. He goes further to provide rich and detailed portrayals of all the main activists who are drawn to socialism. He shows how the experiment fails on economic and political grounds.

The book was written only a few years before the socialist Left came to influence national affairs in the age of the New Deal, and what's refreshing about this study is its complete absence of red baiting. It treats socialism as dangerous and myopic intellectual error that can lead to ruin, but never as some foreign threat. If capitalism were to collapse, he believed, it would be from within. As a novel, *Harangue* is just as competent as his others, but it takes a different angle: it explores the dangers of the intellectual and political world as a contrast to the creative world of commerce.

The New Deal

Within a year of being shot in a speakeasy, Garrett came out with a book of high importance to Austrian economists: *The Bubble that Broke the World* (1931). This book blows away the conventional interpretations of the crash of 1929, not only in its contents, but in the fact that the book exists at all. Garrett ascribes the crash to the piling up of debt, which in turn was made possible by the Fed's printing machine. This debt created distortions in the production structure that cried out for correction.

What is the answer, according to Garrett? Let the correction happen and learn from our mistakes.

Such is the thesis, but take note: this book was a big seller in 1931. In other words, two years before FDR arrived with his destructive New Deal, ascribing the depression to capitalism and speculation, Garrett had already explained what was really behind the correction. It took Murray Rothbard to resurrect these truths decades later, and by the time he did so in 1963, it was a shocking thesis.

We are still fighting an uphill battle to explain the true causes of the crash and ensuing depression. But here in this wonderful book of Garrett's is an actual contemporary account that spelled it out plainly for the world to see. No more can we say that people back then could not have understood. Garrett told them.

Empire

In 1954, Garrett's masterpiece of nonfiction writing appeared: *The People's Pottage*. This was a collection of his previous essays. The first essay, "The Revolution Was", had first appeared in 1938, the burden of which was to show that the New Deal transformed American society to such an extent that it was foolhardy to listen to American politicians and their warnings of dangers from the outside. "There are those who still think they are holding the pass against a revolution that may be coming up the road," he wrote. "But they are gazing in the wrong direction. The revolution is behind them. It went by in the Night of Depression, singing songs to freedom."

Here he chronicles what historians have forgotten, namely, that FDR campaigned for limiting government against the big-spending policies of Herbert Hoover. He shows how the New Deal regimented production to the point of making genuine production impossible. He blasts FDR's monetary policy as nothing short of robbery, and exposes the New Deal as a violation of everything a free country should be.

The second essay is "Ex America" (1951) a shocking look back at what America was and what it had become. The third essay is "The Rise of Empire" (1952):

> We have crossed the boundary that lies between Republic and Empire. If you ask when, the answer is that you cannot make a single stroke between day and night; the precise moment does not matter. There was no painted sign to say: "You now are entering Imperium."

Here Garrett spells out the conditions that signal the move from Republic to Empire, including the dominance of the executive, the rise of the military mind, a "complex of vaunting and fear," the subjugation of domestic concerns to foreign ones, and a system of satellite nations.

The list is an eerie one for us today, for it essentially spells out what drives American policy in the post-Cold War world. With the fear of communism out of the way, we should be better positioned than ever to heed his warnings.

To Garrett, there is no heroism in war, but only in creativity and production, and no folly greater than overthrowing the institutions that make creativity and economic progress possible. He was not just a great writer of fiction, not just a courageous opponent of the planning state and war; he was a prophet of the fate of America under government control, a brilliant intellectual force in the 20th century, and a wise and eloquent spokesman for freedom itself. May he be remembered and appreciated anew, and may he teach all to learn to adore peace and prosperity, and all its creative adventures, as he did.

Bibliography

The Blue Wound (NY: Putnam's, 1921)

The Cinder Buggy (NY: Dutton, 1923; Mises Institute, 2007)

The Driver (NY: Dutton, 1922; Mises Institute, 2007)

Satan's Bushel (NY: Dutton, 1924; Mises Institute, 2007)

Harangue (The Trees Said to the Bramble Come Reign Over Us) (NY, Dutton: 1927; Mises Institute 2007)

A Bubble That Broke the World (Boston: Little, 1932; Mises Institute, 2007)

The People's Pottage (Caldwell, Idaho: Caxton, 1953; Mises Institute, 2007)

The Wild Wheel (NY: Pantheon, 1952; Mises Institute, 2007)

The American Story (Chicago: Regnery, 1955)

56

Albert Jay Nock: Forgotten Man of the Old Right

October 12, 2007

For an earlier generation of American dissidents from the prevailing ideology of left-liberalism, a rite of passage was reading Albert Jay Nock's *Memoirs of a Superfluous Man*, which appeared in 1943. William F. Buckley was hardly alone in seeing it as a seminal text crucial to his personal formation.

Here it is in one package, an illustration of the level of learning that had been lost with mass education, a picture of the way a true political dissident from our collectivist period thinks about the modern world, and a comprehensive argument for the very meaning of freedom and civility—all from a man who helped shape the Right's intellectual response to the triumph of FDR's welfare-warfare state.

It was destined to be a classic, read by many generations to come. But then the official doctrine changed. Instead of seeing war as part of the problem, as a species of socialism, *National Review* led the American Right down a different path. Nock's book was quickly buried with the rise of the Cold War state, which required that conservatives reject anything like radical individualism—even of Nock's aristocratic sort—and instead embrace the Wilson-FDR values of nationalism and militarism.

Instead of Nock's *Memoirs*, young conservatives were encouraged to read personal accounts of communists who converted to backing the Cold War (e.g., Whittaker Chambers), as if warming up to the glories of nukes represents some sort of courageous intellectual step. To the extent that Nock (1870–1947) is known at all today, it is by libertarians, and for his classic essay *Our Enemy, The State* (1935) and his wonderful little biography, *Mr.*

Jefferson (1926). Both are great works. He was also the founder of *The Freeman* in its first incarnation (1920–1924), which held to the highest literary standards and provoked unending controversy by its sheer radicalism.

However, it is with the *Memoirs*, this wonderful little treatise—part autobiography, part ideological instruction—that we are given the full Nockian worldview, not just his politics but his culture, his life, and his understanding of man and his place in the universe. The book makes a very bracing read today, if only because it proves how little today's "conservative movement" has to do with its mid-century ancestor, the Old Right. It is also instructive for libertarians to discover that there is more to anarchism than childish rantings against the police power.

The phrase "Man of Letters" is thrown around casually these days, but A.J. Nock was the real thing. Born in Scranton, Pennsylvania, he was homeschooled from the earliest age in Greek and Latin, unbelievably well read in every field, a natural aristocrat in the best sense of that term.

He combined an old-world cultural sense (he despised popular culture) and a political anarchism that saw the state as the enemy of everything that is civilized, beautiful, and true. And he applied this principle consistently in opposition to welfare, government-managed economies, consolidation, and, above all else, war.

In the introduction to my edition, Hugh MacLennan compares the *Memoirs* to *The Education of Henry Adams*, and expresses the hope that it will "one day be recognized as the minor classic it really is." Well, I can predict that this time is not coming soon. Given its contents, consistency, relentless truth-telling, and, above all, its sheer persuasive power, it is a wonder that the book is in print and that we are even allowed to read it.

To follow Nock, what traits must a man of the Right have? He must be both fiercely independent and believe in the power of social authority; he must love tradition but hate the state and everything it does; he must believe in radical freedom while never doubting the immutability of human nature and natural laws; he must be antimaterialist in his own life while defending economic freedom without compromise; he must be an elitist and antidemocrat yet despise elites who hold illicit power; and he must be realistic about the dim prospects for change while still retaining a strong sense of hope and enthusiasm for life.

I'm not sure I can think of anyone but Murray Rothbard who consistently upheld the Nockian position after Nock's death, and it is Nock's *Memoirs* that provides a full immersion in his genius. Consider his main literary device: to take a commonplace subject, make a casual and slightly quirky observation about it, one that wins your affections, and then surprise and shock by driving the point to score a deadly blow against some great evil that is widely taken for granted:

> Another neighbor, a patriarchal old Englishman with a white beard, kept a great stand of bees. I remember his incessant drumming on a tin pan to marshal them when they were swarming, and myself as idly wondering who first discovered that this was the thing to do, and why the bees should fall in with it. It struck me that if the bees were as intelligent as bees are cracked up to be, instead of mobilizing themselves for old man Reynolds's benefit, they would sting him soundly and then fly off about their business. I always think of this when I see a file of soldiers, wondering why the sound of a drum does not incite them to shoot their officers, throw away their rifles, go home, and go to work.

In the course of his 325-page narrative, he employs this casual device again and again, until you begin to get the message that there is something profoundly wrong with the world, and the biggest thing of all is the state.

In Nock's view, it is the state that crowds out all that is decent, lovely, civilized. He demonstrates this not through deduction but through calm and entertaining tales of how rich and varied and productive life can be when the state does not interfere.

In a society without the state, for example, the "court of tastes and manners" would be the thing that guides the operation of society, and this "court" would have a much larger role in society than law, legislation, or religion. If such a court were not in operation, because people are too uncivilized or too ill-educated to maintain it, there was nothing the state could do to uplift people. No matter how low a civilization is, it can only be made to go lower through state activity.

Though an old-school Yankee of the purest-bred sort, he completely rejected what came to be the defining trait of his class: the impulse to try to improve others through badgering and coercion:

> One of the most offensive things about the society in which I later found myself was its monstrous itch for changing people. It seemed to me a society made up of congenital missionaries, natural-born evangelists and propagandists, bent on re-shaping, re-forming and standardizing people according to a pattern of their own devising—and what a

> pattern it was, good heavens! when one came to examine it. It seems to me, in short, a society fundamentally and profoundly ill-bred. A very small experience of it was enough to convince me that Cain's heresy was not altogether without reason or without merit; and that conviction quickly ripened into a great horror of every attempt to change anybody; or I should rather say, every *wish* to change anybody, for that is the important thing. The attempt is relatively immaterial, perhaps, for it is usually its own undoing, but the moment one *wishes* to change anybody, one becomes like the socialists, vegetarians, prohibitionists; and this, as Rabelais, says, "is a terrible thing to think upon."

Given such views, it is hardly surprising that he had nothing but contempt for politics, which then and now seeks to manage not only society but thought as well:

> My first impression of politics was unfavorable; and my disfavor was heightened by subsequently noticing that the people around me always spoke of politics and politicians in a tone of contempt. This was understandable. If all I had casually seen ... was of the essence of politics, if it was part and parcel of carrying on the country's government, then obviously a decent person could find no place in politics, not even the place of a ordinary voter, for the forces of ignorance, brutality and indecency would outnumber him ten to one.

But, with Nock's infallible flair for radicalism, his logic takes him further down the anarchist road:

> Nevertheless there was an anomaly here. We were all supposed to respect our government and its laws, yet by all accounts those who were charged with the conduct of government and the making of its laws were most dreadful swine; indeed, the very conditions of their tenure precluded their being anything else.

Nock is capable of surprising readers who think they might be able to anticipate the biases of a traditionalist-anarchist. Sometimes old-style, rightist aristocrats who wax eloquent on the virtues of tradition fall into strange left-wing habits of extolling the environment as something glorious and virtuous on its own, and somehow deserving of being left alone. Nock had no interest in this strange deviation. Consider his experience with the woods and nature:

> In those years [living in rural areas] I undoubtedly built up and fortified the singular immunity to infirmity and disease which has lasted all my life; but in those years also my congenital indifference to nature in the wild, natural scenery, rocks, rills, woods and templed hills, hardened into permanent distaste. Like the Goncourts, I can see nature only as an enemy; a highly respected enemy, but an enemy. "I am a lover of knowledge," Socrates said, "and the men who dwell in the city are my teachers, and not the trees or the country."

Nock was thus not an American Tory by any stretch, though his cultural outlook was as highbrow as any landed aristocrat's. What's more, unlike the socialist anarchists and most conservatives of today, Nock believed in and understood the crucial importance, even centrality, of economic liberty:

> If a regime of complete economic freedom be established, social and political freedom will follow automatically; and until it is established neither social nor political freedom can exist. Here one comes in sight of the reason why the State will never tolerate the establishment of economic freedom. In a spirit of sheer conscious fraud, the State will at any time offer its people "four freedoms," or six, or any number; but it will never let them have economic freedom. If it did, it would be signing its own death-warrant, for as Lenin pointed out, "it is nonsense to make any pretence of reconciling the State and liberty." Our economic system being what it is, and the State being what it is, all the mass verbiage about "the free peoples" and "the free democracies" is merely so much obscene buffoonery.

In fact, he understood even technical points of economics that are completely lost on most conservatives today. Here is Nock on the 1920s bubble economy:

> Many no doubt remember the "new economics" hatched in the consulship of Mr. Coolidge, whereby it was demonstrated beyond question that credit could be pyramided on credit indefinitely, and all hands could become rich with no one doing any work. Then when this seductive theory blew up with a loud report in 1929, we began to hear of the economics of scarcity, the economics of plenty, and then appeared the devil-and-all of "plans," notions about pump-priming, and disquisitions on the practicability of a nation's

> spending itself rich.... Ever since 1918 people everywhere have been thinking in terms of money, not in terms of commodities; and this in spite of the most spectacular evidence that such thinking is sheer insanity. The only time I was ever a millionaire was when I spent a few weeks in Germany in 1923. I was the proud possessor of more money than one could shake a stick at, but I could buy hardly anything with it."

And on fiscal policy:

> Another strange notion pervading whole peoples is that the State has money of its own; and nowhere is this absurdity more firmly fixed than in America. The State has no money. It produces nothing. It existence is purely parasitic, maintained by taxation; that is to say, by forced levies on the production of others. "Government money," of which one hears so much nowadays, does not exist; there is no such thing. One is especially amused at seeing how largely a naïve ignorance of this fact underlies the pernicious measures of "social security" which have been foisted on the American people. In various schemes of pensioning, of insurance against sickness, accident, unemployment and what-not, one notices that the government is supposed to pay so-much into the fund, the employer so-much, and the workman so-much.... But the government pays nothing, for it has nothing to pay with. What such schemes actually come to is that the workman pays his own share outright; he pays the employer's share in the enhanced price of commodities; and he pays the government's share in taxation. He pays the whole bill; and when one counts in the unconscionably swollen costs of bureaucratic brokerage and *paperasserie*, one sees that what the workman-beneficiary gets out the arrangement is about the most expensive form of insurance that could be devised consistently with keeping its promoters out of gaol.

A special contribution of Nock's book is his comprehensive critique of the pre–New Deal reform movements that culminated in the Progressive Era. Though he had once identified himself as a true liberal in the Jeffersonian sense, he was a close observer of the early stages of liberalism's corruption, when it came to mean not liberty but something else entirely. He saw the essential error that the liberal movement was making:

> Liberals generally—there may have been exceptions, but I do not know who they were—joined in the agitation for an income-tax, in utter disregard of the fact that it meant writing the principle of absolutism into the Constitution. Nor did they give a moment's thought to the appalling social effects of an income-tax; I never once heard this aspect of the matter discussed. Liberals were also active in promoting the "democratic" movement for the popular election of senators. It certainly took no great perspicacity to see that these two measures would straightway ease our political system into collectivism as soon as some Eubulus, some mass-man overgifted with sagacity, should maneuver himself into popular leadership; and in the nature of things, this would not be long.

In time, of course, the liberal reform movement began to adopt a mild version of the class-war rhetoric of the socialist Left, and the longer this went on, the more the political process came to be a struggle not between liberty and power but between two versions of state domination:

> What I was looking at was simply a tussle between two groups of mass-men, one large and poor, the other small and rich, and as judged by the standards of civilized society, neither of them any more meritorious or promising than the other. The object of the tussle was the material gains accruing from control of the State's machinery. It is easier to seize wealth than to produce it; and as long as the State makes the seizure of wealth a matter of legalized privilege, so long will the squabble for that privilege go on.

From Nock's point of view, the Great Depression and the two world wars saddled America with a new faith in the state, and along with it came a shift in people's loyalties, from themselves, their families, and communities to the Grand National Project, whatever it may be. We see the same thing today on the right and left, when questioning any aspect of the war on terrorism gets you branded as a heretic to the national religion. Nock would have nothing to do with it:

> I am profoundly thankful that during my formative years I never had contact with any institution under State control; not in school, not in college, nor yet in my three years of irregular graduate study. No attempt was ever made by any one to indoctrinate me with State-inspired views—or any views, for that matter—of patriotism or nationalism. I was

> never dragooned into flag-worship or hero-worship, never was caught in any spate of verbiage about duty to one's country, never debauched by any of the routine devices hatched by scoundrels for inducing a synthetic devotion to one's native land and loyalty to its jobholders. Therefore when later the various aspects of contemporary patriotism and nationalism appeared before me, my mind was wholly unprepossessed, and my view of them was unaffected by any emotional distortion."

What, then, is patriotism, if not faith in one's government? Can patriotism be considered a virtue at all to the civilized man, and, if so, in what does it consist? Consider this passage of immense power:

> What is patriotism? Is it loyalty to a spot on a map, marked off from other spots by blue or yellow lines, the spot where one was born? But birth is a pure accident; surely one is in no way responsible for having been born on this spot or on that. Flaubert had poured a stream of corrosive irony on this idea of patriotism. Is it loyalty to a set of political jobholders, a king and his court, a president and his bureaucracy, a parliament, a congress, a *Duce* or *Führer*, a *camorra* of commissars? I should say it depends entirely on what the jobholders are like and what they do. Certainly I had never seen any who commanded my loyalty; I should feel utterly degraded if ever once I thought they could. Does patriotism mean loyalty to a political system and its institutions, constitutional, autocratic, republican, or what-not? But if history has made anything unmistakably clear, it is that from the standpoint of the individual and his welfare, these are no more than names. The reality which in the end they are found to cover is the same for all alike. If a tree be known by its fruits, which I believe is regarded as good sound doctrine, then the peculiar merit of a system, if it has any, ought to be reflected in the qualities and conditions of the people who live under it; and looking over the peoples and systems of the world, I found no reason in the nature of things why a person should be loyal to one system rather than another. One could see at a glance that there is no saving grace in any system. Whatever merit or demerit may attach to any of them lies in the way it is administered.
>
> So when people speak of loyalty to one's country, one must ask them what they mean by that. What is one's country?

> Mr. Jefferson said contemptuously that "merchants have no country; the mere spot they stand on does not constitute so strong an attachment as that from which they draw their gains." But one may ask, why should it? This motive of patriotism seems to me perfectly sound, and if it should be sound for merchants, why not for others who are not merchants? If it holds good in respect of material gains, why not of spiritual gains, cultural gains, intellectual and aesthetic gains? As a general principle, I should put it that a man's country is where the things he loves are most respected. Circumstances may have prevented his ever setting foot there, but it remains his country.

In the early years of the American republic, patriotism and loyalty were primarily directed toward one's town or county, because it was very likely the place where the things one loved were most respected. Something like national patriotism was unknown. It came to be imposed under consolidation. Under today's conservative view of patriotism, that our loves must be dictated by the state, there would be no argument against the idea that we ought to be patriotic toward NATO or the United Nations. Nock had this to say about global consolidation:

> Some of the more adventurous spirits, apparently under the effects of Mr. Wilson's inspiration, went so far as to propose educating all mankind into setting up a World State which should supersede the separatist nationalist State; on the principle, so it seemed, that if a spoonful of prussic acid will kill you, a bottleful is just what you need to do you a great deal of good.

Nock would also be dissident on the right today concerning the freedom of association, which he saw as the very essence of freedom itself.

> I know, however, that the problem of no minority anywhere can be settled unless and until two preliminaries are established. First, that the principle of equality before the law be maintained without subterfuge and with the utmost vigor. Second, that this principle be definitively understood as carrying no social implications of any kind whatever. "I will buy with you, sell with you, talk with you, walk with you, and so following," said Shylock; "but I will not eat with you, drink with you, nor pray with you."

> These two preliminaries demand a much clearer conception of natural as well as legal rights than I think can ever prevail in America.

Nock is sometimes presented as a brooding man who despaired for his country. There seems to be truth in that, but what's most impressive is how he managed to keep his chin up and find personal joy in fighting evil, or at least exposing it as much as possible.

> All I have done towards the achievement of a happy life has been to follow my nose.... I learned early with Thoreau that a man is rich in proportion to the numbers of things he can afford to let alone; and in view of this I have always considered myself extremely well-to-do. All I ever asked of life was the freedom to think and say exactly what I pleased, when I pleased, and as I pleased. I have always had that freedom, with an immense amount of uncovenanted lagniappe thrown in; and having had it, I always felt I could well afford to let all else alone. It is true that one can never get something for nothing; it is true that in a society like ours one who takes the course which I have taken must reconcile himself to the status of a superfluous man; but the price seems to me by no means exorbitant and I have paid it gladly, without a shadow of doubt that I was getting all the best of the bargain."

There are aspects of Nock that call for correction. His views on marriage and the family are highly unconventional, for example, and he sometimes takes his notion of the "remnant" too far, appearing to endorse passivity in the face of rising despotism. He refused to join any antiwar movements, not because he disagreed with their goal but because he didn't believe his participation would do any good.

But here is where his example is more instructive than his theory: Nock fought against the state with the most powerful weapons he had, his mind and his pen. Despite his claim, he was not superfluous at all, but essential, even indispensable, as are all great libertarian intellectuals.

Pass the *Memoirs* on to a twenty-year-old student and you stand a good chance of arming him against a lifetime of nonsense, whether it comes from the tedious Left that loves redistribution and collectivism or the fraudulent Right that is completely blind to the impossibility of reconciling war and nationalism with the true American spirit of freedom.

57

Mark Twain's Radical Liberalism

January 27, 2010

Part of the difficulty of understanding Mark Twain's political outlook is due to terminology and the tendency of politics to corrupt the meaning of everything. As often as you see him called a liberal, he is called a conservative, and sometimes both in the same breath. Critics puzzle about how one person could be a champion of workers, owners, and the capitalist rich, while holding views that are antigovernment on domestic matters, antislavery, and antiwar. They often conclude that his politics are incoherent.

Part of the reason for the confusion has to do with the changed meaning of liberalism as an ideology and the incapacity of modern critics to understand its 19th-century implications.

Twain was born as Samuel Langhorne Clemens in 1835, when the meaning of liberalism was less ambiguous. To be liberal was to favor free enterprise and property rights, oppose slavery, reject old-world caste systems, loathe war, be generally disposed toward free trade and cosmopolitanism, favor the social advance of women, favor technological progress—and to possess a grave skepticism toward government management of anything.

The tradition of thought extends from Enlightenment thinkers like Jefferson through 20th-century Misesians and Hayekians. This outlook on the world might be nearly extinguished from politics today (two flavors of statism), but it was the one embraced by Clemens.

By the time Clemens died in 1910, liberalism was on the verge of transformation. The Gilded Age of capitalist accumulation had come and gone, and inspired envy and ideological fanaticism all around. Liberalism's progressive outlook led to sympathy for socialism and government management, and, later, to the war economy as a means of imposing economic regimentation in the absence of democratic consensus. A half century later, liberalism would have moved full swing toward the very opposite of its 19th-century meaning, while those who opposed government management and favored free enterprise were called conservatives.

It is for this reason that Twain's political views are so frequently misunderstood, as the vast literature on his life and work easily demonstrates. Biographers and critics have had difficulty figuring out how the same person could champion the interests of the Newport capitalist class while founding the Anti-Imperialist League. He loved America's attachment to property and commerce but emerged as the country's most severe critic of the warfare state (he said that the United States should make a special flag for the Philippines: "just our usual flag, with the white stripes painted black and the stars replaced by the skull and cross-bones.")

Nearly alone in the Twain literature, Louis J. Budd's pioneering work *Mark Twain: Social Philosopher*[1] described his outlook as unambiguously liberal in the mold of the Manchester School of Cobden and Bright. "There is no good government at all & none possible," he quotes Clemens in summary of his creed.[2]

It is in the Budd book that we learn that Clemens was a great champion of technological progress and commerce, and never worked up enthusiasm for welfarist measures, for society in the "business age" is governed by "exact and constant" laws that should not be "interfered with for the accommodation of any individual or political or religious faction."[3]

The author of this study doesn't use the term classical liberalism. Instead he called Clemens's outlook a 19th-century, urban, middle-class liberalism. Indeed, Budd himself regrets Twain's political and economic outlook. The author is even aghast that Twain acted as if "supply and demand was a fixed law rather than a debatable theory…"[4]

When the book was reviewed in the *Nineteenth-Century Fiction*[5] Guy A. Cardwell wrote,

> by present standards Mark Twain was more conservative than liberal. He believed strongly in laissez faire, thought

---

[1] Bloomington: Indiana University Press, 1962.

[2] Budd, p. 160.

[3] Budd, p. 160, letter from Aix-Les-Bains.

[4] Budd, p. 39.

[5] Vol. 18, No. 2 (Sep., 1963), pp. 197–200)

> personal political rights secondary to property rights, admired self-made plutocrats, and advocated a leadership to be composed of men of wealth and brains. Among his attitudes now more readily recognized as liberal were a faith in progress through technology and a hostility towards monarchy, inherited aristocracy, the Roman Catholic church, and, in his later years, imperialism.

This review was written many decades ago, when liberals still had faith in technology. This too changed in time, so that now his faith in technology would probably be unclassifiable. His opposition to war would be similarly so, given how unpredictable antiwar feelings are among today's liberals and conservatives.

The party of liberalism that Clemens embraced no longer has a comfortable home in the current age. This problem has led to a general confusion about his outlook on matters of political economy, and thus is his outlook generally disregarded as fuzzy and confused.

Actually, the best way to dispel that impression is by reading Twain's own work. A look at some of his most popular fiction demonstrates that Budd is precisely right: he was a Manchesterite, a liberal of the old school, which, in today's terms, would probably cause him to be classified as a laissez-faire radical or libertarian. He clung to the Whiggism of his family and youth, felt a stronger draw toward Jefferson Davis than Lincoln (but famously and rightly deserted the centrally organized Confederate Army), and championed hard money. He later supported Cleveland in the presidential election of 1884, in part for his support of the gold standard.

Along with Twain's classical liberalism came a strong antiwar position, one which was rooted in Lockean-style love of liberty and opposition to government, not a Leninist-style analysis of the imperialism of finance capitalism.

"Talking of patriotism what humbug it is," he wrote; "it is a word that always commemorates a robbery."

Further: "Patriotism is being carried to insane excess. I know men who do not love God because He is a foreigner."[6]

He was an opponent of the Spanish-American War, believed that Filipinos who were harassing U.S. troops were only fighting for their

---

[6] Quoted in Budd, 182–83.

independence, and might have been the only American who publicly defended the Boxers in China as good patriots.[7]

His general attitude toward political power can be summed up in his account of the transformation of Tom Canty in *The Prince and the Pauper* (1881). Tom was a pauper who finds himself required to act as a stand-in for the prince following an identity mix-up that began in a silly game of changing clothes. The entire story is meant to illustrate the essential artificiality of the caste system that distinguished the nobles from the peasants—a novel filled with bitter vitriol toward the state penal system and overweening police power of the English state.

When Tom Canty comes to know the depredations of power from the inside, he is personally scandalized and sets about making humanitarian reforms. This is the part of Tom usually emphasized in the movie versions. But the original book adds an extra element of complexity, as if to illustrate the universal corruption that comes with power. The formerly sweet, charming, and humane Tom Canty undergoes a radical change once he has power at his disposal:

> When we saw him last, royalty was just beginning to have a bright side for him. This bright side went on brightening more and more every day: in a very little while it was become almost all sunshine and delightfulness. He lost his fears; his misgivings faded out and died; his embarrassments departed, and gave place to an easy and confident bearing.
>
> He worked the whipping-boy mine to ever-increasing profit. He ordered my Lady Elizabeth and my Lady Jane Grey into his presence when he wanted to play or talk, and dismissed them when he was done with them, with the air of one familiarly accustomed to such performances. It no longer confused him to have these lofty personages kiss his hand at parting.
>
> He came to enjoy being conducted to bed in state at night, and dressed with intricate and solemn ceremony in the morning. It came to be a proud pleasure to march to dinner attended by a glittering procession of officers of state and gentlemen-at-arms; insomuch, indeed, that he doubled his guard of gentlemen-at-arms, and made them a

---

[7] Budd, 1983.

> hundred. He liked to hear the bugles sounding down the long corridors, and the distant voices responding, "Way for the King!"
>
> He even learned to enjoy sitting in throned state in council, and seeming to be something more than the Lord Protector's mouthpiece. He liked to receive great ambassadors and their gorgeous trains, and listen to the affectionate messages they brought from illustrious monarchs who called him brother....
>
> He enjoyed his splendid clothes, and ordered more: he found his four hundred servants too few for his proper grandeur, and trebled them. The adulation of salaaming courtiers came to be sweet music to his ears....

Later, as part of the coronation parade, we are told that "Tom Canty gazed abroad over the surging sea of eager faces, and his heart swelled with exultation; and he felt that the one thing worth living for in this world was to be a king, and a nation's idol."

Thus do we see a vivid illustration of the central theme of classical liberalism, that power corrupts. It even corrupts the reformer and those who intend to use their power on behalf of liberty, as indeed Tom Canty had during the early stages of his reign. It is the office and the institution that do this to even the best people, and this power in the hands of bad people can unleash every manner of evil and call it good.

Another central theme of the old classical liberal school was its confidence in the ability of society to manage by itself and the futility of attempting to use the state apparatus as a mechanism for overriding the preferences of individuals. This confidence in the ability of individuals to govern themselves stemmed from an understanding of the creative power of mutual exchange in the absence of the state and the violence against person and property unleashed by its presence.

This theme is returned to again and again in the course of the narrative in both *The Adventures of Tom Sawyer* and *The Adventures of Huckleberry Finn*, two great American novels in which the state is conspicuous for its sheer absence. Indeed, this is part of the great charm and enduring power of these two novels: they describe the affairs of a society that is in evolution apart from the state. The state has only one role in the novels and it is entirely negative: it makes and enforces the fugitive slave laws. It is this fact alone that turns Huckleberry and Jim into outlaws fleeing down the Mississippi to find freedom.

What critics have called the mere sentimentalism of the close relationship between the slave Jim, Tom, and Huck, can be more readily understood as an archetype of the kind of social relations that emerge in the condition of freedom. Their relationship is not characterized by conflict, as people on the Left and Right might have it, but rather by humane and mutual respect for each other as individual human beings. This was Clemens's essentially liberal vision of the capacity that people have for developing friendships apart from the coercion of the state.

Twain's outlook is illustrated in a scene early in *Tom Sawyer*, a case of mutually beneficial exchange in which subjective value is the overriding principle:

Tom and Huck are exchanging banter about their possessions.

Tom says to Huck,

> "Say—what's that?"
>
> "Nothing but a tick."
>
> "Where'd you get him?"
>
> "Out in the woods."
>
> "What'll you take for him?"
>
> "I don't know. I don't want to sell him."
>
> "All right. It's a mighty small tick, anyway."
>
> "Oh, anybody can run a tick down that don't belong to them. I'm satisfied with it. It's a good enough tick for me."
>
> "Sho, there's ticks a plenty. I could have a thousand of 'em if I wanted to."
>
> "Well, why don't you? Becuz you know mighty well you can't. This is a pretty early tick, I reckon. It's the first one I've seen this year."
>
> "Say, Huck—I'll give you my tooth for him."
>
> "Less see it."
>
> Tom got out a bit of paper and carefully unrolled it. Huckleberry viewed it wistfully. The temptation was very strong. At last he said:
>
> "Is it genuwyne?"
>
> Tom lifted his lip and showed the vacancy.
>
> "Well, all right," said Huckleberry, "it's a trade."

> Tom enclosed the tick in the percussion-cap box that had lately been the pinchbug's prison, and the boys separated, each feeling wealthier than before.

Here is an illustration of the principle of mutually beneficial exchange, presented in the most reduced form, with the objects in question being of virtually no value from the point of view of others, and commanding no market price. But through a subtle change in the outlook of each boy, each realizes that he would be somehow better off after the exchange than before.

The tick-for-tooth trade might seem like an irrelevant exchange in terms of the macroeconomy but the principles that drive it and consummate it are the very ones that bring about society itself. "The exchange relation is the fundamental social relation," writes Mises. "Interpersonal exchange of goods and services weaves the bond which unites men into society."[8]

The same subjectivism and cognizance of the gains from trade is at the heart of the story involving the manual labor of fence painting that takes place at the beginning of *Tom Sawyer*. Tom bamboozles a series of kids to do his work for him, on the grounds that it is not really work at all but rather a high calling that he is proud to undertake. Once his friends observe that Tom is enjoying his painting, they decide that they too would like to paint. He refuses pending payment for the chance to do so. Tom then trades the opportunity to paint a fence for a variety of goods: an apple, a kite, a dead rat and "string to swing it with," and more. These items may seem to be worthless at one level, but to their owners, they are highly valuable.

More of a puzzle, the work that Tom's friends purchase with these goods is subjectively seen as more valuable than what they trade for it. This would seem to violate neoclassical dictums concerning the disutility of labor. Tom persuades them otherwise. He persuades them that the joy of immediate gratification of a job well done more than compensates for the disutility associated with the task.

As Rothbard writes,

> A man will expend his labor as long as the marginal utility of the return exceeds the marginal disutility of the labor effort. A man will stop work when the marginal disutility of labor is greater than the marginal utility of the increased goods provided by the effort.[9]

---

[8] *Human Action*, Ludwig von Mises (Mises Institute, 2000), p. 194.

[9] *Man, Economy, and State* (Mises Institute, 2004). p. 42.

The boys did experience disutility from this negative-wage work, but this was outweighed by the desire for the prestige associated with doing the work, clearly a subjective note. And so we read in Tom Sawyer that as each boy became tired of the hard job, there was another worker there to take his place.

Twain writes as follows:

> Tom said to himself that it was not such a hollow world, after all. He had discovered a great law of human action, without knowing it—namely, that in order to make a man or a boy covet a thing, it is only necessary to make the thing difficult to attain. If he had been a great and wise philosopher, like the writer of this book, he would now have comprehended that Work consists of whatever a body is obliged to do, and that Play consists of whatever a body is not obliged to do. And this would help him to understand why constructing artificial flowers or performing on a tread-mill is work, while rolling ten-pins or climbing Mont Blanc is only amusement.

This concept of "play" as a consumable good also finds a mention in Rothbard:

> Those activities which are engaged in *purely* for their own sake are not labor but are pure *play*, consumers' goods in themselves. Play, as a consumers' good, is subject to the law of marginal utility as are all goods, and the time spent in play will be balanced against the utility to be derived from other obtainable goods.[10]

Here is an example of how the economics of *Tom Sawyer* is infused with a sense of the subjective as the determining factor in the decision to trade or work or play. This subjectivism is at the heart of the economic theory that drives the narrative.

An overriding problem that emerged with all this trading among the kids was that it had to be in barter form. What was needed was a medium of exchange, some item that would be universally desirable, divisible, durable, and finally exchangeable for a consumer good. A monetary economy quickly develops that suits the need. The final consumer good was a bound

[10] *Man, Economy, and State*, p. 42.

Bible worth about 40 cents at the time, to be given away at the school to the student who was most adept at memorizing Bible verses.

For each verse learned, a student would get a ticket. The bible could be purchased through ten yellow tickets. One yellow ticket was equal to ten red tickets. One red ticket was worth ten blue tickets. A student could earn a blue ticket by memorizing two verses. Thus was the final consumer good of the Bible priced as 2,000 memorized verses. The downside to this system was that it was planned: the fixed and only way to acquire tickets was through the performance of the single service of memorizing the Bible verses.

Tom and his friends quickly found a way around it. To be sure, not even the final consumer good was enough. As the narrator says, "Tom's mental stomach had never really hungered for one of those prizes, but unquestionably his entire being had for many a day longed for the glory and the eclat that came with it."

Tom asked a friend:

> "Say, Billy, got a yaller ticket?"
>
> "Yes."
>
> "What'll you take for her?"
>
> "What'll you give?"
>
> "Piece of lickrish and a fish-hook."
>
> "Less see 'em."
>
> Tom exhibited. They were satisfactory, and the property changed hands. Then Tom traded a couple of white alleys for three red tickets, and some small trifle or other for a couple of blue ones. He waylaid other boys as they came, and went on buying tickets of various colors ten or fifteen minutes longer.

Eventually Tom enters the church, and comes forward with nine yellow tickets, nine red tickets, and 10 blue ones—and thus was he eligible for a Bible and all the status that came with earning one. The other boys immediately realized that the basis of Tom's fortune was his initial trafficking in whitewashing privileges, and they were bitter and filled with envy. These were, however, ex post feelings that do not impact at all on their ex ante sense of having benefited from the exchanges.

In the end, however, Tom was found out when he was unable to answer a simple Bible question that was asked of him.

This embarrassing failure did not de-monetize the tickets, however, even if they were somewhat devalued. A few scenes later, the reader is witness to another mutually beneficial change.

Tom hailed the romantic outcast:

> "Hello, Huckleberry!"
>
> "Hello yourself, and see how you like it."
>
> "What's that you got?"
>
> "Dead cat."
>
> "Lemme see him, Huck. My, he's pretty stiff. Where'd you get him ?"
>
> "Bought him off'n a boy."
>
> "What did you give?"
>
> "I give a blue ticket and a bladder that I got at the slaughter-house."
>
> "Where'd you get the blue ticket?"
>
> "Bought it off'n Ben Rogers two weeks ago for a hoop-stick."
>
> "Say—what is dead cats good for, Huck?"
>
> "Good for? Cure warts with."
>
> "No! Is that so? I know something that's better."
>
> "I bet you don't. What is it?"
>
> "Why, spunk-water."
>
> "Spunk-water! I wouldn't give a dern for spunk-water."
>
> "You wouldn't, wouldn't you? D'you ever try it?"

What follows is a long discussion of wart-curing methods, which ends with Huck having been persuaded of the merit of spunk-water. But what matters here is that the tickets continue to serve as a medium of exchange. This monetary economy that had developed among the boys emerged in the absence of any kind of formal social pact or state involvement. It was the result of human action rooted in subjective evaluations leading to a complex of exchanges—a microversion of the same process that takes place in the larger economy, where monetary entrepreneurs discover the most highly valued good with monetary properties to serve as a medium of exchange.

The experience of Tom with his attempt to accumulate wealth foreshadows the treasure hunt that leads to a harrowing crime story, the tracing of a treasure, and a near death experience for Tom that ends with both Tom and Huck as very wealthy at a young age.

Nothing about their new-found wealth changes anything about the boys. They do not spend the money or even have much of a consciousness of how the money might elevate their material position. Indeed, Huck gives up his money in *Huckleberry*: "I don't want it at all—nor the six thousand, nuther. I want you to take it; I want to give it to you—the six thousand and all."

And so in this action, Huckleberry reveals a feature of the American entrepreneurial mind, as Twain understands it. Those who have the right mix of passion, creativity, and drive can become enormously wealthy but the wealth alone is not the final goal but rather a means to further accomplishment, whether in the commercial sector or in charitable work. In Tom and Huck's case, they acquired their treasure, but found that possessing was far less interesting than the thrill of discovery.

What drives their search for treasure is not materialism but the pursuit of an ideal, an entrepreneurial push for discovery, adventure, and personal satisfaction. In setting up the story in this way, Twain is offering a perspective on the commercial culture of a society of entrepreneurial freedom: it is driven not so much by the demand for material reward but by the desire for discovery and achievement, with the money serving as a measure of success rather than the end itself.

The unusual treatment of wealth in the *Tom Sawyer* story foreshadowed events of the Gilded Age when large-scale capitalist enterprise created vast wealth and gave rise to a class of entrepreneurs who came to realize that they had more money at their disposal than the European royalty of old. But simultaneous to this was the rise of large-scale professional philanthropy made possible by enormous gifts of this wealth. Like Huck Finn, the so-called robber barons found their treasure but also gave vast sums of it away.

Another profit-making venture makes an appearance in *Tom Sawyer Abroad*, but in this case, the state intervenes to prevent Tom, Huck, and Jim from carrying out their dream. Oddly, Tom, Huck, and Jim find themselves floating in a traveling balloon over the Sahara Desert. Following a sandstorm, they wonder what they will do with all the sand that has built up in the basket.

Jim has the idea first: "Mars Tom, can't we tote it back home en sell it?"

After some reflection, Tom says,

> "Well, the minute people knows it's genuwyne sand from the genuwyne Desert of Sahara, they'll just be in a perfect state of mind to git hold of some of it to keep on the what-not in a vial with a label on it for a curiosity. All we got to do is to put it up in vials and float around all over the United States and peddle them out at ten cents apiece. We've got all of ten thousand dollars' worth of sand in this boat.... And we can keep on coming back and fetching sand, and coming back and fetching more sand, and just keep it a-going till we've carted this whole Desert over there and sold it out; and there ain't ever going to be any opposition, either, because we'll take out a patent."

Tom's excitement soon died out.

> "Boys, it won't work; we got to give it up."
>
> "Why, Tom?"
>
> "On account of the duties."

Jim and Huck ask what he is talking about. Tom explains that a duty "is a tax":

> ...Whenever you strike a frontier—that's the border of a country, you know—you find a custom-house there, and the gov'ment officers comes and rummages among your things and charges a big tax, which they call a duty because it's their duty to bust you if they can, and if you don't pay the duty they'll hog your sand. They call it confiscating, but that don't deceive nobody, it's just hogging, and that's all it is. Now if we try to carry this sand home the way we're pointed now, we got to climb fences till we git tired—just frontier after frontier—Egypt, Arabia, Hindostan, and so on, and they'll all whack on a duty, and so you see, easy enough, we *can't* go *that* road.
>
> ... we're shut off the other way, too. If we go back the way we've come, there's the New York custom-house, and that is worse than all of them others put together, on account of the kind of cargo we've got."
>
> "Why?"

> "Well, they can't raise Sahara sand in America, of course, and when they can't raise a thing there, the duty is fourteen hundred thousand per cent on it if you try to fetch it in from where they do raise it."

Huck says:

> "There ain't no sense in that, Tom Sawyer."...

Jim says:

> "Mars Tom, do dey jam dat duty onto everything we can't raise in America, en don't make no 'stinction 'twix' anything?"
>
> "Yes, that's what they do."
>
> "Mars Tom, ain't de blessin' o' de Lord de mos' valuable thing dey is?"
>
> "Yes, it is."

Jim then goes on to point out that the blessing of the Lord might be considered an untaxed import from heaven. If the government makes no distinctions among imports, wouldn't the government tax a blessing? And if it doesn't do so, and there is equality before the law, why should the state tax any imports at all? Tom has no answer to this point.

The narrator comments:

> [Tom] tried to wiggle out by saying they had *forgot* to put on that tax, but they'd be sure to remember about it, next session of Congress, and then they'd put it on, but that was a poor lame come-off, and he knowed it. He said there warn't nothing foreign that warn't taxed but just that one, and so they couldn't be consistent without taxing it, and to be consistent was the first law of politics. So he stuck to it that they'd left it out unintentional and would be certain to do their best to fix it before they got caught and laughed at.

This passage is a rare intrusion of a direct discussion of the state in books that are so beloved and compelling precisely because they concern themselves with unmanaged human action on a small scale, and readers are invited to share in the mystery and beauty of microcivilizations that result from the casual engagement of people. It is because Twain focused on this social phenomenon and understood its underlying dynamic so well that he is considered such a great American novelist, for he celebrated the human capacity for mutual exchange and understood that order results from liberty and that violent power can only create distortion.

Twain in his books did not create an image of a utopia that would exist in absence of power. There is criminality, clan violence, cruelty, and bigotry—all features of human nature that are not eradicated with a state but only centralized, organized, and legitimized.

But his work does posit that the essential job of developing civilization toward an ideal is to be undertaken by private individuals in their social and economic lives, and not by some mythical institution called the state or an ideology that contradicts the practical experience of people in their communities. A good example comes from his explanation of how the Mississippi came to be discovered in the fullest sense, not merely observed but seen as something economically useful.

Here is Twain from *Life on the Mississippi*:

> After De Soto glimpsed the river, a fraction short of a quarter of a century elapsed, and then Shakespeare was born; lived a trifle more than half a century, then died; and when he had been in his grave considerably more than half a century, the second white man saw the Mississippi....
>
> The mere mysteriousness of the matter ought to have fired curiosity and compelled exploration; but this did not occur. Apparently nobody happened to want such a river, nobody needed it, nobody was curious about it; so, for a century and a half the Mississippi remained out of the market and undisturbed. When De Soto found it, he was not hunting for a river, and had no present occasion for one; consequently he did not value it or even take any particular notice of it.
>
> But at last La Salle, the Frenchman, conceived the idea of seeking out that river and exploring it. It always happens that when a man seizes upon a neglected and important idea, people inflamed with the same notion crop up all around. It happened so in this instance.
>
> Naturally the question suggests itself, Why did these people want the river now when nobody had wanted it in the five preceding generations? Apparently it was because at

> this late day they thought they had discovered a way to make it useful.[11]

Here is the essence of the Austrian idea of entrepreneurship: it is not merely finding a technology or resource. Rather, it concerns viewing a possible economic use of that resource given existing economic realities and making a judgment about the future employment of those resources to serve human ends. It is in this area that the market excels, and the state so completely fails.

As Clemens himself once wrote,

> The mania for giving the Government power to meddle with the private affairs of cities or citizens is likely to cause endless trouble ... and there is great danger that our people will lose that independence of thought and action which is the cause of much of our greatness, and sink into the helplessness of the Frenchman or German who expects his government to feed him when hungry, clothe him when naked ... and, in time, to regulate every act of humanity from the cradle to the tomb, including the manner in which he may seek future admission to paradise.[12]

---

[11] *Life on the Mississippi* (Boston: James Osgood and Company, 1883), pp. 30–31.

[12] Twain's letter to Enterprise on January 24, 1866. Cited in Budd, p. 38–39.

58

The Awful Strife of Nature

November 23, 2007

Environmentalism, it's been said, is the ideological luxury of city dwellers in modern life, for anyone who lives outside an urban or suburban environment knows the truth: nature is vicious and cruel and works relentlessly to make the life of man a living Hell.

I was reminded of this when looking at the horrible, bloody gashes on my brother's domesticated cat, a sweet animal that lives in harmony with his superiors, the human family that owns and cares for him. The violence had been inflicted by another cat, a wild animal that is much bigger and lacks the mirage of conscience that we try to infuse in our pets.

The wild animal arrives at the back porch of this house nestled in the country on the edge of the West Texas desert. When no one is looking, the wild animal terrorizes the domestic cat, stealing food, slashing at his fur and skin, and generally try to rid the world of its competition for survival.

One would think it would be easy enough to kill it, but it is cunning beyond all expectation. I wandered through the mesquite and wild grass looking for him, rifle in hand, but he knew where I was going and hid magnificently. Once I gave up he would appear again as if to taunt me. I would go out with the gun again, and it would start all over.

As my brother and I waited in silence by the reservoir, I noted a skull sitting by the water. Where did this come from? Wild dogs, came the answer. They have been prowling for three months. They target the goats. Three months ago, there were 16 goats, domesticated and happy. Then one day the dogs arrived. At night, they hop the fence and kill them and drag them away. Sometimes they ravaged them to the bone right on the spot, and leave the goat remains to bake in the sun.

Man's best friend!

The goat herd was down to three. One missing goat made everyone particularly sad. It was undersized, born early, white with brown spots. It was brought close to the house and reared in safety. After several months, it was big enough to care for itself and it was allowed to roam with the others. It only lasted a day, however. It was the first one targeted in the season's opening massacre. The baby goat was dinner for dogs.

Such problems as this dominate country life. When it's not dogs and coyotes and wild cats, it's other varmints such as raccoons and hyenas, not to mention snakes and scorpions. Birds devour the fish in the pond. Turtles compete for food. Then there is the plant life, which is far from harmless to the well being of people. Poison plants and thorny bushes dare us to walk outside areas we have tilled. They choked out new plantings. Then there is the weather, which seems to be constantly conspiring to make our lives miserable and foil our plans.

Generally the picture you gain from living in this environment for more than a few days is the very opposite of the "preservationist" outlook you get from environmental propaganda. If we are to survive in this cruel world, the only option is to tame it or kill it. It's them or us. We hear about the precious and delicate balance of nature, how species help each to thrive in a mystical cycle of being, but all we witness is a "natural" kill-or-be-killed practice that is so awful you can hardly watch.

The cruel competition for survival is not limited to animals. It extends to plants, to all things. And it could easily characterize the actions of people, absent the civilizing institutions of exchange, ownership, and the marketplace—the scene of peace in which man uses his reason to create and develop, cooperate and flourish.

And what is war but the very opposite of this impulse, a reversal of reason and an attempt at practicing authentic "environmentalism" in which the choice is to kill or be killed?

As I thought of the lessons here, going through my head were the words of a speech delivered by Absalom Weaver in Garet Garrett's novel *Satan's Bushel*, a book of agricultural life with a speech by Weaver that has profound economic and political significance. For in this speech, he compares what is the same and what is different between man and nature. In so doing, he draws attention to aspects of nature that are completely forgotten amid the propaganda.

The setting is a gathering of farmers, who are being lectured by a government bureaucrat at the turn of the 20th century. They are being told to join the federal effort to coordinate wheat sales among themselves, as a means of driving up prices. The problem, as they see it, is that farmers are fighting for their livelihoods in an age of rising industrialization. How can they survive? The bureaucrat offers one way. Weaver offers another:

"This natural elm," he began, with an admiring look at the tree, "was once a tiny thing. A sheep might have eaten it at one bite. Every living thing around it was hostile and injurious. And it survived. It grew. It took its profit. It became tall and powerful beyond the reach of enemies. What preserved it—cooperative marketing? What gave it power—a law from Congress? What gave it fullness—the Golden Rule? On what was its strength founded—a fraternal spirit? You know better. Your instincts tell you no. It saved itself. It found its own greatness. How? By fighting.

"Did you know that plants fight? If only you could see the deadly, ceaseless warfare among plants this lovely landscape would terrify you. It would make you think man's struggles tame. I will show you some glimpses of it.

"I hold up this leaf from the elm. The reason it is flat and thin is that the peaceable work of its life is to gather nourishment for the tree from the air. Therefore it must have as much surface as possible to touch the air with. But it has another work to do. A grisly work. A natural work all the same. It must fight.

"For that use it is pointed at the end as you see and has teeth around the edge—these. The first thing the elm plant does is to grow straight up out of the ground with a spear thrust, its leaves rolled tightly together. Its enemies do not notice it. Then suddenly each leaf spreads itself out and with its teeth attacks other plants; it overturns them, holds them out of the sunlight, drowns them. And this is the tree! Do you wonder why the elm plant does not overrun the earth? Because other plants fight back, each in its own way.

"I show you a blade of grass. It has no teeth. How can it fight? Perhaps it lives by love and sweetness. It does not. It grows very fast by stealth, taking up so little room that nothing else minds, until all at once it is tall and strong enough to throw out blades in every direction and fall upon other plants. It smothers them to death. Then the bramble. I care not for the bramble. Not because it fights. For another reason. Here is its weapon. Besides the spear point and the teeth the bramble leaf you see is in *five* parts, like one's hand. It is a hand in fact, and one very hard to cast off. When it cannot overthrow and kill an enemy as the elm does, it climbs up his back to light and air, and in fact prefers that opportunity, gaining its profit not in natural combat but in shrewd advantage, like the middleman.

"Another plant I would like to show you. There is one near by. Unfortunately it would be inconvenient to exhibit him in these circumstances. His familiar name is honeysuckle. He is sleek, suave, brilliantly arrayed, and you would not suspect his nature, which is that of the preying speculator. Once you are in his toils it is hopeless. If you have not drowned or smothered him at first he will get you. The way of this plant is to twist itself round and round another and strangle it.

"This awful strife is universal in plant life. There are no exemptions. Among animals it is not so fierce. They can run from one another. Plants must fight it out where they stand. They must live or die on the spot. Among plants of one kind there is rivalry. The weak fall out and die; the better survive. That is the principle of natural selection. But all plants of one kind fight alike against plants of all other kinds. That is the law of their strength. None is helped but who first helps himself. A race of plants that had wasted its time waiting for Congress to give it light and air, or for a state bureau with hired agents to organize it by the Golden Rule, or had been persuaded that its interests were in common with those of the consumer, would have disappeared from the earth."

Garrett provides this speech as a warning to producers tied to the land: they must be fighters or die. The warning to all of us is that we must understand that nature is only provisionally tamed. In truth, we live in the wild, and we are only a step away from being devoured by it.

59

The Works of Leonard E. Read

March 31, 2009

The works of Leonard E. Read, who founded the Foundation for Economic Education (FEE) in 1946, are now online at the Mises Institute. It is probably not the complete collected works, but it is all that he collected in book form. These are books that shaped several generations of activists, donors, writers, and intellectuals. They are the books that kick-started the libertarian movement after World War II. The sons of FEE went on to do great good for the world, and FEE is often called the father of all libertarian think tanks—institutions that work outside official academia to advance radical ideas.

Read did more than merely sponsor lectures and publish. As a matter of fact, others were doing the same. So far as I know, no one has yet noticed that he used a secret weapon in his struggle, something that made him truly different and unusually effective. He eschewed the use of exclusive copyright. That is to say, he encouraged the widest possible distribution of his work and did not forbid others from copying his infinitely reproducible ideas.

Pick up any book or publication from FEE before the 1990s. You will see a remarkable and visionary sentence on the copyright page:

> Permission to reprint granted without special request.

This one sentence is what made it happen. Any newspaper could print a column. Any publisher could include an essay. Indeed, he invited any publisher to take any FEE book and publish it and sell it, owing no royalties and asking no permissions.

The publisher was not even asked to acknowledge its source! So, in this sense, he was even more radical than the Creative Commons attribution license. An FEE book was copyrighted solely so that someone else couldn't copyright it, and then maximum permissions were granted. In effect, Read was putting all of the scholarship of FEE in the public domain as soon as it was published.

This saved on the grueling bureaucratic struggle involved in granting permissions and keeping up with the permissions granted. Asking no fees or royalties meant saving on accounting bureaucracy as well.

Read was no anarchist. He was a believer in "limited government," but regardless, this much is true: he hated the state beyond its most limited form. He saw it as the great enemy of freedom, creativity, and social progress. In fact, he was even more radical: he loathed all restrictions on information. He must have seen that restricting the flow of information through conventional copyright relies upon state interference to make a nonscarce thing—information—artificially scarce. This went against his entire temperament.

As he wrote, "Freedom works its wonders simply because the generative capacity of countless millions has no external force standing against its release!"

But there is a more important point that Read understood. He understood that the critical problem faced by what he called the "freedom philosophy" was not piracy. From his point of view, the ideas of liberty were not "stolen" nearly enough. The problem that he sought to overcome was not too much copying; it was not enough copying. He saw that his number-one goal had to be busting up the obscurity of these ideas and getting them out to the public. Conventional copyright was not a help in this respect; it was a hindrance.

Never forget that Read had a background in business. He was head of the Chamber of Commerce in Los Angeles before founding FEE. He must have seen countless businesses start and fail, not because they didn't have a good product, but because people didn't know about the product enough to go and buy it. The critical problem that every innovator faces, after coming up with the innovation, is getting the word out.

Think of a new hamburger stand in Los Angeles. It doesn't matter how great the burgers are; if people don't know about it, it will not succeed. Imagine if some huge fan wanted to print up T-shirts about the hamburgers. Why in the world would the owner of the joint want to use the government to extract money from the T-shirt printer? That would be nuts.

And let's say that another burger company in town started up that used the same recipe. What then? The answer is to regard the imitation as flattery, and compete in the most aggressive possible way. It keeps you on your toes, keeps you innovating, and the excitement of the competition itself can attract imitation. And who is going to benefit the most from this struggle, the original institution or its copy? The answer is shown to us every day. Originators who continue to innovate benefit from having their products and ideas spread.

In the same way, Read saw himself in the idea business. Why, then, would he turn to the state to restrict the flow of ideas? That would cut into everything he ever wanted to do. Indeed, rather than restricting access to FEE texts, he begged the world to take them and print them and distribute them. He wanted this more than anything else.

You will note that he was very prolific; but why? Because he had a lifetime burning passion to get the word out in every possible way. He stated the freedom philosophy again and again in every way he could imagine and encouraged others to do the same. He was an evangelist spreading the news. He wanted to be pirated so that he could see that he was making a difference.

Reading his books, you will find that he was repetitive, and, if we want to be critical, it could be noted that he rarely dealt in depth with any particular technical aspect of economics or commented much on the news. He eschewed techniques that pass for rigorous analysis today. But we need a greater appreciation for two things:

1. He knew that the most important task of educating was to inspire people to understand the big picture, and

2. On the big-picture issue of the capacity of society to manage itself, he was 100% correct.

He had this gigantic faith in freedom. He often said that he could not and would not predict the outcome of granting liberty to individuals and could not and would not speculate on the shape that society would take under conditions of freedom. But he could say for certain that whatever the results of freedom, they would be more consonant with human rights, more prosperous, more creative, and more orderly than anything that the state could manufacture through coercion.

Taking leaps into the unknown was this man's habit of mind, something he believed in strongly. When people warned him that granting universal reprint permissions would cut into FEE revenue, he would completely dismiss the notion. His view was that, insofar as FEE could do its part to make the universe open-ended, it would do that and trust that the results would be better than restriction.

He shared this faith with people like Bastiat, who is a similar figure in history: these were two men who had a firm conviction about a point of social organization that manages to elude most every living person at any point in history. They believed that freedom was all that was necessary to make the good society happen. They were both tireless in making the point and strove to find every possible way to teach it.

Thank goodness for his vision. But please note what it means. The modern freedom movement depended heavily on open-source materials. It had an effect on the world because it eschewed state means of imposing artificial scarcities and sought above all else to get the word out. The modern libertarian movement was born in the equivalent of Creative Commons and grew through that means.

"Originators who continue to innovate benefit from having their products and ideas spread."Indeed it was true: FEE material was everywhere! It was in newspapers, magazines, monographs, books, and printed by all existing technologies. People in those days report that you couldn't help bumping into it. I'm telling you that Read knew what he was doing. He went against the pack. Everyone else was availing themselves of copyright. He said no. And he stuck to it.

Did this harm FEE? Quite the contrary! It was the best thing that ever happened to the institution and to the ideas it represented. Just as Read said, freedom worked. The implications are profound.

This is all about practicing what you preach, but there is more to it than that: it is about developing an effective tactic for spreading the truth. It's a glorious thing that Read did, if only by instinct. Would that we all had his instinct for how to rise from obscurity into prominence.

60

The Genius of Rube Goldberg

April 28, 2005

Everyone has heard something described as a Rube Goldberg machine, and most of us know what this means: some crazy convoluted way of accomplishing a task that would otherwise be quite simple. That's how Webster's defines it. The phase most often applies to overly complicated software but it was also applied to the Clinton health care plan and might also be applied to emerging Social Security reform.

How fascinating, then, to discover the man and legend behind the expression, and to reflect on his remarkable turn of mind and the light it sheds on the world around us. Reuben Goldberg, born in 1883 in San Francisco, was the son of Hannah and Max Goldberg, who had immigrated from Prussia and lived in New York before moving West.

Rube studied to be an engineer and did that for a while until he could convince his father that his avocation as a cartoonist should be his profession. Rube worked in San Francisco and later in New York. He lived a long and wonderful life as a genius cartoonist and also a writer, actor, and sculptor. Even aside from his contraptions, he was popular for his long-running series called "Foolish Questions," which was turned into a board game. He made animated cartoons and wrote short stories too. He received the Pulitzer Prize in 1948. He died in 1970.

But of course it was his cartoon inventions that made his name. A book called *Inventions* (N.Y.: Simon and Schuster, 2000) collects his most famous material, mostly consisting of hilarious and overcomplicated machinery to accomplish simple tasks like turning a page of music or emptying out sand from shoes or closing a window and swatting a fly or prevent a dinner plate from sliding in the dining room of a rocking boat. In a goofy sort of way, his works celebrates the inventor and innovator, and the problem-solving spirit.

All of it was justly popular during the so-called Age of Invention, and seems to have experienced a revival today.

But there's an edge here too: Goldberg's work ridicules intellectualism unhinged from the market test. As Rothbard wrote about entrepreneurship, and Stephen Carson recently elaborated, it is not enough merely to conjure up an idea; the idea must be backed by real property put at risk in the real world and subjected to the market test. Innovation alone does not make for progress. It is innovation within the framework of a market economy that serves society.

The sheer goofy genius of Goldberg's work also illustrates a Hayekian theme of the error of rationalism detached from reality. Society works not because a single mastermind has preset all the moving parts. It works because people find ways to cooperate through private actions that follow signs and rules that cannot be anticipated but can nonetheless be coordinated. Society and its workings cannot be mapped out, and the attempt to do so can create frameable images but not civilizations.

Each Goldberg contraption takes a few minutes to figure out, as the cartoonist explains to the reader the workings of each part. There's always at least one implausible step that will guarantee failure in real life, but that's also the fun. Sometimes it involves supposing that people will do something they are not likely to do—an Arabian dwarf acrobat reaching for a trapeze at the right moment, for example. Sometimes it involves a problem of timing—I'm thinking here of his fire extinguisher that depends at a crucial point on a frog's leg motions moving a knife that cuts a chain!

Sometimes the whole thing is obviously nuts from the very outset. A good example is "The Latest Simple Flyswatter"

> Carbolic acid (A) drops on string (B) causing it to break and release elastic of bean shooter (C) which projects ball (D) into bunch of garlic (E) causing it to fall into syrup can (F) and splash syrup violently against side wall. Fly (G) buzzes with glee and goes for syrup, his favorite dish. Butler-dog (H) mistakes hum of fly's wings for door buzzer and runs to meet visitor, pulling rope (I) which turns stop-go signal (J) and causes baseball bat (K) to sock fly who falls to floor unconscious. As fly drops to floor pet trout (L) jumps for him, misses, and lands in net (M). Weight of fish forces shoe (N) down on fallen fly and puts him out of the running for all time.

What surprised me—though it should not have—was to discover that Mr. Goldberg seems to have been very solid on politics too. All the drawings in the politics section show government as the most complicated and unworkable machinery of all, that nonetheless does accomplish its primary goal of giving some people power at others' expense.

This drawing is perhaps the best visual description of central planning I've seen.

Goldberg's art exhibits a disdain for supposed experts who have an inflated sense of their own mastery. The class that presumes to rob people for their own good comes under special scrutiny. Thus did Goldberg not spare the state and its minions. Taxes in particular, low by the standards of our own time, came in for hard knocks under his pen. Here, laughing gas is applied in order to keep the working man from noticing how much the government is taking from him.

How charming to discover that the web has an official Rube Goldberg website, and that there is an annual Rube Goldberg Machine Contest at Purdue University and also one for high school students. You don't need to submit or attend to enjoy Goldberg's genius. The book *Inventions* will keep you busy for months, or you can examine many machines at RubeGoldberg.com.

61

A Book that Changes Everything

January 16, 2009

At a taped video interview in my office, before the crew would start the camera, a man had to remove my Picasso prints from the wall. The prints are probably under copyright, they said.

But the guy who drew them died 30 years ago. Besides, they are mine.

Doesn't matter. They have to go.

What about the poor fellow who painted the wall behind the prints? Why doesn't he have a copyright? If I scrape off the paint, there is the drywall and its creator. Behind the drywall are the boards, which are surely proprietary too. To avoid the "intellectual-property" thicket, maybe we have to sit in an open field; but there is the problem of the guy who last mowed the grass. Then there is the inventor of the grass to consider.

Is there something wrong with this picture?

The worldly-wise say no. This is just the way things are. It is not for us to question but to obey. So it is with all despotisms in history. They become so woven into the fabric of daily life that absurdities are no longer questioned. Only a handful of daring people are capable of thinking along completely different lines. But when they do, the earth beneath our feet moves.

Such is the case with *Against Intellectual Monopoly* (Cambridge University Press, 2008) by Michele Boldrin and David Levine, two daring professors of economics at Washington University in St. Louis. They have written a book that is likely to rock your world, as it has mine. (It is also posted on their site with the permission of the publisher.)

With piracy and struggles over intellectual property in the news daily, it is time to wonder about this issue, its relationship to freedom, property rights, and efficiency. You have to think seriously about where you stand.

This is not one of those no-brainer issues for libertarians, like minimum wage or price controls. The problem is complicated, and solving it requires careful thought. But it is essential that every person do the thinking, and there is no better tool for breaking the intellectual gridlock than this book.

The issue is impossible to escape, from the grave warnings you get from the FBI at the beginning of "your" DVD to the posters warning kids never to download a song, to the outrageous settlements transferring billions from firm to firm. It even affects the outrageous prices you pay for medicine at the drug store. The issue of "intellectual property" is a ubiquitous part of modern life.

Some of the police-state tactics used to enforce IP have to make anyone with a conscience squeamish. You have surely wondered about the right and wrong of all this, but, if you are like most people, you figure that copyrights and patents are consistent with the justice that comes from giving the innovator his due. In principle they seem fine, even if the law might be in need of reform.

The first I'd ever thought critically about issues of intellectual property was in reading about it in the abstract many years ago. The Austrian position has traditionally favored copyrights on the same grounds it has favored property rights in general, but has tended to oppose patents on grounds that they are government grants of monopolistic privilege. Machlup, Mises, and Rothbard—as well as Stigler, Plant, and Penrose—have discussed the issue but not at great length and with varying levels of cautious skepticism.

That changed in 2001 with the publication of Stephan Kinsella's article and now monograph "Against Intellectual Property." He made a strong theoretical argument that ideas are not scarce, do not require rationing, are not diminished by their dissemination, and so cannot really be called property. All IP is unjust, he wrote. It is inconsistent with libertarian ethics and contrary to a free market. He favors the complete repeal of all intellectual-property laws.

The argument initially struck me as crazy on its face. As I considered it further, my own view gradually changed: it's not crazy, I thought, but it is still pie-in-the-sky theorizing that has nothing to do with reality. Kinsella's article appeared just before the explosive public interest in this subject. The patent regime has in the meantime gone completely wild, with nearly 200,000 patents issued every year in the United States, and half a million more in other countries—with 6.1 million patents in effect worldwide—and large firms collecting stockpiles of them.

And the copyright issue has led to a massive struggle between generations: young people live by "pirating" music, movies, software, whereas the old consider this practice to presage the end of the capitalist system as we know it. The music industry has spent billions trying to contain the problem and only ended up engendering consumer embitterment and terrible public relations.

Kinsella's article continued to haunt me personally. It took about six years or so, but I finally worked through all the theoretical problems and came to embrace his view, so you might say that I was predisposed to hear what Boldrin and Levine have to say. What I hadn't realized until encountering their book was just how far-reaching and radical the implications of a detailed look at IP really are.

It is not just a matter of deciding what you believe from a theoretical or political perspective. It is not just a matter of thinking that "pirates" are not really violating moral law. To fully absorb what these authors say changes the way you look at technology, at history, at the ebbs and flows of economic development; it even changes who the good guys and bad guys are in the history of civilization.

Kinsella deals expertly with the theoretical aspects, while *Against Intellectual Monopoly* doesn't really go into the theory at great length. What this amazing book deals with is the real-world practice of intellectual-property regulation now and in history. I can make a personal guarantee that not a single objection you think you have to their thesis goes unaddressed in these pages. Their case is like the sun that melts all snow for many miles in all directions.

The implications are utterly shattering, and every day I've turned the pages in the Boldrin/Levine book I've felt that sense of intellectual stimulation that comes along rarely in life—that sense that makes you want to grab anyone off the street and tell that person what this book says. It helps you understand many things that had previously been confusing. The emergent clarity that comes from having absorbed this work is akin to what it must feel like to hear or see for the first time. If they are right, the implications are astonishing.

Their main thesis is a seemingly simple one. Copyright and patents are not part of the natural competitive order. They are products of positive law and legislation, imposed at the behest of market winners as a means of excluding competition. They are government grants of monopolies, and, as neoclassical economists with a promarket disposition, the authors are against monopoly because it raises prices, generates economic stagnation, inhibits innovation, robs consumers, and rewards special interests.

What they have done is apply this conventional model of monopoly to one of the most long-lasting, old-world forms of mercantilist/monopolistic institutional privilege, a surviving form of the mercantilist privilege of the 16th century. IP is like a dam in the river of development, or perhaps very large boulders that impede the flow.

They too favor its total repeal but their case goes far beyond the theoretical. They convince you that radical, far-reaching, uncompromising, revolutionary reform is essential to our social well-being now and in the future.

The results are dazzling and utterly persuasive. I personally dare anyone who thinks that he believes in patent or copyright to read this book and deal with it. For this reason, I'm thrilled that the Mises Institute is now carrying the book to give it the broadest possible exposure.

I'm not sure what aspect of their case is the most powerful. Here are just a few examples:

They show that people like James Watt, Eli Whitney, and the Wright Brothers are not heroes of innovation, as legend has it, but rent-seeking mercantilists who dramatically set back the cause of technological development. These people spent vast resources prohibiting third parties from improving "their" product and making it available at a cheaper price. Instead of promoting innovation and profitability, they actually stopped it, even at the cost of their own business dreams.

The authors show that every great period of innovation in human history has taken place in the absence of intellectual property, and that every thicket of IP has ended up stagnating the industries to which they apply. Think of the early years of the web, in which open-source technology inspired breakneck development, until patents and copyright were imposed with the resulting cartelization of operating systems. Even today, the greatest innovations in digital communications come from the highly profitable open-source movement.

It is impossible to develop software without running into IP problems, and the largest players are living off IP and not innovation. Meanwhile, the most profitable and most innovative sector of the web, the porn sector, has no access to courts and IP enforcement because of the stigma associated with it. It is not an accident that absence of IP coincides with growth and innovation. The connection is causal.

And look at the industries that do not have IP access, such as clothing design and architecture and perfume. They are huge and fast-moving and fabulous. First movers still make the big bucks, without coercing competition. Boldrin and Levine further speculate that IP is behind one of the great puzzles of the last millennium: stagnation in classical music. The sector is seriously burdened and tethered by IP.

Other mysteries are answered. Why no musical composition of note in England after 1750? England had the world's most strict copyright laws. Why was English literature so popular in the United States in 19th-century schoolrooms? It could be imported without copyright restriction—and therefore sold cheaply—whereas American authors used IP and limited their market. And consider the irony that Disney, which relies heavily on IP, got its start and makes it largest profits by retelling public-domain stories!

Examples like this abound. One wonders if the modern history of literature and art needs to be completely rewritten. Examples will occur to you that are not discussed in the book, such as fan fiction. It is technically illegal, so far as anyone can tell, to take a copyrighted character and tell a story about him even if the story is original. And yet Harry Potter fan-fiction sites enjoy tens of millions of hits per month. One hosts 5,000 pieces of fan fiction, some as long as 1,000 pages. Enforcement has been spotty and unpredictable.

And yes, the book covers the poster child of the IP world: pharmaceuticals. Boldrin and Levine muster plenty of evidence that IP here does nothing to promote innovation and widespread availability and is largely responsible for the egregiously high prices of drugs that are driving the system toward socialization.

The authors explore the very strange tendency of capitalists to misdiagnose the source of their profits in a world of IP, spending far more on beating up pirates than they would have earned in a free market. They further demonstrate that IP is a form of exploitation and expropriation that is gravely dangerous for civilization itself.

In short, they have taken what might seem to be merely a geeky concern and moved it to the center of the discussion over economic development itself.

What about the far-flung conclusion that IP should be repealed? The authors take away your fears. The development of IP came about in the 16th century as a mechanism for governments to enforce political control and punish dissenters. The cause of this "property right" was then taken over by individuals in the 18th and 19th century as part of the liberal revolution for individual rights. In the 20th century, it was transferred again, to corporations, who become the effective owners through copyright. The creators no longer own anything, and let themselves be beaten and abused by their own publishers and production companies.

Boldrin and Levine's thesis really steps up this issue. It makes you wonder how long authors and creators will put up with the nonsense that some company has a state-enforced exclusive to use the work of others for longer than 100 years. Fortunately, the digital age is forcing the issue, and alternatives like Creative Commons (roughly akin to what would exist in a free market) are becoming increasingly popular. As the tyranny has grown more obvious, the free market is responding.

No, the authors are not really Austrian, and I'm not even sure that they can be called libertarians, but they understand the competitive process in ways that would make Hayek and Mises proud. As I've thought more about their book, it seems that it might suggest a revision in classical-liberal theory. We have traditionally thought that cooperation and competition were the two pillars of social order; a third could be added: emulation. In addition, there is surely work to do here that integrates Hayek's theory of knowledge with the problem of IP.

If the book lacks for anything, it is precisely what Kinsella provides: a robust theory behind the practical analytics. But since Kinsella has already provided this, the value added of real-world application is enormous. I have a minor nit to pick with Boldrin and Levine on their passing comment on trademarks, which strikes me as wrong. Otherwise, this book moves mountains; A book like this comes along very rarely. *Against Intellectual Monopoly* is a relatively small manifesto on economics that absolutely must be understood and absorbed by every thinking person without exception.

62

Business Cycles, Not Our Fault

November 21, 2008

These are times when you just feel like yelling at the people who write the news, particularly the business press. They are happy to report, word for word, what the Fed and Treasury Department tell them, and their message is always the same: hey, it's not our fault; in fact, we are fixing the problem!

We are told that the economy has tanked because foreigners invested too much in the U.S., that foreigners *saved* too much money, that we all lived beyond our means, that greedy capitalists fed our materialist instincts until we popped, or any combination of the above. Or maybe business cycles are just like weather, cold one season and hot the next. Regardless, it is the government that must come to the rescue with the usual combination of cockamamie schemes.

Discovering the Austrian business cycle theory, then, is a revelation, because through it, you learn how the whole business traces to loose money and credit generated by the Fed. The money is pumped into the capital-goods fashion of the day, in this case housing. The whole sector becomes overbuilt and unsustainable and it turns, tanking many other sectors. The only answer to the problem is not more of the poison that caused the problem but a real liquidation.

This time around, the theory is more in circulation than ever before—thanks to the Mises Institute—but you still don't see evidence of consciousness on the part of "establishment" journalists.

It turns out that this was also true at the onset of the Great Depression. The cause of the crash of 1929 and its effects was not unknown to that generation either. There were people saying the right things. It's just that the press and the establishment ignored them. Here's the evidence: *A Bubble that Broke the World*, by Garet Garrett, published in 1932. Here he lays it all out.

"This is a delusion about credit. And whereas from the nature of credit it is to be expected that a certain line will divide the view between creditor and debtor, the irrational fact in this case is that for more than ten years debtors and creditors together have pursued the same deceptions. In many ways, as will appear, the folly of the lender has exceeded the extravagance of the borrower."

He goes on to explain how the debt overhang of the First World War is the root cause; how society came to accept the idea that if people can't immediately afford stuff, government should provide it; how government came to operate on a bankrupt system; how we came to believe that prosperity came from credit rather than savings; and how the Federal Reserve, working with government, is the root source of the problem.

Beautiful. Magnificently written, as only Garrett can. How could anyone have missed it? He wasn't exactly obscure. He wrote for the *Saturday Evening Post*. Incredibly, he chronicled the New Deal blow by blow in the *Saturday Evening Post*, every rotten law, every goofy plan, every attack on liberty, property, and economic sanity. There was no mystery here. The proof: *Salvos Against the New Deal,* an assembly of his best work from this period.

In other words, the cause, the effects, the folly, the power grabs—it's all here, and all eerily similar to what we are experiencing today. We call it the Great Depression. But had the politicians not intervened, it would have been known as the 1929 crash, and it might have been as memorable as many other crashes in American history. The difference this time was the application of "modern economic methods" to cure the thing, methods which only ended up prolonging human suffering.

Let's talk of two other cases in which the error was pointed out. Lord Lionel Robbins wrote in 1934. His book called *The Great Depression*, much more technical and scholarly than Garrett's own, presents the Austrian theory in a very precise way, and documents how the Fed and the Bank of England inflated the money supply and loosened credit in the latter half of the 1920s, leading to the bust. His is a cautious treatise in some way.

After all, he was blaming the central bank—not exactly a position that was politically wise—and we aren't just talking about the equivalent of a blogger today. He was Lionel Robbins, the most influential economist in Britain until Lord Keynes stole the show with his whiz-bang policy ideas.

And why? Robbins counseled letting the bad investments wash out of the system. Keynes thought you could use the state to rev the bad back to life.

By the way, this is the 1934 first edition, and so it is replete with citations of the Austrians, such as Mises and Menger. A later second edition was gutted and replaced with Keynesian and classical citations, and this was before Robbins later caved in to the Keynesian consensus and repudiated the book altogether. The pressure was on!

As another example, and really the definitive one, Ludwig von Mises himself was writing all throughout the late twenties and early thirties about the business cycle. He nails it all in essay after essay: the credit expansion, the malinvestment, the folly of counter-cyclical policy, the dangers of protectionism and reflation, and so much more. These essays could all be written today, and what is also impressive is Mises's focus on theory. He never makes empirical claims that aren't backed up by an attempt to explain the theoretical apparatus behind the analysis.

What's tragic is that his work on business cycle theory—which inspired Hayek's—was not translated into English until the 1980s and, even then, not distributed in a form that elicited much attention. This is why *The Causes of the Economic Crisis* is such an important book. It collects all of Mises's essays in a single book that is beautifully edited and bound. It shows who precisely was the great master of economics in the 20th century.

All of this leads up to Rothbard's *America's Great Depression*, the book that is often cited as the one to show that the episode was caused not by the market but by the central bank. It is getting new attention today. But if you follow his citations, they lead right back to Garrett, Robbins, and Mises—three of the observers of the time who saw precisely what was happening. They had to be ignored by the New Dealers, for they utterly demolish the case for stabilization policy.

63

Capitalism as Drama

July 20, 2009

Somehow the movie *Wall Street* (1987) still holds up after all these years. Sure, the technology is dated—the cell phones are hilariously huge and the fat-back screens in offices display only green digits—but it hardly matters. The clothing by Alan Flusser is of course amazing and holds up too, but the real merit here runs deeper than appearances alone.

The sensibility of the film, the thrill of commerce and trade, the challenge of the battle between money and morality, and the larger-than-life quality of its main character—the rich, savvy, and unstoppable Gordon Gekko—all combine to make a legendary story that remains strangely inspiring in ways that its maker, Oliver Stone, surely did not entirely intend.

The film ends with a paean to labor unions and governments that save companies from rapacious capitalists, but it seems artificial, like a Victorian novel that had to have a happy ending lest the readers revolt. The overall message concerns the central role of finance and commerce in moving history forward. Even the famed "greed is good" speech gives one pause: he is onto something here, even if it is inelegantly stated.

In the same way that the Godfather movies shaped the culture of organized crime, *Wall Street* continues to influence the way traders and high-flying capitalists understand themselves.

And it's no wonder. The impression one is left with is all about the courage, the thrill of the fight, the riskiness of entrepreneurship, that struggle to obtain vast wealth, and the striving for the status of "master of the universe." It pictures commerce as a gladiator fight, a magnificent and relentless struggle for progress, an epic and massively important setting in which the fate of civilization is determined.

Enticing isn't it? Indeed it is and should be. Not all of commercial life is like this but parts of it are. And some features are universals that don't just apply to high finance. Everywhere and always, the future is uncertain. Those who make good judgments are rewarded. It isn't easy. It isn't for the faint of heart. Competition can be as fierce in a small business setting as in a big business one. Even the tiniest shop faces a daily risk, and this risk affects decision-making in every area. Contrary to what Gekko claims, there is no sure thing, even with inside knowledge and even with all the wealth of the world. Indeed, Gekko is ultimately undone by forgetting that there might be someone out there with even better information.

The thing that levels the playing field in this rivalry in the service of society is the ubiquitous reality that no one really knows for sure what is around the corner. And in the end, whether you win or lose depends on that fickle and uncontrollable thing called consumer volition and its confrontation with the other undeniable reality of scarcity in all things.

I was trying to think of another story that captures that amazing element of drama associated with commercial life. It was this feature of the novels of Ayn Rand that most impressed Ludwig von Mises and Murray Rothbard. She gave voice to their own love of economics as high-drama intellectual battles for and against the progress of man.

My own favorite writer in this genre is Garet Garrett, with his four novels written in the 1920s.

It is not just his novels. It is Garrett's entire worldview. He saw the market as the tableau for the working out of the great struggles in human history. Unlike Oliver Stone, he favored capitalism, for the reason that it was the engine of progress, and a vibrant and wholly cooperative way to work out the competitive spirit in the human person.

The virtues of steadfastness, valor, bravery, and the impulse to make a dent in the universe, and never, never, never give in (Churchill) are tragically associated with the death and destruction of war, but free enterprise provides a means by which these impulses can be channeled toward creative purposes.

And so, for example, in *The Cinder Buggy* we are witness to a titanic struggle within a family over whether the future belongs to iron or steel. And the description of the struggle in the lives of its entrepreneurs causes the heart to race.

> The day of steel was breaking.

> It was not a brilliant event. It was like a cloudy dawn, unable to make a clean stroke between the light and the dark. Yet everyone had a sense of what was passing in this dimness.
>
> Gib, whose disbelief in steel rested as much upon pain memories and hatred as upon reason, was a fanatic; but at the same time great numbers of men with no such romantic bias of mind were violently excited on one side or the other of a fighting dispute. Fate decided the issue. The consequences were such as become fate. They were tremendous, uncontrollable, unimaginable. They changed the face of civilization. Vertical cities, suburbs, subways, industrialism, the rise of a wilderness in two generations to be the paramount nation in the world, victory in the World War,—those were consequences.

And look at this. You have to love this material:

> And all the time, bad as it was, steel kept coming more and more into use, especially, that is to say,—almost exclusively in the form of rails. And the reason the steel rail kept coming into use was that an amazing human society yet unborn, one that should have shapes, aspects, wants, powers and pastimes then undreamed of, was calling for it,—calling especially for the steel rail.
>
> The steel men heard it. That was what kept them in hope. The iron men heard it and were struck with fear.

Even the everyday actions of workers become fascinating:

> The air was torn, shattered, upheaved, compressed, pierced through, by sounds of shock, strain, impact, clangor, cannonade and shrill whistle blasts, occurring in any order of sequence, and then all at one time dissolving in a moment of vast silence even more amazing to the ear. Conversation would be possible only by shrieks close up. The men seemed never to speak at their work. They did not communicate ideas by signs either. Each man had his place, his part, his own pattern of action, and did what he did with a kind of mechanical inevitability, as if it were something he had never learned. They were related not to each other but to the process, kept their eyes fixedly on it for obvious reasons, and stepped warily. A false gesture might have immediate consequences.

Later in the book, the fight between the dynasties revolves around price movements. One side gets into the nail business. The other side dumps nails on the market to lower the price, attempting to drive all competition out of business, even though it proves harmful to the very firm doing the dumping. The action is driven by spite, and the capitalist deems the price paid worth it for his goal of revenge. The action starts his downward spiral toward death. The firm that hopes to make and sell nails moves on to greater things.

So it is in the real world of commerce. No, the profitability is not always the motivation. Self-interest defines a wide category of human impulses, from benevolence to greed to the desire to destroy. This multiplicity of motivation can no more be ended than human nature itself can be permanently changed. The beauty of the market is its capacity for funneling it all in the service of the consumers, and *The Cinder Buggy* shows how all this works. Who benefitted from the struggle? Those who needed nails and were glad to pay a lower price.

Price movements are also central to the drama of *Satan's Bushel*. The reader follows the price of wheat up and down and up again, and watches these price changes shift the fortunes of families, communities, and whole regions. No matter how powerful and rich the players, they are reduced to bit players in the face of larger market trends.

Garrett writes of a wheat speculator what could be said of Gekko in his best moments:

> No rule of probability contains him. To say that he acts upon impulse, without reflection, in a headlong manner, is true only so far as it goes. Many people have that weakness. With him it is not a weakness. It is a principle of conduct. The impulse in his case is not ungovernable. It does not possess him and overthrow his judgment. It is the other way around. He takes possession of the impulse, mounting it as it were the enchanted steed of the Arabian Nights, and rides it to its kingdom of consequences. What lies at the end is always a surprise; if it is something he doesn't care for, no matter. Another steed is waiting. Meaning to do this, living for it, he has no baggage. There is nothing behind him. If he has wealth it is portable. He is at any moment ready.

It is the same with *The Driver* and with *Harangue*: the wonders of market-based inevitabilities sweep all dreams before them. Whether that dream in for some whacko socialist utopia, a Manichean experiment in living off the raw products of nature, or the goal of reigning in market forces through regulation in order to benefit a few at the expense of the many, the market's love of reality is triumphant. Those who know this in advance are the long-run winners.

In the movie *Wall Street*, we are told that we should all love unions and their desire to keep wages as high as possible and fix jobs in place for generation after generation. And yet look around and see: the unions have destroyed the American car companies and they have put a serious dent in the profitability of airlines too. Their wishes are unsustainable because they are not the market's command.

In the end, who is the real destroyer: Gordon Gekko or the unions he fought? The movie ends with the unions and the government on top. History ends with the capitalists on top.

64

The Film Noir Moment

September 21, 2009

Film noir is not riding any wave of popularity, so it is the perfect time to anticipate a trend. These movies from the 1940s are not only brilliant and beautiful but also entertaining in their own right. They look completely different to us now from what they must have looked like then, and I don't mean merely to inspire a sentimentalism for days gone by.

These were times when Mises's was writing *Human Action* in English, Hazlitt was working at the *New York Times*, and Ayn Rand was marketing *The Fountainhead* to Hollywood. These authors, writing on manual typewriters and submitting the results only in hard copy, were the champions of markets and technological progress. They saw what others did not, namely, that the innovations of the time, as wonderful as they seemed, were only the beginning of what was possible under freedom.

The film noir of their period beautifully illustrates the strange way in which the operation of society itself was limited by the existing technology as compared with our own digital age. Because none of us can live two lifetimes, we depend on media like this to provide us insight in this area and many others.

The plots of many of these hundreds of films turn on the ability of people to change identities and get lost in the thick of things, with tricks and turns that would be completely unimaginable today in the information age. What is especially interesting is that the characters in the movies are unaware that they are living in what seems like prehistoric times to us. For them, the ability to call house-to-house, to listen to the radio in the car, to communicate with others from phone booths might have been dazzling.

Watching today, we see a society radically hobbled by the limits of technology, people whose decisions and course of life is determined by this fact, even without their knowing it. The biggest limit concerns the absence of information about people's backgrounds and hence core character. Evildoers masquerade as respectable people, while respectable people turn to evil and are oddly successful at hiding it even from intimates.

The Detour, for example, is about a hitchhiker—talk about an anachronism!—picked up by a driver who hasn't contacted his parents in many years; nor do they have a way to contact him. The driver unexpectedly dies and the hitchhiker, fearing blame, dumps his body, takes his money and clothes, and assumes a new identity. He even plans to sell the car, since there was some disconnect between the owner and the car registration. Then a girl he picks up turns to him and demands to know where the body is, a terrifying moment simply because one person knows something that was previously hidden. The lack of communication and knowledge is the core plot device, so that information is the source of terror.

There are other features of this film that turn on technological limits. Many people seem strangely displaced, without a known past, and they can float around from place to place with anonymity, appearing and disappearing from the social fabric. The newspapers were the way you heard the news, but gossip was generally more reliable. You had to be standing right by the phone to get a call. The phones were necessarily connected to the wall, so if you wanted to make a private call, you had to grab the phone and take it into another room. In *Detour*, when one person pulls on the cord to get the phone back, he inadvertently strangles a girl in the next room.

Not even credit checks are very efficient, which is why the lead in *Quicksand* was able to buy a watch on a borrowed $100 and resell it for $30 a little while later, so that he could return the $20 that he borrowed from the cash register at work, which no one would have noticed was gone until the weekly accountancy check. By the way, in this particular film, his misdeed is discovered, and he has to return the $100 the next day, which requires that he mug a drunk, which then leads to being blackmailed for $500 by someone who saw him do it, and so on until he is on the run for auto theft and murder. It's like a metaphor for financing the U.S. government.

Sometimes the information asymmetry is extreme, as in *Double Indemnity*. An insurance investigator is checking into an exorbitant insurance claim with a partner who in fact is the perpetrator of the very crime he is investigating. The insurance man is romantically pursuing a woman, who he does not know plans to kill him once the scheme is complete. She is, in turn, married to a man who doesn't know that his current wife is the killer of his previous wife. And the daughter of the woman befriends the insurance man without knowing that he is the killer of her father. Meanwhile, the daughter's boyfriend doesn't know that her stepmother is lying to him and probably setting him up to take the fall for this grisly mess.

In *The Man Who Cheated Himself*, the entire plot turns on a confusion about whether the car that dumped a body at the airport is blue or green, a problem that would have been solved with a color camera at the scene of the crime.

In a personal favorite of mine, *The Strange Love of Martha Ivers*, the details of a murder some 20 years ago had been forgotten so that a stranger in town has to go to the deepest archives of the local newspaper to discover that the heiress who runs the local industry conspired with her now-district-attorney husband to frame up an innocent man, who went to the chair for a crime he didn't commit. This plot wouldn't have gone anywhere in an age of Google.

Nor would the scenario of *The Scar*, in which a gangster assumes the identity of a psychoanalyst by murdering him following a casino robbery gone bad, be plausible in the slightest today. Our faces are on the tiniest piece of our identities, and they count for very little as compared with our digital data trail. Nor would the crook be surprised to find that the seemingly respectable psychoanalyst whose identity he assumed was in even deeper trouble with the law than he was.

The naive bride in *Dangerous Crossing* would not have inadvertently married a man who planned to murder her to steal her fortune, which he believes should have been inherited by her father's brother. Nor would she have lost track of him on the cruise ship they boarded together on their honeymoon. And surely the doctor examining the sick passenger would have quickly figured out that this was the same man who was missing!

There is a series of strange apartment break-ins in *I Wake Up Screaming*. Several times, the plot turns on the uncanny way in which people can easily break locks on doors and windows. Not infrequently, people wake in the middle of the night to find someone standing over them asking questions. The absence of reliable alarm systems and secure locks gives the film a strange quality: everyone is vulnerable; no one is safe from prying eyes, whether they are doing good or evil.

So on the one hand, the level of privacy is far beyond what we imagine is possible today. Who today can disappear, sneak away, be out of touch for any length of time, much less change identities or travel anonymously? On the other hand, there is no security against physical invasion of one's home, car, office, or personal records, none of which are password-protected and all of which exist only in the physical world. As much as people bemoan the absence of privacy today, the current inversion of the film-noir world is far to be preferred.

The ability to disappear and inability to be secure fosters the world of relentless suspicion and danger that is inherent in the film noir genre. Women fall into two general categories: black widows whose secret pasts lie in hiding as they pursue their next victim in a nefarious plot, or fallen angels who pine for stability and get hooked up with bad men before being rescued from a life of desperation. Surely we have here a reflection of the deep anxieties of women in a time when men were being snatched away by the draft and sent away to foreign lands to kill and be killed.

In many plots, a moral ambiguity is pervasive, as one small and regrettable decision turns out to have disproportionately bad results, which then require an attempt at coverup that involves the further suppression of conscience and a further trip down the road to ruin. The viewer is never entirely sure when to stop sympathizing with the evildoer, who often seems to have bad choices imposed on him because of the imperfections of the world around him. The small steps towards dishonesty don't trouble us until we find ourselves traveling with him to perdition.

What's more, many of the small steps toward wrongdoing have a rationale rooted in a distrust of the justice system. The judge will never believe me if I say that I didn't commit this murder, so I'd better make a break for it! The police will throw me in the slammer for decades for this petty theft so I'd better cover it up! and on it goes: no one quite believes that the state's system of justice really works fairly and accurately. Despite the censor's attempts to bolster civic mythology in the final scenes of such movies, a deep distrust of all official institutions is their political infrastructure.

And this fact is very striking given the portrayal of police and police investigators in the film, who don't seem to be entirely on the other side of the divide from mere civilians in film noir. They are not jackbooted or heavily armed or otherwise tasing people for showing the slightest bit of resistance. They seem like people with different jobs to do, and that's about it.

And they always have time, as when the poisoned man in *D.O.A.* comes stumbling into the investigations bureau and says, "I'm here to report a murder. Mine." He then takes a couple of hours out of the time of five officers to explain how he ended up being poisoned by a dangerous gang of racketeers.

It can sometimes be hilarious to our generation when the criminals are trying to head for the border, where presumably the law then cannot reach them. We know nothing of this strange assumption today.

Even if individual policemen themselves are decent and conscientious, these films are replete with cynicism toward law—toward the system, with lies leading to more lies and deceptions and coverups in all aspects of life. They were made in the 1940s, in a time we are all taught was defined by the great struggle between obvious good and obvious evil, embodied in the "greatest generation," which fought the "good war." How could these themes of deeply complicated moral ambiguity and official corruption really connect with audiences?

Well, reading Jeff Riggenbach's *Why American History Is Not What They Say* provides a richer picture of a time when people did not, in fact, trust government.

It was widely believed (or understood) that there was something fishy about that whole Pearl Harbor thing and the drive to war, widely believed that officials in Washington were just improvising during the Depression, widely believed that the expansion of the state and its vast new powers were not really about science but were rather a power grab.

In fact, one looks in vain for evidence from film noir that any viewers were predisposed to believe anything from on high.

In other words, there was a veneer of naiveté but growing distrust beneath the surface—times, in other words, very much like our own. It is in the writings of Mises, Hazlitt, and Rand that we discover the secrets to understanding the strange world of film noir. It is a feast for the eyes and ears, a look at how dramatically and sweepingly different our times are in so many ways, and yet how the themes of corruption, deception, and lies are persistent wherever public and private violence against person and property rears its ugly head.

65

Who Was Beowulf?

November 22, 2007

It took twice through, but I'm finally convinced; *Beowulf* is a wonderful film. There would be plenty to recommend it, even if it had stuck to the original plot line.

Nearly every frame is beautiful and riveting. The visuals seemed to have borrowed from the field of gaming, so you can never quite tell if what you are looking at is real or animated. The music is a kick. Beowulf is himself thrilling to watch, as are the monsters, dragons, swords, and, above all, the time: it is set in the 10th century Scandinavia. The viewer is convinced that it must have been something like this.

Having read the newest translation several years ago, by Seamus Heaney, I was not prepared for how the film would change the plot, which is rather linear and boring in the original, but, hey, it's the 10th century, so who can complain? A monster vexes a town. Beowulf arrives and kills it, kills the monster's mother, and becomes king and then does other amazing things before he dies a hero's death.

In the new film version, there is a remarkable undercurrent. Hrothgar, the king that comes before, has a hidden secret and it concerns the monster's mother. It seems that Grendel is Hrothgar's offspring, and the witch, played by Angelina Jolie, is irresistible to him, and, later, to Beowulf. Beowulf kills Grendel and then sets out for the mother, who seduces him into giving her yet another offspring that returns to torment the community many years later. Beowulf lies, however. He has given in to her, but tells everyone that he killed her.

His secret is known only to a few: his wife and his closest associate. Both decide not to pass it on. He is a hero and generations will sing his praises. So declare the court historians, and so it was to be, in the official version. And so the official version has stood.

There is a profoundly moral story here, much like Faustus. What we see are the dreadful consequences of sin visiting themselves on many more than just the sinner. The family is destroyed. The community is destroyed. The path of history is distorted from its rightful journey toward justice and truth onto another path of betrayal, hurt, suffering, violence, degradation, and ruin.

The moral can be described as Christian, and rigorously so. Indeed, there is an overtly Christian theme in the movie. In an early scene, the king is asked whether the people should pray to the new Roman God named Jesus Christ. No, he says, they don't need Jesus; they need a hero. Later in the film, the man who asked the question carries a crucifix, and, even later, becomes a Christian monk, working to convert the community, and successfully so. (Why the Christian Right isn't heralding this movie is unclear.)

Is this just another case of hero-debunking in an age of cynicism, in which authentic virtue is a myth and there is no one to admire? I don't think so. What's at stake here is the reputation of leaders, who are a special breed. The state organizes itself in order to celebrate itself. It rules with the consensus of society, which also desires to celebrate the state and its leaders. The head of state has to work very hard not to emerge from this conspiracy as a hero.

We don't have to look far for examples. See Mount Rushmore. Are we really suppose to believe the maniac, power-mad Theodore Roosevelt is godlike? And let's consider people who in private life would be considered gangsters, thieves, liars, and murderers, men such as Abraham Lincoln and Franklin Roosevelt. How is it that they came to have their images on our nation's money, that their glorious stories are taught to all American schoolkids? That their lives are held up to us as models of virtue and glory?

The underside of government leadership is the primary subject of all revisionist history, and this form of history is something we should always give some benefit of the doubt. It is the official story of the heroism of leadership that we should suspect. This is true even with such untarnished demigods as George Washington, who, by all revisionist accounts, was an incompetent general, a man who had no sympathy for the original American idea, who jumped at the chance to send in the troops to put down a tax rebellion. The father of our country? Come on.

Have you visited the Lincoln Memorial? Pure paganism, wrapped in state worship. There he sits in the Temple of Democracy, with his hands on the fasces, ruling us from the Heavens to which he clearly ascended after his martydom—the glorification of power on display for all of us. The tourists come and the tourists go. They figure that Lincoln must have been pretty marvelous, and think nothing more about it.

So it might have been—must have been—with Beowulf, the great warrior who became the king. We know and do not question the version of history handed down to us. We take his ancient hagiographers at their word. But what was the truth? The film provides a credible alternative history, but whether or not this is the true story, the message is one we need to hear: power corrupts. If we care about truth, we need to look at this corruption in its face, and learn from it, and not merely believe what the court historians, from our time or the 10th century, have told us.

66

Spidey's Forgotten World

May 15, 2007

An unexpected pleasure of watching any Spider-Man movie—and the new release of the third is no exception—is that it allows the viewer to be a voyeur of a largely abandoned ideology, the perspective of the Old, Old Left. The film, and the ideological structure of Spiderman's world, not only shows us how wrong the Left was way back then; it reveals just how much the class-conflict view of economics has had to adjust in order to stay viable at all.

In this Old-Left view of the social order, the essential conflict driving history was between the wealthy capitalistic barons who live in unrestrained opulence at the expense of the working poor, and the members of the working class who never get a break and never advance socially or economically.

In this unreconstructed version of leftism—which reached its height from the thirties through the sixties—issues like the environment, disability, sexual orientation, and the unmitigated evil of the European mind play no role at all. This was the Left of yesteryear that believed in socialism as a tool for economic development, the remedy for the intractable plight of the working poor. This is a view that has a dwindling presence in the world today.

Spider-Man is, of course, the archetype of the oppressed proletarian. He has all the makings of someone who should excell. He is smart, hard working, charming, and, by the way, possessed of amazing powers to climb buildings and dash around on webs. But he does not get justice: he still lives in a dingy, dumpy, broken-down apartment and can barely pay his rent. Whatever job he happens to find, he loses rather quickly. Bosses are arbitrary and uncaring. He takes great photos but has to sell them to J. Jonah Jameson at a fraction of what they are really worth, and hence the media mogul enjoys the surplus value. Part of his passion for social justice stems from his own consciousness of his economic class. Thus says the *Socialist Worker*: "Spider-Man is a superhero we can all identify with."

Why he has to remain poor is not explained very well. He complains that the door on his apartment doesn't work right, but he doesn't think to hop over to Home Depot and pick up a new knob. The paint in his apartment is cracking and dingy but he somehow can't take a Sunday afternoon off to do some renovation work, and neither can his proletarian landlord across the hall. He has to use a payphone to make calls when he could just Skype (actually, it is rather interesting: I can't recall any computers in the film at all). He keeps selling his photos at below market rates, without thinking to offer them to a newspaper besides the *Daily Bugle*.

Get a life, Spidey! But for reasons that are unclear, he just can't. Nor can those in his immediate circle. His girlfriend can't get a break either. She lands a singing job on Broadway but (we saw it coming) she loses it rather quickly. Even though she is beautiful and talented, she ends up having to wait tables in a jazz club—an appropriate venue for her since jazz mavens can be counted on to embrace one of their own. Spidey's aunt is in a similar situation, always on the verge of some economic disaster. None of this makes any sense unless you are willing to buy into the old socialist view that the capital owners are running everyone else into the ground via some kind of logic of history.

The third film in the series highlights the strange way in which Spider-Man's villains are unusually sympathetic creatures. Look at the life of The Sandman as the movie presents it. He was a perfectly normal working-class guy but he was faced with the terrible reality of a daughter who was desperately in need of some medical attention that he couldn't afford. So, he decided to steal the money—which, we are led to believe, is perfectly understandable. But during the robbery he became scared, and in an ill-fated moment of snap decision-making, he pulled the trigger on the guy he was robbing. The victim happened to be Spider-Man's uncle, but once Spidey comes to understand the background here, he too is sympathetic.

The Sandman is caught and goes to jail, but then escapes. On the run from the police, he runs through a field and falls into a hole that is being used for some nuclear molecular-decompression blaster thing. His body and sand are fused together and he somehow lives on to continue his search for money to help his daughter. So while he is ostensibly Spider-Man's enemy, they really share the crucial thing in common: class interest. The

Sandman might steal, kill, and destroy without compunction but if you focus too much on these facts, you are blaming the victim!

The class interest issue arises again in connection with Harry Osborn (the New Goblin), the son of Norman Osborn, a.k.a. the Green Goblin, who is the ultimate Marxian prototype of the wealthy capitalist villain, who himself inherited wealth from his father Amberson Osborn. Here we have the capitalistic dynasty, which, despite living in a marbled-floored mansion, is rife with every pathology one can imagine, each brought on by the desperate struggle to retain possession of vast wealth. Harry is ostensibly friends with Peter Parker (Spider-Man) but is secretly involved in a private war to kill Spider-Man in revenge for Harry's father's death.

Tellingly, *Spider-Man 3* has a period in which Harry and Peter are genuinely friends. In this period, Harry is sincere, charming, and truthful. How does this come about? Harry has lost his memory, enough such that his *class consciousness is changed*. His is temporarily freed from his attachment to wealth and class. Once he recovers his memory by looking at an image of his father, his nastiness comes back again.

And so on it goes. Not that any regular viewer would recognize any of the underlying ideological dynamics at work here. Nor is this presentation particularly effective, since the old-line Marxist notions are about as fantastical as the whole superhero concept itself. It posited that capitalism was driving the working poor into the ground; but as it turns out, capitalism is undeniably the best thing that ever happened to the working poor. In the sweep of history, capitalism has, in fact, been the sole source for economic advance. When this became obvious even to the Marxists at the turn of the 20th century, there ensued a clamor to reformulate the historical dynamic that Marx had dreamed up.

But what is most interesting here is how far removed the movie has to be from reality in order to project this Marxian vision. People are not quite responsible for their social positions but rather come to inhabit them in some sort of Rawlsian way, and they live out their appointed roles as if controlled by some hyper-historical force operating in the world.

In the movie, moreover, one sees none of the real institutions that truly do serve the working poor. Peter Parker is never shown shopping at Wal-Mart for example. Indeed, it is capitalism that has created in reality all that the socialists of old imagined their revolution would achieve: an unbelievable variety of food, clothing, and life-style luxuries at rock-bottom prices. So you might believe that the socialists would cheer. On the contrary, they loathe Wal-Mart more than any existing institution and implausibly claim that it is somehow an exploiter. The passage of time in the real world has also revealed the reality of what the working poor really want: not revolution against the capitalist class but more free ring tones on their cell phones.

It was only after it became perfectly obvious to every living person that the market was serving the poor that the socialist Left abandoned its goal of material prosperity of the working poor. Now they tell us that material prosperity itself is the problem (and actually Rothbard took note of this ideological turn in the late 1950s). If we want true justice, the new view went, we must all learn to live without. What should concern us is the destruction of the environment, the exploitation of cultural minorities, the hidden costs of industrialization, and even such bogeymen as warm weather.

What the Spider-Man movies show us is a simpler time when the socialists made a strong but empirically testable claim: socialism would serve proletarian interests whereas capitalism is always contrary to proletarian interests. That claim turned out to be 100% false. The movie makes one nostalgic for such simple-minded and easily refutable views. Perhaps it is appropriate that such a vision live on only in comic books and the movies based on them.

67

Neither Brown Nor Red

May 12, 2009

For reasons I don't entirely understand, conservatives bitterly attacked the movie *Reds* when it came out in 1981. After all these years, the movie holds up as one of the most intellectually interesting and visually powerful portrayals of lost history that I've seen.

The movie stars Warren Beatty playing John Reed, the great communist journalist who wrote *Ten Days that Shook the World*, a journalistic account of the Bolshevik revolution that whipped up a great deal of sympathy for the Bolsheviks in the United States. Diane Keaton plays his girlfriend and eventual wife, Louise Bryant.

The film is unforgettable in so many ways. It includes some of the best romantic fight scenes I've ever seen, not least because they paralleled the actual off-screen lives of Beatty and Keaton. The portrayals of legends like Max Eastman, Eugene O'Neill, and Emma Goldman are very convincing.

In terms of culture and politics, the film provides a richer education than you can get from 50 books on the topic of the Progressive Era, the Great War, the Russian Revolution, and the heady brew of interwoven cultural issues like women's suffrage, birth control, abortion, free love, and the beginnings of the organized socialist movement in the United States.

The account of the many splits on the American Left in those days helps people understand why the history of the I.W.W. (Wobblies) is something that needs to be understood.

I've never been sympathetic to the Bolsheviks as versus the old regime in Russia, but the scenes here from the revolution are completely inspired and touch the heart of anyone who agrees with Jefferson on the positive need for revolution from time to time. The portrayals of both Lenin and Trotsky seem authentic, and thrillingly so.

That sense you get that you are watching the real thing is enhanced by the extended interviews with people who actually knew both Reed and Bryant. They all have strong opinions. They are wise. They are insightful. We hear from communists and anticommunists, socialites and politicians, working-class philosophers and credentialed academics. It is a beautiful mix.

From a political perspective, the film offers a devastating turnaround judgment on the results of revolution. Emma Goldman tries to talk some sense into Reed in the years following, and explains that millions have died from starvation, that nothing works right, that the vanguard of the proletariat has become a centralized police state. Reed won't listen. He explains back to her that the socialist revolution requires terror, murder, and firing squads.

Here is the exchange (Maureen Stapleton as Emma Goldman):

Goldman:

> Jack, we have to face it. The dream that we had is dying. If Bolshevism means the peasants taking the land, the workers taking the factories, then Russia's one place where there is no Bolshevism.

Reed:

> Ya know, I can argue with cops. I can fight with generals. I can't deal with a bureaucrat.

Goldman:

> You think Zinoviev is nothing worse than a bureaucrat. The soviets have no local autonomy. The central state has all the power. All the power is in the hands of a few men and they are destroying the revolution. They are destroying any hope of real communism in Russia. They are putting people like me in jail. My understanding of revolution is not a continual extermination of political dissenters. And I want no part of it. Every single newspaper has been shut down or taken over by the Party. Anyone even vaguely suspected of being a counter-revolutionary can be taken out and shot without a trial. Where does it end? Is any nightmare justifiable in the name of defense against counter-revolution?

The dream may be dying in Russia, but I'm not. It may take some time, but I'm getting out.

Reed:

You sound like you are a little confused about the revolution in action, EG. Up 'till now you've only dealt with it in theory. What did you think this thing was going to be? A revolution by consensus where we all sat down and agreed over a cup of coffee?

Goldman:

Nothing works! Four million people died last year. Not from fighting war, they died from starvation and typhus in a militaristic police state that suppresses freedom and human rights—where nothing works!

Reed:

They died because of the French, British and American blockade that cut off all food and medical supplies. And, counter-revolutionaries have sabotaged the factories and the railroads and telephones. And the people, the poor, ignorant, superstitious, illiterate people are trying to run things themselves just like you always said they should, but they don't know how to run them yet. Did you honestly think things were going to work right away? Did you honestly expect social transformation was going to be anything other than a murderous process? It's a war EG, and we got to fight it like we fight a war: with discipline, with terror, with firing squads. Or we just give it up.

Goldman:

Those four million didn't die fighting a war. They died from a system that cannot work.

Reed:

It's just the beginning EG. It's not happening like we thought it would. It's not happening the way we wanted it to, but it is happening. If you walk out on it now, what does your whole life mean?

And here we come to understand something of the strange mind of the dedicated communist, so dogmatic in his adherence to a creed that nothing can shake the faith, not even the deaths of millions and millions of people.

Reed's doubts about the revolution and the Communist Party crystallize only when one of his speeches is edited. So he can turn a blind eye to holocaust but a violation of his freedom to speak becomes an intolerable act. Some moral compass!

At the same time, we are given a more complicated picture at the ground level of what drove the actual events of the Bolshevik Revolution. The film narrative focuses heavily on the Russian war on Germany and what the draft and massive death meant for the Russian people. It prepared them to embrace radical solutions. Lenin in particular was more hardcore than anyone else on the need to end the war. In real life, there was another complicating factor here: hyperinflation had wrecked the economy. Hopelessness is what drove the Russians into the hands of the communists.

Stateside, we discover that World War I, the gigantic military machine erected in the United States to fight it, the betrayal of the antiwar cause by Woodrow Wilson, and the emergence of a capitalist class working together with the state machinery were the issues that emboldened the socialist movement in the United States.

Let's consider militarism, the draft, and the government-business partnership of war to be pieces of what we can call right-wing government. The film brilliantly portrays how the Right prepares the way for the Left—in both the United States and Russia. The Right gives the motivation and creates the sense of desperation and moral outrage that leads people to embrace utterly implausible solutions like socialism and communism.

Had there been no war and inflation in Russia, there would have been no revolution, and we would have been spared 80 years of communism. In the United States, the communists and socialists would have remained a small group of activists with no rallying cry, no victim story, no tale of capitalist evil to tell to the public and the workers.

The entire story makes an interesting parallel with our own times. Show me an Obama fanatic, someone for whom this man can do no wrong, no matter how brainless his economic policies or how violent his foreign policies, and I'll show you a person who hates George W. Bush's guts—and mostly for the right reasons.

We all saw this coming for the last eight years. Bush took power with Republicans by his side, and rather than using the opportunity to bring about the humbler foreign policy he had promised, or reduce the role of government in our lives, he used his power the way Republicans always have: to betray election promises, explode spending, start pointless wars that garner global enemies, vastly increase regulatory power, and attempt a regimentation of cultural life that impinges on people's civil rights and liberties.

It was a mix of policies that seemed designed to embolden the Left. By the time the election rolled around, Obama-style socialism was a ripe fruit dangling from a tree. In this sense, a good name for the American Left would be *reactionaries*, since that seems to be the dominant mode of these people.

This process of right-wing statism giving way to left-wing statism, and back again, provides a summary narrative of the last 100 years of political history, and it is a particularly maddening one for old-style liberals and libertarians, since we see how the two work together, often unbeknownst to the partisans, to build the leviathan state step by step.

It is surely not a far-flung hope that someday societies will learn to reject the militarism and regimentation of the Right without embracing the collectivism and violence against property offered by the Left. And someday perhaps there will come a time when the tide of history will turn back the advances of the Left without emboldening the violence of the Right.

In other words, the goal isn't reaction but progress through liberty.

68

Catch the Libertarianism If You Can

May 28, 2003

There are some great libertarian themes in *Catch Me If You Can*, the DVD of which was released earlier this month. Leonardo DiCaprio stars in the more or less true story of Frank Abagnale, Jr., a kid and master of deception who managed to work as a teacher, a physician, an attorney and prosecutor, and an airline pilot, all before his 18th birthday.

Frank sets out on his life of lies after a family tragedy, draws the attention of the FBI for his financial scams, and eludes agent Carl Hanratty (played by Tom Hanks) for a very long time. Then he cuts his prison term short by agreeing to work for the FBI in its financial crimes division.

Before we get to the libertarianism implied in the film, there is a downside. The film is no more or less complicated that the three sentences above. There are no interesting twists or turns. It is a linear story, and the plot, sequence of action, and ending are known by viewers from the outset. It's a fine story for an hour-long show or perhaps 100 minutes. But to drag this out to 2 hours and 20 minutes is painful, excruciatingly so.

There is no such thing as a captive audience, as Steven Spielberg surely knows. The problem is that he is the director and producer, and also owns Dreamworks, which released the film. There must not be anyone at the studio in a position to tell him that this movie needed to be cut by half. So, I cannot entirely recommend this movie for these reasons alone.

That said, the movie is packed with insights concerning the relationship of the individual to the state. For starters, Frank's family life is shattered by the IRS, which begins to hound his father for tax evasion. There is no indication that his dad did anything other than attempt to keep the money he made. He was found out and financially ruined, the family house, car, and income all taken by the state. (Throughout the ordeal, Frank's dad issues idle threats to sue the IRS.) Seeking financial security, Frank's mom then runs off with Frank's father's boss.

Young Frank is overcome with shock that his father, once a corporate bigshot and pillar of the community, is being ground down by the government into the status of a pauper, that his family that was once so stable is no more, that he himself, once a privileged child of wealth, is suddenly thrust into the public-school miasma. Thus begins the cynicism and the perception that life is all a racket anyway, that we live in world in which what we think is true turns out to be a fragile construction. Social and professional standing can be granted or taken away by arbitrary edicts issued by powerful people.

Being 17 years old, he doesn't adopt a political ideology, but there is a tacit force at work in his later decisions to deceive the world: he is setting out to prove that a world so imposed upon by state edict is something of a hoax and hence easy to trick. He wants to do the honors as a way of showing that his father was not so much guilty as unlucky. In this way, he seems to be working to avenge his father's humiliation at the hands of the government.

The life of deception begins in public school. Treated rudely by the other students on the first day, he decides to affect the manner of a teacher and rules over the French class as a substitute teacher for a full week. Next he tries the same trick to become an airline pilot by merely having the right badge and uniform, then a doctor by merely forging a diploma, and finally an attorney through forgery and various distraction tactics. He finances his operations through check fraud, turning pieces of paper into spendable cash through elaborate financial trickery.

The choice of these professions is significant. They are all professions in which the government exercises an unusual degree of control over who is in and who is out. To understand the difference between these professions and others, imagine a person who attempts to fool people by pretending to be a software designer. Now, if such a fellow designs great software, who is to say that he really isn't a software designer? He has a marketable skill and markets it. If he doesn't design useful software, he is fired and that is the end of the story. If he lied in his application, he is a jerk but not a criminal.

In a free market, what a person *is* is determined by how well a person does. But it's different in state-controlled professions. You can be a great doctor but without the license to practice, you are guilty of a serious crime. The same is true in aviation and law. It is not enough to be good at what you do. You must jump through hoops held by politicians and bureaucrats. The fraud at the heart of pretending to be a lawyer is not that you are not a good one but that you have not obeyed the regulations that govern who is in and who is out. What's more, the film doesn't encourage us to be scandalized by Frank's deceptions but rather to admire his ability to work within and around the system.

The FBI is after him mainly for his financial crimes. He forges checks and cashes them, being careful to time his activities in such a way that he gets the cash before the fraud is revealed. The film makes no comment on the activities of the Federal Reserve, but when this institution buys bonds from the government, it is merely creating the money out of thin air and pumping it into the economy via its preferred bond dealers. Is what Frank is doing privately really that much more shocking than what the Fed does as a matter of its own daily operations? After all, it was a Fed official who only recently bragged of the institution's ability to engage in a kind of alchemy.

Eventually, of course, Frank is caught, but the story doesn't end there. He has become so skilled at forgery that his services at spotting the real from the fake are sought out by the FBI. His prison term is lessened in exchange for his agreement to work for the state. By agreeing to help the government, presto, he goes from world-class criminal to respectable bureaucrat, one who is helping enforce the law. His shift from jailbird to jailer is officially sanctioned and hence not considered deception.

The switch seems to be the mirror image of the switch in his father, who went from respectable professional to an impoverished member of the working class, also at the stroke of a pen. When the state defines who is rich and who is poor, who is a lawyer and who is not, who is a criminal and who is a criminal catcher, we enter into a world driven by the arbitrariness of power, and that power has real and shocking effects on people's lives: making and breaking the human will itself.

Spielberg is a specialist at Americana, and with this film he has captured the hidden resentment that many feel toward the regimentation of life that has come with the hegemony of state over society. The distinctions between real and phony, even between criminal and crime-stopper, become blurry and fleeting. Frank Abagnale, Jr., was brilliant at playing a game that the state plays on an ongoing basis.

69

Time and Justice

June 20, 2001

Hit-in-the-head movies are usually pathetic. Some guy takes a fall and learns to see the world a new way, which invariably involves becoming more politically correct and marrying a feminist, or some such thing. *Memento* is not to be confused with one of these. It is surely one of the most brilliant and innovative films to come along in years.

I can only compare my reaction to *Memento* to the first time I saw *The Godfather*: here is something completely new and unexpected, yet completely integrated and successful, that sheds all new light on the medium and the subject. That subject is time and how we perceive it. But it goes beyond that to touch even on the moral universe. This movie is so good, and so smart, that you want to watch the whole thing over again just as it ends.

Memento is a thriller that tells the story of Leonard Shelby (played by Guy Pearce), who has the mission of finding and killing the survivor of two men who broke into his home and raped and killed his wife. Leonard suffered a head injury in the attack, so now he has this "condition": he has no short-term memory. He knows who he is and where he is from. He knows that he was a happy husband and a claims investigator for a life-insurance company. But he cannot remember anything after the terrifying night when his wife was attacked. He does know that he has this memory problem and that he must seek vengeance.

Despite this crippling problem, he is determined to carry on. Because he cannot form new memories, he must snap photos of things he wants to recall later on. He carries pictures of the hotel he is staying at, the car he drives, and people he meets. He must make judgements about the characters of people and write them down, because he knows that the next time he sees them, he will not remember their name or face. Once something is written down on a photo, or tattooed to his body, it is fixed in place. If it is not written down, the information is lost.

Each day he wakes up unsure about where he is and what he is supposed to do. He must reorient himself completely, not to remind himself of what he knows but to form a complete impression from scratch. He looks in the mirror to read that his purpose in life is to find the man or men who killed his wife. He finds notes, written the previous day, that tell him where to go and who to meet, and why he should meet them and whether he can trust them. His memory fades far more quickly than 24 hours, however. It appears to last about 10 to 15 minutes, so Leonard has to rush to keep himself on track, and so does the viewer of this film.

Leonard explains that there are advantages to living this way. Memory is notoriously unreliable as a guide, he says. But we can trust facts, and he records facts about the attacker as he finds them. This, he says, puts him in the same position as a police investigator who must put emotional distance between himself and the crime. He discovers the facts and, with the aid of the police report, he pieces together the mystery to find the person he is after. He seems to get closer and closer to solving the mystery.

Leonard is once asked why he wants to kill the attacker, since, after all, even if he finds the guy and kills him, Leonard is not likely to remember it. Leonard responds very intelligently. It's true, he says, that he may not remember. But vengeance is not a subjective state of mind but rather a fact of reality. So it doesn't actually matter whether he carries with him the subjective sense. What matters is that justice is done, period.

We cheer. In fact, we admire him because, all in all, Leonard seems to manage very well with his condition. We follow him in hot pursuit of the bad guy through many very intense scenes, and in this respect the film is old-fashioned. In one very funny scene, he is fleeing a man who is trying to gun him down and suddenly his memory fades. He thinks to himself: "Okay, what are we doing here? I'm chasing this man … no, wait, he is chasing me!"

Oh, but there's a bit more to it. You see, the film is cut up into some 30 or 40 separate pieces, and the viewer watches the film in backwards chronology, starting with the last scene first. At each scene, we find ourselves in a completely unfamiliar setting, which we then must back out of to discover how we got there in the first place. As the action proceeds, or recedes, we know only what Leonard knows and only a fraction of what everybody else in the film knows about the same people and events.

To keep the story line stitched together the viewer must juggle scenes and dates, remembering places and characters from previous scenes that are actually in the future. This technique places the viewer in something like the same state of mind as Leonard: a radical disorientation of time and place. We struggle to orient ourselves at roughly the same pace as Leonard. To top it off, there is a parallel story line that runs underneath (shown in black and white) that moves in forward chronology, until the forward and backward stories meet in the end (which is the beginning of the story).

The overall effect is spectacular. I know of no movie that is more flattering to the intelligence of the viewer. But I don't want to create an impression that this is some typical art-house psychodrama about the human condition. It's a corkscrew of a movie, but it truly works from top to bottom with not a hint of pseudo-profundity. You can't help but be intensely curious about every aspect of Leonard's life and how he handles it. You have to be, for if you turn your attention away even for a moment, you could miss some crucial piece of information.

What do we gain from this film? We come away with an understanding of how central the passage of time, and the gathering of information, is for our subjective impressions of the world. The ability to gather information differs from person to person, and our own personal sense of the passage of time has the most powerful effect on how we behave, on how we regard our place in the social and moral order.

If that were all this movie was about, we might just dismiss the film as a typical lefty effort to say that the world is no more or less than what we make of it in our own minds. But no, this film doesn't stop there: it shows that no matter how we perceive time or events, there is an objective world, even an objective ethic, out there that we must confront and cannot avoid. There is truth, whether we or not we see it and even if we choose not to see it–even if we cannot see it.

There's a political dimension here too. We learn that artificially shortened time horizons (which is what Leonard had and what government imposes on society through, e.g., inflation and welfare) creates internal panic and external chaos. We come to understand the degree to which civilization depends on the ability to plan for the long-term, accumulate information, make sound judgements based on that information, learn from error, and reverse our course of action if the need presents itself.

You sometimes hear it said of a great movie that you must rush to see it on the big screen. It's probably not true with this one. You can wait until the DVD comes out. It is a low-budget number from Newmarket Films, and has no special visual effects and no sex scenes and very little violence (but it is still rated R).

But judging by its numbers, audiences have warmed to it right away. After 14 weeks it has grossed $17 million and stayed in the top 15. The number of theaters in which it is released increases by the day. Writer/director Chris Nolan has done something spectacular here, and he deserves to be rewarded with commercial success.

70

It's a Jetsons World

January 11, 2002

It occurred me last weekend that children should not grow up without a thorough exposure to the great cartoon from 1962, *The Jetsons*. Its celebration of technology and commerce, its retro-style optimism, its hilarious dovetailing of bourgeois normalcy with gizmo-crazed futurism, its complete absence of political correctness (excluding, of course, the atrocious 1990 movie by the same name)—all combine to make this one of the great cartoon achievements of any time.

The answer was simple: obtain a set of DVDs that have the complete series, all 80 episodes made over time. What a dream! It turns out, however, that such a thing doesn't exist. Well, there's always video, but it turns out that these are very hard to find. Where to start? Amazon.com. Search. Nothing. I'm told that the Cartoon Network runs them, but I don't have cable.

But wait. Here's a private individual in the Midwest advertising on Amazon who has one to sell. One click. Moments later, the owner sends an email, telling me that he has *two* episodes on video, at $3 each, no shipping charges. I Paypal him $6, and the videos arrive by UPS three days after it became clear that *The Jetsons* was indispensable. I thank him, he thanks me, and everyone is happy.

What a world we live in, where such transactions can take place with such ease! No slogging through downtown and looking through racks of videos. No checks or cash or even credit cards. And it's all private, just a slight peek into the magical, wonderful world of the market economy that allows me to obtain in minutes an obviously rare copy of a cartoon made thirty years ago and show it to my kids in my own private home.

The fellow who sent these videos isn't officially designated by the statistics collectors as a retailer. He probably didn't go to business school or take marketing classes. He's just a guy with a good video collection; the service ethic he displays was something taught to him by the dictates of the market economy itself and its relentless insistence that the interests of the consumer come first.

Now, please don't accuse me of "worshiping at the altar of the market." Worship is something owed to transcendent beings. In heralding the magic of the marketplace, I am simply recognizing that there is nothing on this earth as wonderfully productive and service-oriented as commercial society, and its glories are never more obvious than when contrasted with the work of government. Let government brag about its ability to raze whole countries; the impossibly wonderful ability of the market to coordinate the needs and desires of billions, while exceeding the expectations of everyone, is far more inspiring.

And don't say that market is merely delivering trivial junk like *The Jetsons*. First, it's not trivial; it's fun. Second, by the same methods, my family obtains DVDs that teach French and Latin, rare books on ancient civilization and history, CDs featuring music from the High Renaissance, and clothing that is cheaper and of higher quality than anything available locally. In addition to providing entertainment, the market is serving humanity in all of its highest aspirations.

In any case, the *Jetsons* videos did not disappoint. In the first episode, George is feeling a financial pinch because his son wants to go to spaceball camp and his daughter needs a new gown for the prom. Meanwhile, his wife is stepping up her usual spending habits. George begins to moonlight as a taxidriver and is nearly fired from his day job (again!) for doing so. Fortunately he wins the Venus lottery (in currency units valued at 75 cents on the dollar), but unfortunately his family then goes on a wild spending spree even before the payoff arrives.

Meanwhile, his company, Spacely Sprockets, is faced with a takeover attempt by some corporate raiders from Venus, which is apparently enjoying economic boom times. Mr. Spacely appeals to George to help him buy more stock to keep the company from falling into Venusian hands.

The plot thickens in every which way until the devastating news arrives that Venus's economy has collapsed and the currency has been devalued. It is now worth a tenth of a penny on the dollar. The takeover attempt is held back but George is now faced with a mountain of debt. The whole story of the inflated Venusian currency sounds like Argentina today!

In the other episode, the main competition of Spacely Sprockets, Cogswell Cogs, moves next door in an apparent attempt to spy. Mr. Spacely hands George the plans for the property and demands that George figure out a way to build a high wall. George's son Elroy notices that the Cogswell Cogs building is six inches over the property line! Mr. Spacely celebrates the news and demands that Cogswell move his building.

A beaten Cogswell goes along until he notices that George had the plans upsidedown, and that it's Spacely who is over the property line! Now Cogswell demands that Spacely move. George is fired (again) until one day, when poking around his old office space, George notices a city zoning inspector measuring the Cogswell building to find it six inches higher than regulations permit. The zoning police decree that the Cogswell building be torn down! George delivers the great news to Mr. Spacely, only to have Spacely announce the news that instead of moving his building, he had agreed to buy Cogswell's now-worthless property!

Of course both episodes feature the technologies that made *The Jetsons* famous: the fold-up flying cars, the space boots that walk on walls and ceilings, the floating and moving sidewalks, and every manner of robot. There are also plenty of old-tech items, like cigars, which are used as a prop to signify prosperity. The *Jetsons* cartoons foresaw the day when huge numbers of workers would sit at terminals with screens. Note too that while there is a massive amount of personal freedom in the world of *The Jetsons*, there are also many government-caused annoyances like zoning regulations and financial bubbles.

Some of the advanced technology in *The Jetsons* looks old-hat by today's standards. Jane's facsimile dress selector looks like a 1970s movie projector that merely broadcasts an image. Nothing special there. And Elroy's enviro-simulator is impressive but no more so than today's video games. The mail is fast, but it is physical!

Other episodes I recall from childhood that are apparently unavailable: the contest between Astro the real dog and Lectronimo the robot dog; the episodes featuring the menacing cat burglar; the one where Jane gets fed up with public transportation and decides to take driving lessons.

And this episode as detailed on the unofficial Jetsons site sounds great:

> G.I. Jetson: Private Jetson is drafted, as George is a family man he gets a full two minutes to report for duty. They're all given an aptitude test, and one not-so-bright recruit jams a square peg into a round hole, whereupon the automated

> grading program determines that his *"original thinking shows leadership potential"* and makes him a general.

Alas, I can't yet obtain it. Someday perhaps. The free market's work is never done. In honor of this great show and the family-friendly market it celebrates, listen to its exhilarating theme song (http://www.cybercomm.nl/~ivo/download/jetsons_theme.mp3).

71

Nixon!

January 14, 2009

Some personal history on my impressions of Richard Nixon:

My earliest memories of Nixon involve Watergate, and my father's outrage that a third-rate burglary would be the stuff of national scandal. He figured it was a racket.

The public school distributed copies of the *Weekly Reader*, packed with pious propaganda and high dudgeon over the entire incident. I was alone in my elementary school to rise in his defense, thereby outraging teachers and administrators.

It was years later that I threw myself into reading the prehistory: the Hiss/Chambers trials of 1949 and Nixon's role as the leader of the prosecution. Later I learned of his horrible role in creating the EPA and making the dollar pure paper, as well as instituting price controls. As I came to understand war as a species of socialism, the ebb flowed again with appreciation for his role in opening up China and for starting arms talks with the Soviet Union.

So is Nixon someone I respected? Yes. His good-government critics have always disgusted me. At the same time, one has to agree with Rothbard that his impeachment/resignation was a great moment, if only because it demonstrated the vulnerability of the presidency. It discredited the power elite and finalized the break with the old world in which everyone was supposed to love and adore and obey the commander president.

One the one hand, on the other hand ... in *saecula saeculorum*.

This is a summary of my own view, so I'm completely dazzled by Oliver Stone's extraordinary 1995 film *Nixon*, which I hadn't seen until this week. The film further complicates the picture of this man with a portrayal that is brutally honest about his flaws but also surprisingly affectionate in the end. In the course of telling the story, Stone also manages to telescope a revisionist political history of the last fifty years.

I can easily imagine that the Stone haters are already screaming at this article: "This film is nothing but a smear rooted in wacky conspiracy theories. The film strongly suggests that Nixon had something to do with the Kennedy assassination, for goodness sake! How dare you try to shore up the credibility of this Stone loon and his stupid movies!"

Well, you know what? The Stone rendition is not made up. It is drawn from published accounts from people who don't accept the official view of things, and it draws together many threads from different narratives that tell a story that is not entirely implausible. In fact, the workings of power that are portrayed here have much in common with an ancient narrative we associate with Shakespeare's telling of the history of Rome. It also fits with everything we know about power and Washington.

Stone's version of history has Nixon making a deal with the CIA and a powerful group of Cuban exiles in the early 1960s. Following the Bay of Pigs invasion, which the exiles believed was botched because Kennedy was not wholly on board, the exiles arranged for Kennedy's assassination. Nixon was their chosen man for whom they hoped to gain the White House, but they had to clear a path for him to achieve this goal. The group that put him in the White House adored his war on Vietnam but turned on him furiously over his overtures first to China and then Russia, and so unleashed the hell that ended up bringing him down.

That's the theory. But even if you reject it, there is a solid reason for watching this. Folks today know virtually none of the essential political history behind the Nixon story. This is a great way to be introduced to it all, from Hiss/Chambers through the 1970s and following, even up to Reagan's revenge against Nixon's peace overtures. You will discover important moments in postwar history that are hardly ever mentioned in public school; actually, they are darn near forgotten.

There is even much to learn here about Vietnam, the student protests, the end of the war and how strangely uneventful it was, and so much more about the political culture of the time. The presidents' men look and behave exactly the way I remembered from when I was a child. The whole movie for me personally is a blast from a past that lives in my mind as only a vague shadow.

Anthony Hopkins does an amazing job playing Nixon, and many of his speeches and press conferences are true-to-life recreations. The impression of the man is highly sympathetic to him personally. He comes across as a disordered person, touched by paranoia and vexed by fear. But he was also a victim in many ways—though not in as many ways as he believed. His character in power was frightening; his character as a man was fearful and confused and cold but pathetically likeable in the end.

Young people who demand an explosion every 10 seconds and a sex scene every 15 minutes will find the movie boring, no question. It is heady, smart, and detailed, and the real action here is very subtle and bound up with intrigue and plot. The picture of life in the White House is unforgettable. It is beautifully filmed, but I can easily see why mainstream audiences wouldn't just drink it up. It is a profoundly serious movie.

Call this film fiction if you want, but something tells me that there is more truth here than official histories admit. Mostly what this film teaches is something about the nature of power. Oliver Stone's greatest gift is his refusal to treat the American system as something supernaturally protected from the corruption that has been endemic to all regimes in the history of the world. For daring to reject the civic religion, he is routinely castigated as a Marxist lunatic.

Watch this and see if that reputation holds up in light of this film, which strikes me as a modern classic.

Index

About the Author

Jeffrey Tucker is editorial vice president of the Ludwig von Mises Institute, editor of its website Mises.org and its monthly newsletter *The Free Market*, an adjunct scholar with the Mackinac Institute, a lecturer at Acton University, managing editor of Sacred Music, author of *Sing Like a Catholic* (2010), writer for many diverse venues including *Markets and Morality* and *Dappled Things*, and contributor to many blogs including the New Liturgical Movement.